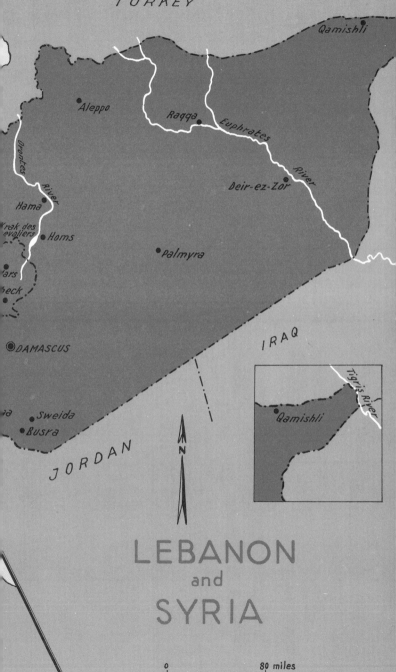

TURKEY

Qamishli

Aleppo

Raqqa

Euphrates

Orontes

River

Deir-ez-Zor

River

Hama

Krak des
Chevaliers   Homs

Palmyra

Baalbeck

DAMASCUS

IRAQ

Tigris River

Qamishli

Sweida

Busra

JORDAN

N

LEBANON
and
SYRIA

0   80 miles

COMPLETE REFERENCE GUIDE
TO THE ARAB MIDDLE EAST

COMPLETE REFERENCE GUIDE TO

THE ARAB MIDDLE EAST

LEBANON • SYRIA • JORDAN EGYPT • IRAQ

By Kay Showker

PAN AMERICAN AIRWAYS

First Edition
First Printing.

ACKNOWLEDGMENT

This book was made possible through the cooperation and assistance of Pan American employees and agents. We also wish to acknowledge the helpful assistance given by the Tourist Offices of the countries represented. Inquiries and comments should be addressed to Gerald W. Whitted, Publications Editor, Pan American Airways. Pan Am Building, New York, N.Y. 10017. NOTE: While we have made every effort to provide current and accurate information, there are frequent changes in hotel rates and other facts relating to travel abroad; and we can accept no responsibility for inaccuracies and omissions.

LIBRARY OF CONGRESS CATALOG CARD NUMBER: 67-19408
MANUFACTURED IN THE UNITED STATES OF AMERICA
CLIPPER, PAN AM AND NEW HORIZONS, TRADE MARKS, REG. U. S. PAT. OFF.
TRADE DISTRIBUTION IN U.S. AND CANADA BY SIMON & SCHUSTER
630 FIFTH AVENUE, NEW YORK, N. Y. 10020

TRADE DISTRIBUTION ELSEWHERE
BY FEFFER & SIMONS, INC.
31 UNION SQUARE, NEW YORK, N.Y. 10003

TABLE OF CONTENTS

SOURCES OF INFORMATION

LEBANON

Pan American Offices
Phoenicia Inter-Continental Hotel and Riad-El-Solh Square, Beirut (Tel. 221934)

U.S.A.
Tourist Attaché, Embassy of Lebanon
Sheraton Park Hotel, 2660 Woodley Road, N. W., Washington, D. C. 20008
(Tel. CO 5-5100)

SYRIA

Khoury Bros. (Pan Am representative)
al Nasr Street, Damascus (Tel. 12500)

U.S.A.
Arab Information Center
757 Third Avenue, New York, N.Y. 10017 (Tel. 421-5353)

JORDAN

Jordan Tourist Bureau
Jebel Amman, Amman, Jordan (Tel. 41462)
Salah ed-Din Street, Jerusalem, Jordan (Tel. 2295)
Halaby Building, 2nd floor, Beirut, Lebanon (Tel. 247642)

U.S.A.
Jordan Tourist Bureau
530 Fifth Avenue, New York, N. Y. 10036 (Tel. PL 5-3431)

EGYPT

Pan American Office
Continental Hotel, 10 Opera Square, Cairo (Tel. 911233)

U.S.A.
United Arab Republic Tourist Office
630 Fifth Avenue, New York, N. Y. 10020 (Tel. CI 6-6960)

IRAQ

Pan American Office
Saadun Street, Baghdad (Tel. 87709)

U.S.A.
Embassy of Iraq
1801 P Street, N. W., Washington, D. C. 20036 (Tel. HUdson 3-7500)

Castle of the Sea, Sidon.

CHAPTER I

LEBANON
TRAVEL FACTS

WEATHER IN BEIRUT—Lat. N33°55'—Alt. approx. sea level

	JAN.	FEB.	MAR.	APR.	MAY	JUNE	JULY	AUG.	SEPT.	OCT.	NOV.	DEC.
Average temp.	57°	58°	61°	66°	72°	78°	82°	83°	81°	76°	67°	61°
Inches of rain	7.3	5.7	3.9	2.2	.8	.1	0	0	.3	2.1	5.3	7.5

LOCATION . . . Lebanon, land of the ancient Phoenicians, lies at the eastern end of the Mediterranean and is bordered by Syria on the north and east.

CHARACTERISTICS . . . This wonderful little country is a fascinating mixture of old and new. Within its boundaries are some of the most magnificent sites of antiquity in the world, while modern cities with excellent hotels, restaurants, night clubs and beaches make it the favorite vacation spot of the Middle East. The delightful climate is another attraction. After a sunny Mediterranean swim in early spring you drive only a short distance to high mountains for excellent skiing. Lebanon is the Biblical "Land of Milk and Honey," with orange and olive groves, banana plantations, beautiful wild flowers and clear rivers gushing from grottos. The famous Cedars of Lebanon are the country's most prized possession. The Lebanese are gay and exuberant and famous for their hospitality. A visitor will quickly feel at home with them.

POPULATION . . . 2,200,000; the country has a slightly larger population than Philadelphia. The Lebanese people are an interesting mixture of races, ethnic origins and religious affiliations.

SIZE . . . About 130 miles long and varying from 30 to 35 miles in width, Lebanon has a total area of 4,015 square miles (about the size of Connecticut). One mountain range, the Lebanon Mountains, extends the length of the country parallel with the coast, and another range, the Anti-Lebanon, forms its eastern border with Syria. Between these two great ranges is the Bekaa, a high fertile valley, once the bread basket of the Roman Empire.

CAPITAL . . . Beirut, with a population of about 700,000.

GOVERNMENT . . . An independent republic with a unicameral legislature, elected by a system of proportional representation based primarily on religious affiliation.

HOW TO GET THERE . . . By Pan American Jet Clipper Service from New York to Beirut, only 13½ hours. You may fly directly to Beirut or stop over in Europe en route without extra charge. New excursion fares enable you to fly from New York to Beirut and visit four other countries of the Middle East for as little as $535 round trip. By ship the trip from the U.S. takes from 14 to 21 days, depending on the steamship line.

ACCOMMODATIONS . . . Best by far in Beirut is the new *Hotel Phoenicia Inter–Continental,* completely air-conditioned; every room with a balcony and a view; restaurants, night clubs, swimming pool. Rates, $13 to $17 single, $16 to $20 double. Other good hotels: the *St. George,* which has a bathing beach, the *Excelsior, Riviera, Bristol, Coral Beach, Carlton* (last two have swimming pools), from $11 single, $12 double the year round. Also the air-conditioned *Alcazar, Commodore, Le Beryte, Normandy* and *Biarritz,* with rates about $8 single and $12 double. Good second-class hotels are the *Palm Beach, Pacific,* and *Charles;* about $6 single, $9 double. In tourist class the *Mayflower* and the *Bliss* begin at $3.50 to $5 single and $6 double. A few hotels include breakfast and service charges in rates, but usually a 12% service charge is added to the bill. Breakfast may be served in your room with no extra charge for room service. Smaller hotels in the mountain resorts are open only during the summer season, June 1 through October 31. Summer hotel rates usually include full pension. More information on Beirut hotels in Chapter III; on other hotels in Chapter IV.

ARTS . . . The National Museum, Sursock Museum, and the Museum of the American University of Beirut. *L'Orient* newspaper lists exhibits of local artists daily. Gallery One, Phoenicia Street, maintains a permanent collection of works by leading Lebanese artists. The Museum of Contemporary Art holds three exhibitions of Lebanese artists each year, and the government sponsors several yearly competitions. Beirut also has an Academy of Fine Arts. One of the most interesting exhibits is an open-air museum of sculpture by the Basbous brothers at their home in Rachana, 30 miles north of Beirut.

BALLET . . . The Baalbek Festival (July 15–August 31) offers famous theatrical troupes, orchestras, ballet and folklore. Lebanese folk dancing may be seen the year round at the Phoenicia Hotel Theater. During the season the Theatre du Liban usually includes a well-known foreign ballet company on its program.

BANKS . . . Because of its free money market Beirut is one of the world's great banking centers. American banks include Chase Manhattan, First National City Bank, Bank of America, Manufacturers Hanover Trust, American Express, Bankers Trust, Irving Trust, and Morgan Guaranty Trust Co. of New York.

CALENDAR OF HOLIDAYS . . . There are 23 legal holidays in the year. Government offices and banks close on all national and major religious holidays. So do many stores, but museums stay open. Museums close on Mondays. National holidays include New Year's Day—January 1; Founding of the Arab League—March 22; Labor Day—May 1; Martyrs Day—May 6; Independence Day—November 22. The dates of many religious feasts vary from year to year, depending on the calendar used by the community—i.e., Roman Christian (Gregorian), Orthodox Christian (Julian), Moslem (Hejira). Major Christian feasts are Good Friday (Roman and Orthodox); Easter Monday (Roman and Orthodox); Ascension Day; Assumption Day—August 15; All Saints Day—November 1; Christmas, Roman—December 25; Orthodox—January 7. Moslem feasts are Muharram 1—New Year; Id al-Fitr (2 days)—at the end of the month of Ramadan; Id al-Adha (2 days)—at the end of the pilgrimage to Mecca; and Moulid al-Nebi—Prophet Muhammad's birthday.

CIGARETTES AND TOBACCO . . . Most leading American brands are available and cost 165 piasters (52¢) per pack. Local cigarettes cost from 40 to 110 piasters.

CLIMATE . . . There are four distinct seasons, but it is almost always warm near the sea and cool in the mountains. April through November is the best time to visit Lebanon. From May to November you can count on dry weather and clear skies.

CLUBS . . . Lions, Masonic Lodge, Propellor, Rotary, St. George's and Skal. At these clubs tourists should be accompanied by a member. There are many swimming and beach clubs to which tourists may go without membership. Also chapters of YMCA and YWCA.

COMMON COURTESIES AND LOCAL CUSTOMS . . . The Lebanese are extremely hospitable. A guest is a sacred trust. Say *Marhaba* for "hello," *Shookran* for "thank you." There are no particular taboos about which you need warning. The Lebanese are quite sophisticated and are accustomed to foreigners. A great number of them travel frequently to Europe and the United States and are often well informed. You will seldom meet a Lebanese who does not have at least one relative in America.

In Lebanon, as in all the Middle East, time is not as important as gracious hospitality. You will be served the inevitable cup of coffee, and considerable chitchat about health and weather will precede any discussion of business. To a Lebanese, this is not wasting time. Rather, it is a matter of common courtesy.

COMMUNICATIONS . . . A 3-minute phone call to New York is L.L.45.90 ($15); a 10-word cablegram is L.L.14.80. Airmail postage to the U.S. is 70 piasters for 10-gram letters, 50 piasters for a postcard. The main post office, near Bab Edriss, is open 24 hours a day. Telephone calls to cities outside Lebanon must be placed within a specific time period. Check with the hotel switchboard for details.

CURRENCY . . . There are 100 piasters in the Lebanese pound or lira (L.L.). The average rate is $1 United States equals L.L.3.05, but the open market for exchange fluctuates daily. Because Lebanon has a free money market, there are no restrictions on the amount of money you bring into or take out of the country. Lebanese currency appears in coin denominations of 5, 10, 25, 50 piasters, and banknotes in 1, 5, 10, 25, 50, 100 pounds (lira). Currency values are written in French and Arabic words and numerals on all coins and banknotes.

CUSTOMS REGULATIONS AND DOCUMENTS REQUIRED FOR UNITED STATES CITIZENS . . . Passport and visa required. For passengers holding visas for countries beyond, a transit visa for 15 days is issued on arrival. Vaccination certificate against smallpox. Duty-free allowance: 1 quart of liquor; up to 200 cigarettes, 50 cigars or 250 grams (¼ lb.) of smoking tobacco. (From June 1 to October 31, the quantity is increased to 500 cigarettes, or 100 cigars, or 500 grams of tobacco). The importation of firearms, except by special permit, and narcotics is strictly forbidden. Recorded tapes and film reels must pass security approval, which may involve considerable delay, especially if these items arrive in unaccompanied baggage.

DRUGSTORES . . . All pharmacies are well stocked with American and European products. Many drugs may be purchased in Beirut without prescription. Cosmetics and toiletries are also available in specialty shops and department stores.

ELECTRIC CURRENT . . . The current in Beirut is 50 cycles, 110 volts, A.C. No transformer is necessary for radios, electric razors or American electrical appliances that run on 50-cycle current. Wall plugs are the round two-prong European type. Adapters for American plugs are available in Beirut for 75 piasters.

FAUNA . . . Principally the mule, Arab horse, sheep, goats, and cattle in general, as well as poultry, migratory and local birds. Fish of various forms common to the Mediterranean.

FLORA . . . Lebanese flora is similar to that of southern Europe. Lebanon is rich in flowers, and the mountains are covered with beautiful cedars, olive trees and umbrella pines.

FOOD . . . Lebanese food is among the best and most varied in the world, but it is rich in oils and exotic herbs, so don't get carried away the first day. If you like the food, which most foreigners do, you are likely to overburden your system. The main thing to try is *mezzah*—the Lebanese version of hor d'oeuvres but much more generous. A typical *mezzah* will have 30 or 40 different dishes to sample. A majority of restaurants also serve continental food of considerable sophistication. Milk is bottled and pasteurized; you can drink it with safety in the better restaurants and hotels.

GAMBLING . . . The *Casino du Liban,* reached by a 10-mile scenic drive north of Beirut, has all games similar to Monte Carlo and Las Vegas and superb floor shows. Beirut's race track is set in a grove of umbrella pines and flowering gardens. Races are held every Saturday and Sunday at 1 P.M. Betting is pari-mutuel.

LANGUAGE . . . Arabic is the mother tongue and official language of the country, but a large percentage of the people speak French and English. In hotels, restaurants, shops and on the tourist track, you should have no difficulty in speaking only English.

LAUNDRY AND DRY CLEANING . . . Laundry is good and moderately priced. Dry-cleaning establishments are modern. Average rates: shirts, 50 to 85 piasters; suits cleaned and pressed—from L.L.3.

LIQUOR . . . *Araq* is the national drink, made from grape alcohol and anis, and served as an aperitif. Drink it cautiously. Most restaurants and hotels serve cocktails and European liqueurs. A drink costs about L.L. 4 or 5. Local beer is excellent. Best known are Almaza and Laziza. Some popular European beers are also available. Local wines are very good, especially the rosé. The best wines are Musar, Ksara and Domain des Tourelles. Most restaurants have a variety of fine imported table wines.

MEDICAL FACILITIES . . . There are excellent hospitals with English-speaking doctors, such as the Hospital of the American University, St. Joseph's Hospital, St. Charles Hospital. The American University Hospital has a modern laboratory, X-ray equipment and a blood bank. Student nurses and interns are supervised by experienced American doctors and nurses. There is also a wide range of specialists and good dentists.

MOTION PICTURES . . . Theaters show mostly American films in English with French and Arabic subtitles. The theaters in

Beirut include: Byblos, Radio City, Dunia, Roxy, Capitole, Rivoli, Al-Hamra, Empire, Metropole, Saroulla, Edison, The Strand, Starco and Colissé.

MUSIC . . . The recently created National Symphony performs regularly in the winter season, and concerts by local and visiting artists are given frequently at schools and universities and at the Academy of Music.

NIGHT CLUBS . . . Lebanon has some of the best night clubs in the world, ranging from small, cozy bistros to big, brassy cabarets. A drink at the bar from where you can usually watch the floor show is L.L. 5 to 6. Leading night clubs with floor show include the glittering *Casino du Liban,* which features dinner and an excellent European floor show for L.L.40 per person. In the Casino's smaller night club, *Baccarat,* you dine and dance in elegant surroundings of crystal, velvet and gold. The chic *Le Paon Rouge* (Hotel Phoenicia Inter–Continental) offers dining, dancing and an international show. *La Casbah* (Hotel Commodore) has something of everything—Oriental décor, European orchestra, show, and belly dancer. *Eve, Kit-Kat* and *Lido* on Avenue des Français, *Jockey* on Rue Phoenicia and *Venus* on Rue Chouran are cabarets with long, brassy girlie shows and usually a belly dancer on the program. The orchestras play European and Latin American music for dancing.

Without floor show the most popular clubs are *Les Caves du Roy* (Hotel Excelsior), one of the best night clubs in the eastern Mediterranean, and the *Beachcomber* (Coral Beach Hotel). The lively atmosphere of both clubs is contagious. There is also an endless variety of stereo clubs (discothèques), such as the *Stereo* and *Epi Club,* Phoenicia Street; *Le Reverbère,* on the Raouché; *L'Esterel,* France Street; and *Bacchus,* George Picot Street. *Grenier des Peintres,* Phoenicia Street, is not a night club in the strictest sense but a night spot for a relaxed evening in a quaint setting. Then, too, there are numerous sidewalk cafés and little bars.

PHOTOGRAPHY . . . You can purchase all types of cameras and films—color, black and white for both still and movie cameras. Prices are about the same as in the United States. Developing is good and speedy. Kodak is at Place de l'Etoile, Beydoun Bldg., Beirut. The scenery and antiquities of Lebanon are wonderful subjects to photograph.

RELIGION . . . Approximately half are Christians, the other half Moslems. Each of these major religious divisions is subdivided into many smaller sects. There are churches of all denominations. Major ones are: All Saints Church (Anglican), Avenue des Français; American University of Beirut Chapel (inter-denominational); Community Church (Presbyterian), M. Barres St.; Lutheran Church, Abel Aziz St.; Quaker Meeting, Ras Beirut; Redeemer Church, Abdel Aziz St.; St. Elie Cathedral (Greek Catholic), Maarad; St. George

Cathedral (Maronite), E. Bechir St.; St. Francois Church (Roman Catholic), Hamra St.; and University Baptist Church, Bliss St.

RESTAURANTS . . . In this gourmet's heaven, there are about 3,000 restaurants, cafés and clubs, and about half of these are in Beirut. Most of the better restaurants have both Western and Oriental food. Many specialize in one or the other. In Beirut, *Le Panache* at the Phoenicia Inter–Continental for European selections and American steaks and *St. George Grille* and *Chez Temporel* for French food are outstanding. Wonderful fish at *Seven Seas, Nasr* and *Sinbad;* Spanish dishes at *Espagnol;* Italian specialities at *Quo Vadis* and *Fontana de Trevi;* Hungarian selections at *Bucharest;* German favorites at *Rhenania;* American snacks at *Starco* and *Uncle Sam's;* fondue at *Taverne Suisse* and *La Chandelier.* For local specialties, especially *araq* and *mezzah,* try *Barmaki, Bahri, Grotte aux Pigeons, Faysal, Yildizlar* or *La Gondole.*

Restaurants usually serve lunch from noon to 3 P.M. and dinner from 7 P.M. to midnight. For lunch, the *plat du jour* in most restaurants costs about $1 to $1.50. Dinner in the best restaurants will average $3 to $5 per person.

SHOPS AND STORES . . . Many of the narrow, winding bazaars which typified Beirut as a Middle Eastern city were torn down years ago and have since been replaced by new shops where you can buy almost anything from the four corners of the globe. You should bargain in the bazaars but not necessarily in the better places.

Most shops are open daily, except Sunday, from 9 A.M. to 7 P.M. Some close from 1 to 3 P.M. Major shopping districts are located at the intersection of George Picot and Weygand Streets, Avenue des Français and Hamra Street.

SPECTATOR SPORTS . . . Horse racing, soccer, basketball, wrestling, boxing. Matches are held frequently at the American University, and important sports events take place at the Cité Sportive Stadium, which has a seating capacity of 100,000.

SPORTS . . . Few countries in the world offer the climate, geography and facilities for so many sports in such a small area. You may enjoy swimming, snow·skiing, water skiing, fishing, shooting, tennis, golf, deep-sea diving, sailing, motorboating, water polo, volleyball, football, basketball, ping-pong, bowling, horseback riding, cycling, sports-car racing, camping, mountain climbing and even ice skating (at the Bristol Hotel Rink).

Beirut has two bowling centers. You may ride horseback in Beirut at the Turf Club. Sailboats and motorboats are available at the St. George Beach Club. For snow skiing you may rent skis and boots in Beirut or at the Cedars. The ski season is approximately from December through April. The main ski areas (with distances from Beirut given) are the *Cedars* (3½ hours' drive, 80 miles north, altitude 10,000 feet at the top); *Laklouk* (1½ hours drive, 43 miles north, altitude 5,085 feet); *Dahr el-Baidar* (22 miles, 5,069 feet); *Faraya* (34 miles, 4,100 feet); and *Sannin* (26 miles, 8,622 feet).

Beaches, where you may picnic and swim, stretch north and south of Beirut, yet most people swim at seaside clubs, such as *Longbeach, St. George, Sporting Club, Saint Michel, Saint Simon, Riviera, Acapulco, Sands, Coral Beach* and *Beach Club*. Tourists may swim by the day for 65¢ to $1. Each club has a restaurant, bar, and changing facilities and showers. Also several leading hotels have swimming pools. The swimming season begins in April and ends in November, though some people swim the year round.

THEATERS . . . Well-known European theatrical troupes appear throughout the year at the *Theatre du Liban*. A school of Modern Dramatic Art, begun under the wing of the Baalbeck Festival, presents original plays in Arabic and translations of European ones. Other local groups of professional and semi-professional standing give plays in French and English. The *American Repertoire Theatre* is an amateur group of high quality which draws from the talents of the large English-speaking community. *Theatre du Beirut* is a newly established, permanent theater where well-known American, British, French and Arabic plays are presented regularly.

TIME . . . 7 hours later than U. S. Eastern Standard Time. No daylight saving time.

TIPPING . . . Hotels and restaurants add 10% to 12% service charge to your bill. Tip shoeshine boys and washroom attendants 25 piasters; 50 piasters to the doorman; L.L. 5 for the concierge. Otherwise, a L.L. 1 tip is very generous for everybody from parking-lot attendants to baggage porters. For normal tipping try this formula: Upon departing from a hotel or restaurant your *total* tips should not exceed 10% of your bill before the service charge is added.

TRANSPORTATION . . . Lebanon is such a small country that it does not cost very much to see a lot of it. You can take a taxi for 10 miles for about $2. See Transportation, Chapters II and III, for details.

WATER . . . Good and safe. Bottled Vichy water and soft drinks are available in restaurants throughout the country.

WHAT TO BUY . . . The most popular things are the beautiful brocades (which can be bought for about $8 per yard and cost $25 per yard in the U.S.), rugs, brass objects, inlaid ivory furniture, gold and silver filigree jewelry, and leather goods. Some of the best shops for Oriental goods are in or near the major hotels. The prices might be slightly higher, but the selections are good. English is spoken in these shops, and the proprietors are familiar with mailing goods to the States. Lebanese handicrafts worthy of

Bay of Jounie, 14 miles north of Beirut.

notice are *Jezzine ware,* a unique, stainless-steel cutlery with designed bone handles, made in the south of Lebanon for over a century; fine, hand-embroidered table and bed linens, lingerie and children's clothing displayed at l'Artisanat Libanais, Place de l'Etoile; women's and children's knitted apparel at Malek & Co., next to the Alcazar Hotel, and at Adrian's, Hamra Street. Prices start at $25 for a dress and $50 for a suit.

Beirut is one of the best places in the world to buy gold. The *Gold Souq,* which has a wide selection of fine jewelry, is a must to visit. Well-made, elegant leather handbags and shoes are among the best buys in Beirut. Shoes have European lasts.

Products from other Middle Eastern countries available in Beirut include Damascene brocades and table linens, mosaic inlay tables, cigarette and jewelry boxes, copper and brass trays, vases, pots, trivets from Syria, Egyptian camel saddles, handbags, slippers, brass and copper works, cotton, Hebron glass and beads, olive wood, mother-of-pearl and silver religious items from Jordan, and Persian rugs. If you plan to ship a rug directly to the States, buy it at the Port of Beirut and save the Lebanese customs tax. All major rug dealers of Beirut have shops in the free-port area.

Leading department stores are: *ABC* (equivalent to the U.S. "5 and 10" stores), *Fontana, Lebanese Supply Company, Orosdi-*

Back, Starco Center and *Grand Magazine Byblos*. The better Oriental shops are: *Asfar, Sarkis* and *Elie Nseir*.

Bookshops are well stocked with the latest English and American books and magazines.

WHAT TO WEAR . . . Take along your best clothes. Select the same weights as you would wear in New York City for the corresponding season. Swimming suits are essential from April through October. The beaches are beautiful and the water excellent. A raincoat is necessary from November through April. Snow is heavy at winter resorts in the mountains, so you'll want ski clothes. In winter bring suits and wool dresses with sleeves for daytime and evening, and carry a stole or sweater, as some places do not have central heating. From May to October you may want a lightweight jacket for evenings, especially in the mountains. Miracle fabric clothes and nylon lingerie are comfortable most of the year, but in the hottest summer months cotton is preferable in Beirut. Comfortable walking shoes are essential for sightseeing. Sunglasses are advisable all year and indispensable in summer.

WHERE TO GO—SIGHTSEEING . . . You could round up the major sites of Lebanon by the five "Bs"—Beirut, Baalbeck, Byblos, Beit-eddin and Beit-Meri, and in that order. Other important places are Tripoli, Tyre, Sidon and the Cedars. For details, see Chapters II and III.

The main organization to facilitate tourism is the *National Council for Tourism,* Najjar Bldg., Rome Street, Phone 220285. Generally, travel agents in Beirut offer similar programs at comparable prices. Because Lebanon is a small country with good roads and transportation facilities, you can cover the major sites of interest in a few days. The most convenient plan is to use Beirut as base and arrange your trips daily in one direction—i.e., north, east or south of Beirut. If you are traveling alone or on unscheduled itineraries, *United Lebanese Tours* have regularly scheduled tours with guides to all the major sites. Lebanon is so rich in natural beauty that you should not fail to take at least one trip through the mountains. From April to November be sure to allow enough time for a Mediterranean swim at one of Beirut's many seaside clubs.

SOURCES OF FURTHER INFORMATION . . . Pan American offices in the Phoenicia Inter–Continental Hotel and Riad-El-Solh Square, Beirut (Tel. 221934). For full details and practical information on Lebanon, read *Travel Lebanon* by Kay Showker (Librairie du Liban, Beirut, 1965). Other suggestions for background reading are *Phoenicia and the Phoenicians* by Dimitri Baramki (Khayat's, Beirut, 1963); *See Lebanon* by Bruce Conde (Harb Biggani Press, Beirut, 1960); and *The Modern History of Lebanon* by Kamel Salibi (Weidenfeld and Nicholson, London, 1965).

Phoenicia Inter-Continental Hotel, Beirut.

CHAPTER II

LEBANON: THE COUNTRY AS A WHOLE

TYPES OF ACCOMMODATIONS

HOTELS

Beirut has over 300 hotels, and in all Lebanon there are more than 600. Because Lebanon is a year-round vacation center, you should reserve a hotel room in advance. Hotels are officially classified by the government, and a full list is published annually by the National Council for Tourism. Hotels add 10% to 12% service charge. Reduction in price is usually available for groups. Most hotels in the mountain resorts are open from June to October only, but those which remain open the year round offer off-season rates. In general, hotel prices throughout the country are reasonable, and in smaller mountain resorts they are cheap. Standards of cleanliness and service are high. Rooms in new hotels usually have private baths—and rather elegant ones at that. Almost always you will receive a warm and friendly reception from the management and staff.

PENSIONS

In Beirut there are a few good pensions, while in the mountains most hotels, except for the largest ones, are run on a pension basis.

Generally in a pension you can eat and sleep for $4 to $5 a day in Beirut and $3 to $4 in the mountains.

YOUTH HOSTELS

Hosteling as it is done in Europe is still fairly new in this part of the world, although in fact the institution began here centuries ago. The caravanseri was a way of life for all travelers until this century. If the town or village did not have a *khan,* the mayor or leading family of the village offered lodging to a stranger.

CAMPSITES

The Lebanese, except for scout groups, are not campers. But as a result of requests from abroad, several campsites have been established in the past year.

The fee for camping is L£1 per person per night. There is no fee for children under 10. No fee is levied on cars or trailers. For more information contact the National Council for Tourism, Najjar Bldg., Rome Street, Beirut, tel.: 252940, or the Tourist Police, tel: 253642.

The following sites meet international camping regulations:

Amchit (Byblos): 27 miles from Beirut. Tel.: Jbeil 940322. The site is situated between the sea and the main highway at the crossroads of the village of Amchit. Nearby is the archaeological site of Byblos.

Khalde: 5 miles from Beirut. Tel.: Choueifat 62. Situated between the sea and the main highway at the crossroads of the Sidon autostrade and the Choueifat road (near the radio towers). Nearby are beaches and the archaeological site of Khalde.

Sarafand (Saida): 33 miles from Beirut, 6 miles after Sidon in the direction of Tyre. Situated on the beach near the first café after the Shell station. Nearby are beaches. Tyre is 15 miles south and the Beaufort Castle 15 miles south-southeast.

Zouk Mousbeh (Jeita): 9 miles from Beirut. Situated behind the Total gasoline station on the way to Jeita Grotto, 1½ miles before the crossroad of the Tripoli autostrade. Nearby is the archaeological site of the Dog River.

Baalbeck: 54 miles from Beirut. Tel.: 22.

Beirut: Chayla Stadium, Damascus Street, Tel. 233578.

Deir Zeinoun: 33 miles from Beirut at the Syrian frontier. Situated on the left of the Damascus road behind the Shell station. In the vicinity are the green fields of the Bekaa and the springs and antiquity site of Anjar. Damascus is 33 miles east, and Baalbeck is 18 miles north.

Chtaura: 23 miles from Beirut. Tel.: 29. At 50 yards after the Massabki Hotel, take the road (bordered with weeping willows) on the left and go 200 yards. The site is located in the heart of the Bekaa. Lake Karaoun is 15 miles south, Baalbeck 27 miles north, and the town of Zahle 5 miles north.

TOURING

AUTOMOBILES AND MOTORCYCLES

If you bring a car or motorcycle into Lebanon for a temporary visit, you need a "triptych" or *carnet de passage en douane,* an international driving license (your U.S. driver's license, when stamped by Lebanese police, may be used for three months) and an international certificate and valid license plate for your vehicle. With a triptych you may use your own license plates up to six months from the date of entry. Car insurance is not compulsory but is strongly recommended.

Major highways on the coast and in the mountains are good, and secondary roads in the mountains are being improved constantly. Excellent direction signs in French to towns and villages are posted all over Lebanon, but very few caution signs are posted anywhere. Gasoline stations identical to those in the States are found in Beirut and on major highways. Gasoline is plentiful but expensive— L.L. 1.50 per gallon. Almost any American or European car can be serviced in Beirut at reasonable prices.

BICYCLES

Very rarely used by tourists and not recommended.

AFOOT

Beirut has very few name signs for streets, which makes finding your way around the city difficult at first. If you are not timid about asking directions you can learn the major parts of town in a few days, and you will find the Lebanese very helpful. Good maps are available from Hertz, Librairie du Liban, Pan American Airways, Middle East Airlines and the National Council of Tourism. Because of the mountainous terrain, walking in parts of the country other than the coast becomes a rigorous hiking expedition.

TRAINS

Trains are very slow, and since transportation by other means is good and inexpensive, visitors and Lebanese seldom use them. The train from Beirut to Aleppo connects with the Taurus Express to Istanbul and Baghdad.

BUSES

Sightseeing buses are available through Unitours, at hotels and travel agents. Buses to the mountain villages leave regularly from downtown Beirut, but for a newcomer the taxi-service (described on page 27) is preferable.

TRANSPORTATION TO NEARBY COUNTRIES

Daily air service is available from Beirut to most neighboring Middle Eastern countries. Because roads are good and distances between major cities are not great, overland travel by car is pleasant. The drive from Beirut through the Lebanese mountains and the Bekaa Valley to Damascus is beautiful. From Damascus, a good road leads south to Amman and Jerusalem in Jordan. A view of the countryside on this drive is a delightful introduction to the Holy Land. Driving time from Beirut to Damascus is two hours, from Damascus to Amman 4 hours, to Jerusalem 5 hours. An additional one to two hours should be allowed for border crossings. If you are visiting Syria and Jordan and plan to return to Lebanon via Syria, be sure to get multi-entry visas for both countries.

The least costly means of travel to neighboring countries is by taxi-service. These are five-passenger cars with fixed rates which leave regularly from downtown Beirut for Damascus, Amman and Jerusalem. Service to Homs and Aleppo in Syria is available from Tripoli.

MAJOR EVENTS

If you are in Lebanon between mid-July and late August, attending the Baalbeck Festival could be the highlight of your visit. It is the main cultural event of the year in Lebanon and the Middle East. Famous performers from Europe and the United States come to the historic setting at Baalbeck to participate in a truly exciting program. The temple ruins provide one of the world's most dramatic and inspiring settings for the performing arts. In Bruce Conde's words, the performances "are unforgettable souvenirs of modern Lebanon's tasteful blending of classic and contemporary cultures of the Orient and of the Western World. Fortunate indeed are those visitors who are privileged to see Baalbeck's stupendous ruins spring to life again once each year during Lebanon's now world-famous Festival." In the past, the festival has featured such famous groups as the Comédie Française, the Old Vic Company, the New York Philharmonic, Opera da Comera di Milano, and the Royal Ballet.

Lebanon's foremost singers, along with other outstanding artists, give an annual performance of Lebanese folklore, an operetta inspired by the folklore of the mountains. The dancing—the main attraction of the performance—is based on the *debki,* an ancient dance of the eastern Mediterranean.

The festival schedule is available in advance from the National Council for Tourism and Middle East Airlines offices abroad. Transportation to Baalbeck by bus or taxi can be arranged through travel agencies and taxi companies in Beirut. The drive from Beirut to Baalbeck takes approximately two hours. Take a warm wrap or blanket as nights are chilly in Baalbeck even in the hottest summer months.

Other annual events include the International Bridge Festival in late September, the International Film Festival in October and the Miss Europe Contest in June. Throughout the spring and summer, villages hold feasts and festivals but not on regular schedules. Inquire locally at the National Council for Tourism for specific information on any special events which might be taking place during your visit.

MENU TRANSLATOR, see Chapter **XXII**.

Temple of Jupiter ruins, Baalbek.

CHAPTER III

BEIRUT

BEIRUT INTERNATIONAL AIRPORT

The routes of over 30 international airlines from the U.S., Europe, Asia and Africa converge on Beirut, which is the air center of the Middle East. The city is served by a modern airport located only 5 miles from downtown. Taxis are always available, and the fare to a downtown hotel is L.L. 4.50 ($1.44). Tip the porter L.L. 1 for two bags and L.L. 2 for three suitcases. The National Council for Tourism has a representative on duty in the arrival lounge.

HOTELS

Beirut has hotels to suit every taste and pocketbook. The Phoenicia Inter-Continental offers comfort and luxury on a par with the best American hotels. The St. George is the darling of the international set and enjoys an excellent reputation of thirty years' standing. The Excelsior and Coral Beach are also very good in the deluxe category. Many new, medium-priced hotels are springing up all over the city, especially along the south coast. Prices in the best hotels are moderate by American standards. You will enjoy your visit the most if you stay in a good, moderate-priced or better hotel.

The following list gives the hotel class set by the government. Several new hotels with relatively high prices are not listed. Four stars indicate de luxe; three stars, first class; two stars, second class and one star, third class. The letters indicate refinements of ratings within each class.

Hotel (Tel.)	Class	Single	Double	Rooms/ Baths
Aladdin 251770 Minet el-Hosn	***B	$ 5.00	$ 9.33	30/30
Alcazar 251340 Minet el-Hosn	****B	$ 7.00–$10.00	$13.00	75/75
Alumni Club 220817 Maamari Street	**A	$ 4.00	$ 6.67	21/21
Aoun House 229843 Makdissi	**C	$ 3.17	$ 5.67	27/14
Bacchus 257573 Wadi Abou Jmil	**A	$ 3.67	$ 6.67	25/25
Beirut Commodore 240400 Commodore St.	****B	$10.25	$13.00	153/153
Biarritz 220320 Chouran	***C	$ 4.67–$ 5.67	$ 6.67	48/46

Hotel (Tel.)	Class	Single	Double	Rooms/Baths
Bliss 250296 Bliss St.	**A	$ 5.00	—	19/19
Bristol 221400 Mme. Curie	****A	$10.00	$13.33	162/162
Byblos 251030 George Picot	****B	$ 7.33	$10.67	51/51
Carlton 221400 Mme. Curie	****A	$11.67–$15.00	$19.00	150/150
Cedar Land 220031 Abdel-Aziz	***A	$ 5.00–$ 6.00	$ 6.67–$10	85/85
Charles' 250790 Rustom Pacha	***A	$ 5.83	$ 8.33	37/37
Continental 252620 Chouran	****B	$ 8.33–$10.00	$13.33	96/96
Coral Beach 290788 Jinah	****B	$ 8.33	$15.00	81/—
Dolphin 240160 Chouran	***A	$ 6.00	$10.00	56/56
Excelsior 221440 Minet el-Hosn	****B	$11.66–$13.33	$15.00	104/104
Hotel Pacific 240082 Rustom Pacha	***A	$ 5.00–$ 5.83	$11.67	62/54
Le Béryte 250870 Phoenicia	***A	$ 7.00	$13.00	47/47
Lord's 222323 Manara	***A	$ 5.92	$10.00	47/47
Marble Tower 295260 Makdissi	***A	$ 6.33	$11.33	47/43
Mayflower 240680 Sidani	**A	$ 3.33	$ 6.00	25/21
Myr-Town House 226068 Mexique	**C	$ 2.50	$ 4.33	20/3
Normandy 220540 Ave. des Français	***A	$ 6.67	$11.67	66/48
Orient Prince 250680 Lyon	***C	$ 5.00	$ 9.33	41/41
Palm Beach 220060 Minet el-Hosn	***A	$ 8.33–$ 9.33	$11.33	113/95
Phoenicia **Inter-Continental** 252900 Minet el-Hosn	****A	$10.00–$17.00	$13.00–$20	306/306
Plaza 231458 Hamra	***B	$15.00	$ 8.33	55/55
Riviera 221480 Corniche	****B	$ 9.16	$11.66	123/123
Saint George 220560 Minet el-Hosn	****A	$10.00–$15.00	$19.00	92/92
Sands of Lebanon 291526 Ouzai	****B	$ 8.33–$10.00	—	138/128

Hotel (Tel.)	Class	Single	Double	Rooms/ Baths
Staff House 226590 Makdissi	**A	$ 2.87	$ 5.00	35/29
Strand 296148 Hamra	***B	$ 7.33–$ 8.33	$10.00–$12	60/60

YHA HOSTELS

The Lebanese Youth Hostel Association has one establishment in Beirut located on the Mazraa Corniche. Tel.: 290899/248777. There are sleeping accommodations for 16 persons in three dormitories. Price: L.L. 1.50 per night. You must show evidence of membership in the YHA in your home country.

CAMPSITES — See Chapter II

CITY TRANSPORTATION

Brace yourself for Lebanese driving. It is quite an experience. The drivers pay little attention to rules and regulations—in fact, they seem to get a fiendish glee from scaring the daylights out of you. Be reassured, though, that the Lebanese are excellent drivers. They have to be; otherwise they would all be dead.

Beirut is amply served by convenient and cheap public transportation. A bus ride costs 15 piasters and takes you from one end of Beirut to the other. The taxi-service (pronounced *serveece*) are five-passenger taxis which run along specified routes, picking up and discharging passengers at any place along their routes. Taxi-service to almost any place in the city, to most mountain villages and to coastal towns is available from downtown Beirut. Inside the city, the fare is 25 piasters per person. To outlying areas the fare is based on distance. Metered taxis are available by phone (no extra charge for the phone call). In addition, there are dozens of other taxis which operate without meters. All taxis and service have red license plates. Tariffs are set by the government, and a rate book is available from the National Council for Tourism. *But,* if you want to save yourself an argument, be sure to set the price before entering the cab. Taxi drivers do not expect tips except perhaps those in metered taxis. The average fare to most places within the city is L.L. 1.50–2. All taxi charges increase by 50% between 10 P.M. and 4 A.M.

Hertz, Avis and Auto-Europe have rent-a-car service in Beirut. Also, you may hire a taxi and driver by the day for use in town, a trip to the mountains, to Damascus or Tripoli, or for sightseeing. Such rentals may be arranged through a travel agent, hotel, cab company, or simply by approaching any cab stationed in front of a hotel. Taxi drivers in Beirut speak a smattering of English, French,

German, Italian and Greek, but don't count on their understanding anything except Arabic.

CITY SIGHTS

Beirut is a city in Technicolor, spread across a peninsula jutting into the Mediterranean Sea. Behind the city rise pine-covered mountains bathed in sunlight or capped by winter snows.

Beirut stands on a very ancient site. Throughout most of its history it has centered around the Bay of St. George, the name of which is taken from the city's patron saint, who, legend says, rescued the goddess Beroe from the sea dragon.

In Roman days Berythus, as it was then called, was the seat of a famous law school. In modern times, Beirut developed gradually from the late 18th century as the commercial and administrative center of the country. Today it is Lebanon's most important city and the major commercial and cultural center of the Middle East. Although most of Beirut's old quarters were demolished by the Turkish governor during World War I, the city's atmosphere is permeated with history which gives it a special blend of Oriental and Mediterranean charm.

The few historic sites in Beirut can be visited in a half day.

National Museum is located on Damascus Street. Hours open: 9 A.M. to 12 noon and 2 to 5 P.M. daily except Monday. Admission: L.L. 1, except Saturday afternoon free. The museum houses artifacts found in Lebanon, some over 100,000 years old. The main hall contains the Alphabet, the Galleries of Ramses II, Echmun, Hygiea, and Jupiter. In the middle of the hall stands a model of the reconstructed Temples of Baalbeck. Other exhibits include Phoenician jewelry and pottery, Greek figurines, and interesting displays of ancient furniture and funerary art. The 3,000-year-old stone sarcophagus of Ahiram, King of Byblos, bears one of the world's earliest alphabetic inscriptions in Phoenician script.

Sursock Museum, Sursock Street, Ashrafiya. Open daily from 9 to 11 A.M. and 4 to 7 P.M. The mansion of Nicolas Sursock was willed to the Lebanese Government to be used as a museum. Art and other exhibits are held there throughout the year.

El-Umari Mosque, Place d'Etoile . . . The only well-preserved historical monument in Beirut is known as the *Grand Mosque,* which was originally the Church of St. John, built in the 12th century by the Knights Hospitallers on the foundations of an earlier Byzantine church.

En-Noufara Mosque, Riad Solh Street . . . Built in the early 17th century by the Emir Munzir al-Tanukhi, it is typical of the Lebanese architecture of the 16th century.

El-Khodr Mosque, Abbatoirs Street . . . Originally the Crusader

Church of St. George. Legend claims that on this spot St. George, patron saint of Beirut, slew the dragon.

American University of Beirut, Ras Beirut . . . Founded in 1866 by an American Presbyterian mission, it has grown to be the largest private American educational institution outside the U.S. The university has schools of Arts and Science, Medicine, Engineering and Agriculture and a modern library with over 70,000 books and 1,000 manuscripts. Its Archaeological Museum has an extensive collection of Phoenician pottery, vases, sculpture, lamps and a unique exhibit of ancient coins. Since its founding the American University has played a very important role in the history of the modern Middle East.

Oriental Library, St. Joseph University . . . The French Jesuit Mission, founded in 1843, became a university in 1875. Its library contains over 3,000 original Arabic manuscripts collected by the university's distinguished Orientalists.

EXCURSIONS

Within a few miles of Beirut, now almost the suburbs of the city, there are several sites of historical importance and touristic interest.

On the coastal road south of Beirut at *Khaldeh* (5 miles) is a site which some authorities believe to be the location of ancient Beirut. The site, unearthed in 1964, covers 3,000 years of Lebanon's history, beginning with the 13th century B.C. and continuing with subsequent occupation by the Phoenicians, Greeks, Romans and Byzantines. The exciting finds have included fine Byzantine mosaics and about 350 tombs.

On a new autostrade, partially built with U.S. aid, you motor along the seashore north 9 miles to the mouth of the *Dog River* (Nahr al-Kalb). Here carved on a cliff by the road overlooking the Mediterranean Sea are nineteen different inscriptions of conquerors who passed through Lebanon and ruled it. The earliest plaque is that of Ramses II, Pharaoh of Egypt in the 13th century B.C. Nebuchadnezzar, King of Babylon, inscribed his deeds in the 6th century B.C. Assyrians, Egyptians, Greeks, Romans and Mameluks, too, left their records. In the 20th century, six plaques were added —the last to commemorate the country's independence and the withdrawal of foreign troops in 1946.

On the shores of the Mediterranean Sea near the site of the historic plaques is the *Dog River Motel and Tourist Resort Center.* The center includes a hotel and 95 bungalows which rent for about $5 per person per day with breakfast and one other meal and use of all facilities. The center has tennis and squash courts, bowling, swimming pool, gardens, restaurants, night club and regular shuttle-bus service to and from Beirut.

A mile north of the Dog River a road on the right leads up the mountain along the gorge of the river to the *Grotto of Jeita*. The grotto is the source of the Dog River, from which the city of Beirut gets its water supply. Expeditions have explored the grotto as far as 6,200 meters. The first 800 meters are artificially lighted, enabling you to see the fairyland of stalactites and stalagmites as your boat cruises the subterranean lake. The grotto is open from May to December. Hours: 8 A.M.–6 P.M. daily except Monday. Entrance fee: L.L.2.

Three miles east of Beirut near the village of Mkalles stand the remains of a 787-feet-long Roman aqueduct. By local tradition the ruins have come to be known as the *Aqueduct of Zbeida*—a later Arab queen often confused in popular legend with Zenobia of Palmyra. From the road at Mkalles you can see the aqueduct in the valley on the southeast. In the vicinity of Mkalles there are two well-known restaurants: *Caesar's Gardens,* which serves good Italian cuisine, and *L'Os,* an arty, bohemian hideaway.

Parliament Square, Beirut.

Beit ed-Din Palace, 28 miles from Beirut.

Byblos (Jebeil), 24 miles from Beirut.

CHAPTER IV

LEBANON
TOWNS AND SITES:

NOTE: While local hotels are listed, all sites in Lebanon are within an easy one-day round trip from Beirut and many visitors prefer to return to their hotel in Beirut each evening.

AFQA: 52 miles northeast of Beirut . . . At Jebeil, the mountain road via Beylat proceeds to Tourzaya, where the road divides: the left one leads to the year round resort of Laklouk; the road on the right continues to *Qartaba,* 43 miles from Beirut, altitude 4,429 ft. where these hotels are located.

Hotel (Tel.)	Open	with full board		Rooms/ Baths	
		Single	Double		
Villa Rivoli (2)	all year	$ 3.67	$ 7.00	15	13
Palma (11)	all year	$ 3.50	$ 6.33	16	9

The road continues to *Aqura* (2 miles), an enchanting little village nestled on the mountainside. From here you turn for a short drive to Afqa. From the sacred springs of Adonis at the *Grotto of Afqa* the waters cascade over a precipice 600 feet high to form the River Ibrahim. The setting is often described as one of the most beautiful in the world. The remains of a Roman temple dedicated to Venus are nearby. Curious religious traditions arising from the myth of Adonis and Venus are still preserved by local inhabitants.

AIN-ZHALTA: 28 miles east-southeast of Beirut, altitutde 3,993 feet, population 3,000 . . . At Sofar on the Beirut-Damascus highway, a road leads south to Ain Zhalta, a resort famous for its waterfalls and landscape. Some Assyrian ruins and a temple dedicated to the ancient Syrian god Hadad

Hotel (Tel.)	Open	with full board Single	Double	Rooms/Baths

are located nearby. On the road to Ain Zhalta, the *Cedars of Baruq* are visible on a mountain slope in the distance.

Victoria (1)	summer	$ 5.30	$10.33	31	12

ALEY: 9 miles east of Beirut, altitude 2,800 feet, population 10,000 . . . Between June and September the Lebanese of Beirut move en masse to the mountains, either returning to the villages from where their families originate or to their newly built homes in the major resorts. Many of the main summer resorts lie on the Beirut–Damascus road. The first of these, Aley, perched on a hill overlooking Beirut and the coast, is known all over the Middle East as a lively vacation spot. Its population of 10,000 is multiplied twelvefold in summer by vacations from Beirut and from the surrounding Middle Eastern countries.

Casino Aley (550760)	summer	—	$14.33	43	23
Panorama (550262)	summer	$ 7.67	$14.33	64	64
Montania (550863)	summer	$ 7.33	$19.67	63	63
Rond Point (550803)	all year	$ 7.67	—	72	63
Tanios (550662)	all year	$ 7.67	$14.33	115	93

Ain el-Remaneh, Baroudi, Dafouni, Matam al-Matam, Farouj el-Mishwi and *Ras el-Jebel* are restaurants specializing in *araq and mezzah* and other Lebanese dishes. Aley night life includes cabarets such as *Piscine, Shaheen, Tanios and Villa,* featuring brassy, girlie shows and belly dancers, and café-stereo clubs, such as *Chandelle, Gitan, Pierrot* and *Tam-Tam* for dinner and dancing.

ANJAR: 35 miles east of Beirut . . . The ruins of a palace, walls, streets and shops at Anjar were probably the summer residence of the Umayyad Caliph el Walid in the 8th century. The origins of the site are not clear, as Roman and Byzantine remains have also been uncovered. Some authorities believe that Anjar is the location of ancient *Chalcis.*

On the Damascus road near Anjar there is a rustic tavern called *Relais de Chasse,* which serves Lebanese and European food.

BAABDAT: 14 miles east of Beirut, altitude 2,588 feet, population 2,500 . . . A small village, fast growing as a summer resort. The scenery from all directions is splendid. The night club of the Chalimar Hotel is quite lively in summer.

*** **Chalimar** (145)	summer	$ 8.33	$15.33	54	54

BAALBECK: 53 miles east-northeast of Beirut, population 12,000 . . . Baalbeck is one of the most important historic sites in the world. Its temples are the most colossal monuments handed down from the Roman period. The first temple of Baalbeck was built to honor the Syro-Phoencian god Baal. The Phoenicians called it *Baal Bouqas,* city of Baal. After its conquest by Alexander the Great, the town was named *Heliopolis* (town of the sun), from the Greeks' identification of their sun god with the Semitic god, Baal. After the Roman conquest the town became a colony. The god Baal was identified with Jupiter, to whom the Romans built a magnificent temple. During the Christian period Theodosius built a church

Hotel (Tel.)	Open	with full board		Rooms/Baths
		Single	Double	

in the middle of the Roman temple. In A.D. 634 the Arabs, under the Caliph Umar Ibn al-Khattab, occupied the city; the temple area was later converted into a fortress. The city changed hands many times over the succeeding centuries and each time it was beseiged and pillaged, but the greatest destruction was caused by severe earthquakes in the 17th and 18th centuries.

The whole group of temples form what is called the *Acropolis*. They are entered by a 150-foot-wide monumental stairway which leads to the Propylaea, decorated with a façade of 12 Corinthian columns flanked by two towers. The Propylaea takes you into the hexagonal, colonnaded Forecourt, which in turn leads to the Great Court of Sacrifice. The court was surrounded on three sides by 84 granite columns which supported a wooden roof. From the Court of Sacrifice a monumental staircase in three stages leads to the *Temple of Jupiter*, consecrated to the triad of the three divinities of Baalbeck: Jupiter (Hadad), the god of heaven; Venus (Atargates), his wife; and Mercury, their son. The temple was originally surrounded by 54 collossal stone columns, each measuring 65 feet in height and seven feet in diameter. Only six of the original columns remain standing. These are the largest columns of the Roman period still standing anywhere in the world.

Next to the Temple of Jupiter is the *Temple of Bacchus*, originally surrounded by 50 Corinthian columns, many of which have been restored to their original position. The elaborate carvings on the walls and columns are remarkably well preserved. East of the Temple of Bacchus is the small, circular *Temple of Venus*. Its design was unlike any other temple found in Baalbeck. In the early Christian era the temple was converted into a sanctuary dedicated to St. Barbara.

Hours: 8 A.M. to 12 noon and 2 to 4 P.M. in winter; 8 A.M. to 1:30 P.M. and 2:15 to 5:30 P.M. in summer. *Admission:* L.L. 1. Guides are available at the entrance. Pay the guide L.L. 5 for an hour for one to four persons.

From May through October a "Sound and Light" program is presented each Sunday evening at 7 P.M. in English. Entrance fee: L.L. 3. (See Major Events Section for information on the Baalbeck Festival.)

**A	**Palmyra** (1)	all year	$ 7.33	$13.33	33	18

In the dining room of the Palmyra Hotel hangs a picture of the temples of Baalbeck as they might have looked during Roman times. From this you can have a clear idea of the Acropolis.

BEAUFORT CASTLE (Qalaat esh-Shaqif): 52 miles south-southeast of Beirut, at *Arnun* . . . On a sheer cliff 1,000 feet above the Litani River stand the remains of the Crusader Castle of Beaufort.. Early in the 12th century the castle was taken from Emir Shebab ed-Din by Foulques of Anjou, King of Jerusalem. Subsequently, it was occupied by the Lords of Sayette, by Saladin after a two years' siege and by the Knights Templar. In 1268 the castle was captured by the Mameluk Sultan Baybers. It was last used in the 17th century by Fakhr ed-Din as a fortress to withstand a Turkish siege.

| | | with full board | | |
Hotel (Tel.)	Open	Single	Double	Rooms/Baths

BECHARRE: 80 miles north of Beirut, altitude 4,800 feet, population 4,400 . . . Becharré is situated near the Cedars on the slopes of Mt. Makhmal. The water supply, obtained from ten different springs, and the healthy climate and landscape make the village a popular summer resort. The tomb of Khalil Gibran, Lebanon's outstanding poet and painter and author of *The Prophet,* is located here. A village museum houses some of his paintings and drawings.

Becharré Palace (5)	summer	$ 5.00	$ 9.00	25	10

BEIT ED-DIN: 29 miles south-southeast of Beirut, population 800 . . . Emir Beshir Shehab (1788–1840) ruled Mount Lebanon for over thirty years. For reasons of defense he moved his capital from Deir al-Qamar to the opposite side of the valley at Beit ed-Din. Today his imposing palace is one of the country's main showplaces and its best example of classic Lebanese architecture. The palace was used as the residence of the Lebanese governors until 1914 and is sometimes used now as the summer residence of the President of the republic. The palace, with its richly decorated ceilings, multicolored mosaic floors, graceful arcades, Turkish baths, formal gardens and fountains, has an Arabian Nights splendor about it. A folklore museum is installed in one wing.

BEIT MERY: 9 miles east of Beirut, altitude 2,600 feet, population 1,500 . . . Once a small village and summer resort, Beit Mery is fast becoming a suburb of Beirut. From the village there are magnificent views of Beirut and the coast. On a hill overlooking Beirut and the Metn Valley, the ancient site of *Deir el-Qalaa* was apparently an important place of worship in past centuries. The present church, built in the 16th century, stands on the foundation of a Roman temple which was preceded by an earlier one dedicated to Baal Marqod, Phoenician god of the dance. Nearby are smaller temples, the earliest of which dates from the 4th century B.C. Other ruins include a fine mosaic floor of a 5th-century Byzantine church, an olive press and storage tank, and a Roman villa and baths from the 2nd century.

****B   **Grand Hotel Beit Mery** (opening date 1967).

Accacias (3)	summer	$ 5.00	$ 9.33	29	15

BEKAA: 28 miles east of Beirut, approximately 100 miles in length . . . The Bekaa, a high fertile plain between the Lebanon and Anti-Lebanon Mountains, was known as the "bread basket" of the Roman Empire. It stretches from the Plain of Homs in the north to a rocky gorge on the Syrian border in the south. From ancient times this vast plateau was a caravan highway. Today, ruins from all the great civilizations of the past are in evidence in the valley. From Beirut on the Damascus road after the *Dahr el-Baidar Pass,* 22 miles east of Beirut, the descent begins into the Bekaa. The scene of this valley, with Mount Hermon in the south background, is one of the loveliest in the Middle East. At the crossroads in Chtaura, a road on the north leads to Zahleh and Baalbeck, and the road on the east continues to Damascus.

| Hotel (Tel.) | Open | with full board | | Rooms/Baths |
		Single	Double	

BHAMDOUN: 14 miles east of Beirut, altitude 3,600 feet . . . After Aley on the Beirut–Damascus road, the next major summer resort is Bhamdoun. Here Mt. Sannin towers in the northeast and below is the picturesque valley of Hammana. Like Aley, Bhamdoun is very lively and fun in summer, when its population multiplies tenfold.

Hotel (Tel.)	Open	Single	Double	Rooms	Baths
Ambassador (301)	summer	—	$16.00	92	74
Bhamdoun Palace (213)	summer	—	$10.00	52	22
Esplanada (366)	summer	$10.00	$16.67	66	60
Green House (244)	summer	$ 4.33	$ 8.67	44	22
Shepherd's (281)	summer	$10.00	$16.67	97	80
Splendid (327)	summer	$10.00	$16.00	60	46

Leading restaurants in Bhamdoun include *Monte Rosario,* a huge outdoor pavillion specializing in *mezzah,* and *Arlequin,* a branch of a well-known sweetshop in Beirut. Among the best night clubs are *Flamingo* and *Las Cuevas* for dinner and dancing.

BIKFAYA: 21 miles north of Beirut . . . Summer resort famous for its fruits and its hot springs. Each year a national flower festival is held here in August.

Hotel (Tel.)	Open	Single	Double	Rooms	Baths
Al-Amirieh (83)	all year	$ 6.00	$11.00	41	30
Luxe (185)	all year	—	$ 8.67	14	10

BROUMANA: 13 miles east of Beirut, altitude 2,500 feet, population 4,000 . . . Broumana, one of the leading summer resorts in Lebanon, has a sizable year-round population. One of the best high schools in the country, Broumana Friends (Quaker), is located here. Annually in July and August national and international tennis tournaments are held on the high-school courts. The area around Broumana is covered with graceful umbrella pines, and the views of the Mediterranean coast and of the mountains are magnificent.

Hotel (Tel.)	Open	Single	Double	Rooms	Baths
Printania Palace (322)	all year	$11.33	$20.00	76	76
Park (2)	summer	—	$11.67	32	15
Broumana (20)	summer	$ 6.00	$11.00	62	55
Villa des Pins (14)	summer	$ 5.50	$10.33	31	13
Cedars (1)	summer	$ 6.00	$10.67	22	19
Russli (16)	all year	—	$10.00	19	10
Le Grillon (77)	all year	$ 5.50	$10.33	21	19
Claridge (136)	summer	—	$ 5.50	30	7
Green Wald (6)	all year	$ 6.00	$11.33	21	18

The leading restaurant in town is *Tivoli,* which offers excellent Lebanese specialties. *Chez Paul's,* a popular Beirut patisserie, moves up to Broumana for the summer. The night club of the Park Hotel is attractive and gay in summer.

BYBLOS (Jebeil): 24 miles north of Beirut, population 2,000 . . . According to local tradition, Byblos is the oldest inhabited town in the world. The god El, whom the Greeks identified with Chronos, was said to have lived here from the beginning of time. The name of Byblos is derived

| Hotel (Tel.) | Open | with full board | | Rooms/Baths |
		Single	Double	

from the Greek word meaning papyrus or book—hence, Bible. As early as 4,000 B.C. Byblos was an important commercial and religious center. The Egyptian gods Osiris and Isis, and later the cult of Adonis, were worshiped here. Like the other ancient cities of the Lebanese coast, Byblos witnessed the passing of many civilizations which controlled the eastern Mediterranean.

In Byblos you will see monuments of Amorite, Egyptian, Hyksos, Phoenician, Greek, Roman, Byzantine, Arab and Crusader origin. The Citadel, by which you enter the site of the ancient ruins, dates from the 12th century. Excavations on the south side of the site uncovered ruins from the Neolithic period and a temple of obelisks from the Middle Bronze Age. On the west side is a small Roman theater and colonnade and the royal necropolis of the Phoenicians, where the sarcophagus of King Ahiram (12th century B.C.) was found. It bears one of the earliest alphabet inscriptions in the world. North of the site you can visit the 12th-century Crusader Church of St. John the Baptist, which is still in use. *Hours:* The antiquities site at Byblos is open daily until a half hour before sunset. It is closed at lunch time, 12:30–2:00. *The Byblos Fishing Club,* one of the best restaurants in Lebanon, is situated in an old building next to the ancient harbor.

THE CEDARS: 80 miles north of Beirut, above Becharré . . . Lebanon's most treasured possessions are the "Cedars," which once covered the mountains in forests. About 400 old ones, varying in age between 200 and 1,500 years, are still standing on the slopes of Mt. Makhmal, 6,000 feet above sea level. The largest of them is over 87 feet high. These trees are the national emblem of Lebanon and are pictured on the Lebanese flag, stamps and coins. Wood from the Cedars of Lebanon was imported by Egyptian Pharaohs of the First Dynasty (c. 4,000 B.C.) for construction of their solar boats and royal coffins. Many subsequent kings in the eastern Mediterranean, including Solomon, also made use of cedarwood from Lebanon.

The Cedars is the main skiing resort in the country. The skiing season runs from approximately mid-December to mid-April. Good facilities are available, and skis and boats can be rented for very reasonable fees. The chair lift is 7,550 feet long over a difference in level of about 4,000 feet, and there are also two tows.

A trip to the Cedars is very rewarding, not only to see the Cedars or to ski but also to view the spectacular scenery en route, especially the view down the Qadisha Gorge north of Becharré.

Hotel	Open	Single	Double	Rooms	Baths
St. Bernard	all year	$10.00	—	50	50
Mon Repos (4)	all year	$ 5.33	$13.33	36	14
Cortina (95)	all year	$ 6.00	$10.67	16	6
Le Chalet (27)	all year	$12.67	$21.33	17	14
Rancho Grande (1)	all year	$ 6.67	$12.00	40	23

CHTAURA: 28 miles east of Beirut . . . On the road to Damascus, after passing Dahr al-Baidar, the road descends into the Bekaa Valley. The main resort of this region is Chtaura, famous for its cheese and wine, and a favorite spot for honeymooners. The *Akl Restaurant,* one of the

| Hotel (Tel.) | Open | with full board | | Rooms/Baths |
		Single	Double	

best known and most popular eating places in Lebanon, is open the year round.

Hotel (Tel.)	Open	Single	Double	Rooms	Baths
***A **Park** (120)	all year	$11.33	$20.00	80	80
Massabki (4)	all year	$ 6.00	$11.33	28	24

DEIR AL-QAMAR: 25 miles south-southeast of Beirut, altitude 3,000 feet, population 2,000 . . . When Emir Fakhr ed-Din al-Ma'ani (1585–1635) came to power as Prince of Mt. Lebanon, he moved the capital of his domain from nearby Baaklin to Deir al-Qamar (Monastery of the Moon). For two centuries to follow, this picturesque village was the residence of the governors of Lebanon. Around the main square you may visit several palaces, a mosque and other buildings dating from the 17th and 18th centuries which recently have been restored.

DHOUR EL-CHOUEIR: 18 miles east of Beirut, altitude 4,100 feet, population 2,000 . . . The clear air and magnificent vistas make it one of the most popular summer resorts in the Metn region. Nearby, *Chateau du Bois* is a rustic mountain tavern and restaurant by day and a swinging discothèque by night.

Grand Hotel

Kassouf (1)	summer	$ 8.33	$15.33	67	23

EHDEN: 48 miles north of Beirut, altitude 4,755 ft. . . . A summer resort whose setting is enhanced by numerous mountain streams. A modern church in the town contains the tomb of Joseph Karam, a hero of Lebanon's struggle for independence who was killed by the Turks near the village. Also in the area are ruins of the medieval Church of St. George and a Byzantine chapel. Ehden claims to be the Eden of the Bible. Three miles east of Ehden are the *Cedars of Wadi Firan.*

Belmont (92)	all year	$ 6.83	$10.67	46	30

FARAYA: 34 miles northeast of Beirut, altitude 4,100 feet . . . Because of its proximity to Beirut (1¼ hours' drive), Faraya has become one of the main ski resorts in Lebanon. There is a ski tow and a new hotel. Other accommodations are available in Faraya village below the ski area.

Faraya Mzaar (228453)	all year	$ 8.33	$23.33	—	—

HAMMANA: 20 miles east of Beirut, altitude 3,000 feet, population 2,000 . . . At Sofar the Damascus road forks north into the valley of Hammana. This picturesque valley has been romanticized by the writings of the French poet Lamartine. Hammana and its surrounding area are leading summer retreats. You can enjoy many scenic drives and walks in this area.

Chaghour (5)	summer	$ 5.00	$ 9.00	26	15

HARISSA: 15 miles north of Beirut, altitude 1,700 feet . . . On the summit of the mountain overlooking the Bay of Jounie and the Mediterranean Sea stands the enormous statue of *Our Lady of Lebanon,* erected in the late 19th century. A cable-car ride from Jounie takes you up the mountainside to Harissa, from where you will see one of the most fabulous views anywhere on the Mediterranean.

Hotel (Tel.)	Open	with full board Single	Double	Rooms/Baths

JEZZINE: 24 miles south-southeast of Beirut, altitude 2,625 feet, population 3,000 . . . The high altitude, vistas and waterfalls of Jezzine have made it a popular summer resort, but the village is best known for the bone-handled cutlery made here. You may watch craftsmen at work in any of the village's small factories. Jezzine is one of the oldest villages in Lebanon and was an important center during Crusader days. Legend holds that in the grotto by the waterfalls Fakhr ed-Din, the rebellious Prince of Mt. Lebanon during the early 17th century was finally captured by the Turks.

JOUNIE BAY: 14 miles north of Beirut, population 4,000 . . . The bay, resting against a backdrop of towering mountains, is one of the loveliest coast settings in Lebanon. On the southeast end of the bay, high on the mountain at Harissa, stands a gigantic statue of Our Lady of Lebanon. At Ma'ameltain on a cliff at the north end of the bay overlooking the Mediterranean Sea is the dazzling *Casino of Lebanon*. New cable cars have been installed at Jounie to carry you to the top of the mountain at Harissa. The ride takes nine minutes and costs L.L. 1.50 one way. There is a restaurant at the cable-car station at the top. One mile beyond Jounie a road on the left leads to Tabarja Beach, where there is a lovely new beach resort.

Tabarja Tourist Motel of Liban

Bungalow		$12.83	$16.67	92	92
Hotel (235426)		$10.83	$11.50	102	102

KSARA: 31 miles east of Beirut on the road to Baalbeck . . . Some of Lebanon's best wines are made by the Jesuit fathers at their monastery in Ksara. You may visit the caves where the wine is produced. The monastery also has an observatory open to visitors.

LAKLOUK: 43 miles north-northeast of Beirut, altitude 5,085 feet . . . The invigorating air and the peaceful surrounding of Laklouk can be enjoyed the year round. For winter skiing there is a chair lift and tow. For summer the Nirvana Hotel has a lovely swimming pool. Nearby at Ehmej are the Maronite Monastery of Meshmish and ruins of an ancient temple dating from about the 1st century A.D.

Shangri-la (16)	all year	$10.00	$16.67	54	29
Nirvana	all year	$ 7.33	$12.00	45	25

MOUNT HERMON: 62 miles south-southeast of Beirut on the Syrian border . . . The peaks of Mt. Hermon rise to 9,055 feet and are the highest in the Anti-Lebanon mountain range and among the highest points in the Levant. Mt. Hermon was a sacred landmark in ancient Palestine and is mentioned in the Bible. From it spring the waters of the Jordan River. The ascent of Mt. Hermon is best made from Hasbeya or Rachaya and takes about six hours. The trip should be made in June or July after the snows have melted.

RACHAYA: 53 miles south-southeast of Beirut, altitude 4,430 feet, population 1,500 . . . The town is especially significant because of its connection with Lebanon's struggle for independence against the French. In 1925

| Hotel (Tel.) | Open | with full board | | Rooms/Baths |
		Single	Double	

during the Druze revolt against the French, Rachaya was the scene of heavy fighting. The Citadel, a medieval fortress of the Shehab family, was garrisoned with French troops. Only because the palace was so well fortified were the French able to hold out until reinforcements arrived on November 22. On the same date in 1943 Lebanese President Bechara al-Khoury and other nationalist leaders, who had been imprisoned at Rachaya Citadel by the French, were released. The date ·is used as Lebanon's Independence Day. Nearby at *Deir al-Ushayir* are the ruins of an Ionic temple.

SIDON (Saida): 28 miles south of Beirut, population 40,000 . . . Sidon is one of the oldest continuously inhabited cities in the world. It came consecutively under Egyptian, Assyrian, Persian, Greek, Roman, Byzantine and Arab rule. In A.D. 1111 the town was seized by the Crusaders, who held it until Saladin recaptured it in 1187. Twice again the Crusaders took the town, but finally abandoned it in the late 13th century. Four centuries later, Fakhr-ed-Din had the town partially rebuilt, but it never regained its ancient glory.

At Sidon you may visit the *Castle of the Sea,* a 13th-century Crusader fortress built on an islet at the mouth of the north harbor. Near the castle in the winding alleys of the old city you will see the 17th-century *Khan el-Franji,* once the residence of the French Consul. Today it houses a girl's orphanage. Also in the old town is the *Great Mosque,* previously the church and fortress of St. John of the Knights Hospitallers.

On the south side of the ancient port stand the remains of the *Castle of St. Louis,* where Louix IX of France stayed during his brief rule over the Kingdom of Jerusalem (1250–54). Near the castle is the *Hill of Murex,* named after the small shell, murex, from which the Phoenicians extracted their famous purple dye.

Sidon was the northernmost point in the Holy Land where Jesus Christ is known to have visited and preached. St. Paul on his way from Caesarea sailed from Sidon to Rome.

Saida, as it is called today, is the administrative center of south Lebanon and an important shipping center for the oil industry. The Trans-Arabian Oil Pipeline (TAPLINE) installations may be visited.

Hotel (Tel.)	Open	Single	Double	Rooms	Baths
Tanios (720409)	all year	$ 7.67	$14.33	34	18

EXCURSIONS

On the outskirts of Sidon, in the 'Ain el-Hilwy area near the Tabloun caves (known as the Caves of Apollo), excavations of a Phoenician settlement once as important as Tyre and Byblos have uncovered tablets of Phoenician alphabetic writing, navigation equipment, dyes, agricultural tools, pottery and sarcophagi. Recently a Phoenician grave dating from about the 4th century B.C. was discovered accidentally. The grave contained the skeleton of a woman wearing a golden crown studded with multicolored jewels. Her body was adorned with rings, earrings, necklaces and bracelets of gold. Stored in the tomb were such items as a jar of kohl (mascara) and a small golden statue of Astarte, Phoenician goddess of love. This was the first Phoenician grave ever found intact and untouched by robbers.

| | | with full board | | |
Hotel (Tel.)	Open	Single	Double	Rooms/Baths

In the same area the coffin of Ashmon Azr II (King of Sidon about 280 B.C.) was discovered in 1855. It bears the longest Phoenician inscription ever found. The coffin was given to Napoleon III by the ruling Sultan of Turkey and now rests in the Louvre Museum.

Three miles from Sidon on the road east into the mountain is the Phoenician *Temple of Echmun* dating from about the 5th century B.C.

SOFAR: 16 miles east of Beirut, altitude 4,100 feet . . . A quiet and aristocratic summer resort dotted with luxurious villas. The view from here into the Hammana and Metn valleys is magnificent.

Hotel (Tel.)	Open	Single	Double	Rooms/Baths
Casino Sofar (27)	summer	$ 8.33	$15.83	75	38
Chateau Bernina (154)	all year	$ 7.33	$10.00	27	15

TRIPOLI: 53 miles north of Beirut, population 90,000 . . . Tripoli (*Trablus* in Arabic) is the second largest city in Lebanon and the administrative center of north Lebanon. It is a shipping and trading center and the terminus of the Iraq Petroleum Company pipeline from Kirkuk, Iraq.

At the time it was founded in 846 B.C., Tripoli was merely a trading station. Later it became the capital of the Phoenician Confederation of Tyre, Sidon and Aradus (hence the name "Tripolis"). The city flourished under the Seleucids, the Romans and the Arabs, but its most glorious epoch was under the Mameluks—and most of its old monuments date from this period.

In Tripoli you may visit the hilltop Crusader *Castle of St. Gilles,* which dominates the city. It was built in the 12th century by the Count of Toulouse, first Count of Tripoli, and rebuilt in the 14th century. Also from the Crusader period are the portals of the *Grand Mosque,* once St. Mary's Church of the Tower. The mosque was built by the son of the Mameluk Sultan Qalawun, who captured Tripoli in 1289. The *Teinal Mosque* is a 14th-century structure in the purest Arab style. The *Mosque of Emir Qartawi,* with its beautiful marble mosaic façade, is also from the 14th century. *The Izzedine Baths* were built in the late 13th century, while *Khan as-Saboun, Khan al-Khayyatin, Khan el-Misriye* and the *Azm Baths* are survivals of the Turkish era. In the port area a small fortress, the *Tower of the Lions,* is a good example of 15th-century Moslem military architecture.

Hotel (Tel.)	Open	Single	Double	Rooms/Baths
Villa Faddoul (626488)	all year	$ 7.33	$13.33	7	5
Royal (622794)	all year	—	$ 7.33	20	8
New Royal (621783)	all year	$ 3.67	$ 6.67	20	4

EXCURSIONS

Two miles east of Tripoli near the main Lattakia highway is a small monastery of dervishes known as *Qubbet el Beddawi.* The oldest part is believed to date from the time of the Crusaders. The basin of a fountain in front of the ancient sanctuary contains many fish which are considered sacred by local inhabitants.

About eight miles from Tripoli stands the *Abbey of Belmont* (Deir al-Balamand), a Greek Orthodox convent, perched on a 1,000-foot cliff between two ravines overlooking the Tripoli–Beirut Road. Belmont was

		with full board		
Hotel (Tel.)	Open	Single	Double	Rooms/Baths

founded as a Cistercian Abbey in 1157, although it probably replaced an earlier Byzantine one. The Orthodox apparently reclaimed it about the 13th century. The bell tower dates from the 13th century, while the silver processional cross in Gothic style is believed to have come from Cyprus in the 15th century.

TYRE (Sour): 52 miles south of Beirut, population 12,000 . . . Tyre was one of the great cities of ancient times and the master city-state of the Phoenician domain. From Tyre, Phoenician seamen set out to establish the first commercial empire of the ancient world. As early as 1100 B.C. they had sailed beyond the Straits of Gibraltar, and by 900 B.C. they had founded Carthage.

The most famous king of Tyre was Hiram, who furnished his friend King Solomon with cedarwood for his temple and palace. Another Tyrian king of Biblical fame, Ethbaal, gave his infamous daughter, Jezebel, in marriage to Ahab, king of Israel.

The ancient city of Tyre was built on an island off the mainland probably as early as 2750 B.C. (The island is now connected to the mainland by a half-mile causeway created from silting around the mole built by Alexander the Great.) In Arabic Tyre is called *Sour,* meaning "fortress wall"—and not without reason. The powerful Nebuchadnezzar could not take the city after thirteen years of siege, while the armies of Alexander, after a seven months' blockade, had to build a causeway to conquer it.

Excavations at Tyre are only now beginning to bring to light the archaeological wealth of this area. At the site of ancient Tyre, Phoenician, Greek, Roman and Byzantine ruins have been uncovered. Hours: 8:30 A.M.– 12:30 P.M. and 2 to 5 P.M.

EXCURSIONS

Recently a spectacular cemetery dating from the 2nd century A.D. was discovered a few miles from Tyre. About 6 miles southeast of Tyre is the so-called sarcophagus of King Hiram. (Actually it post-dates Hiram by about four centuries.) Nearby a sanctuary tomb bears the emblem of Tanit, goddess of Carthage. This was the first evidence ever uncovered that indicated that the Carthaginian emblem came originally from Tyre. About 8 miles south of Tyre at *Ras el-Ain,* spring waters fill reservoirs and aqueducts which, according to tradition, were built by Solomon in payment for the cedarwood and workmen supplied by Hiram for building the Temple of Jerusalem.

ZAHLEH: 31 miles east-northeast of Beirut, altitude 3,250 feet, population 15,000 . . . The picturesque village of Zahleh, built on two mountain slopes overlooking the Bardawni River, is the capital of the Bekaa district and third largest city in Lebanon. Its sizable year-round population is greatly increased in summer, especially because the cafés along the river-banks are the leading places in Lebanon for *araq* and *mezzah.* The best restaurants in the group, *Casino Wadi,* has one of the most beautiful settings in Lebanon.

Hotel (Tel.)	Open	Single	Double	Rooms/Baths	
Kadri (116)	all year	$ 6.83	$12.00	66	41
d'Amerique (137)	all year	$ 4.50	$ 8.00	21	3

El Azm Palace, Damascus.

CHAPTER V

SYRIA

TRAVEL FACTS

WEATHER IN DAMASCUS—Lat. N33°31′—Alt. 700′

	JAN.	FEB.	MAR.	APR.	MAY	JUNE	JULY	AUG.	SEPT.	OCT.	NOV.	DEC.
Average temp.	46°	49°	52°	51°	70°	75°	80°	82°	77°	68°	56°	47°
Sunny days	27	23	28	24	31	29	31	31	30	26	25	26

LOCATION . . . Syria lies on the eastern Mediterranean, bounded on the north by Turkey, on the east by Iraq, on the south by Jordan and on the west by Lebanon. In the northwest corner the coast stretches for 200 miles along the Mediterranean Sea. Along the border which Syria shares with Lebanon are the Anti-Lebanon Mountains rising to 9,232 feet at Mount Hermon.

CHARACTERISTICS . . . Syria is predominantly Arab in character and culture, though the urban Syrian is adopting Western dress and habits to an increasing extent. Syria is honeycombed with ruins of ancient civilizations and historical monuments, reflecting the imprint of a hundred conquerors. It's a fantastically old land of Biblical fame, and traces of its exotic past may still be seen behind the modern façade of its cities.

POPULATION . . . 5,500,000, largely of Arab origin. The two major minorities are the Druze, who live in the south, and the Alawites in the northwest.

SIZE . . . 71,228 square miles (about the size of South Dakota).

CAPITAL . . . Damascus, with a population of 600,000.

GOVERNMENT . . . A republic. Divided into twelve administrative provinces (*muhafazat*): Damascus, Aleppo, Homs, Hama, Latakia, Deir-ez-Zor, Hasakah, Dera'a, Sueida, El Raqqa, Idlib and Quneitra.

HOW TO GET THERE . . . Damascus is served by direct international flights from Europe. Pan American Airways has daily flights from New York to Beirut, from where connecting flights to Damascus may be included in a tour for Beirut, Cairo and Jerusalem without extra charge. Syria is served internally by Syrian Arab Airlines, which connects Damascus with other cities in the Middle East. Many visitors arrive in Syria by car from Beirut. It is a delightful two-hour drive over the Lebanese mountains into the Barada Valley to Damascus. An increasing number of travelers are discovering the pleasant drive by car from Turkey to Aleppo and south to Damascus. By ship the trip takes 18 to 21 days.

ACCOMMODATIONS . . . Among the better hotels in Damascus are the *New Omayad, New Semiramis, Orient Palace* and *Cattan Hotel.* In Aleppo the *Baron* and in Latakia the *Casino Hotel* are best. First-class hotel rates are about $8 single, $15 double, including meals and service.

ARTS . . . The National Museum in Damascus is a storehouse of art treasures from the beginning of history. The museum also has a permanent collection of paintings by contemporary Syrian artists.

BANKS . . . No American banks, but the principal banks have U.S. affiliations.

CALENDAR OF HOLIDAYS . . . Friday is the official weekly holiday, though many offices, businesses and stores observe Sunday. Government offices and banks close on all national and major religious holidays. Shops do not always close for all of these. The national holidays are New Year's day, January 1; Unity Day, February 22; Arab League Day, March 22; Evacuation Day, April 17; Tree Day (the last Thursday in December). Christian feasts include Easter (Catholic and Orthodox); Christmas, December 25; Feast of the Virgin in Seidnaya, September 8, attended by hundreds of pilgrims from Syria and Lebanon; Feast of the Holy Cross in Maloula, September 14; St. George Feast in Deir Al-Humaira, October 7, a fair for the villages neighboring St. George's Monastery near the Krak des Chevaliers and held for about one week.

Moslem feasts are based on the lunar calendar and vary from year to year. The main ones are New Year (Muharram 1), Id al-Fitr (3 days) at the end of the fast of Ramadan, Id al Adha (3 days) at the end of the pilgrimage to Mecca; Moulid al Nebi— Prophet Muhammad's birthday.

CIGARETTES AND TOBACCO . . . American cigarettes cost 50¢ a pack. Local brands (a mixture of Syrian and Turkish tobacco) such as Star, Orient and Alhamra are cheaper.

CLIMATE . . . The climate of Syria varies with its terrain. It ranges from mild Mediterranean weather on the coast to desert conditions in the east. Summers are hot but dry in Damascus, while winters are mild. On the other hand, Aleppo winters can be wet and cold. In the desert summers are very hot, winters cool, and year round the temperature between noon and evening might change 30 to 40 degrees.

The best time to visit Syria is spring and fall. Yet in winter Damascus climate is ideal for traveling, and in summer good hotels are air-conditioned. The summer air of the mountain resorts near Damascus and in northern Syria is excellent.

CLUBS . . . The most important clubs in Damascus are the Orient Club (Al Chark) and the Family Club. There's also an Orient Club in Aleppo. Lions and Rotary in both cities.

COMMON COURTESIES AND LOCAL CUSTOMS . . . A traveler from the States will be very much surprised by the modernization of Damascus and Aleppo, as well as the apparent Westernization of Syria in general. Yet the cultures are different. You will enjoy many of the old customs and traditions which prevail, and none should present any difficulty so long as your actions are circumspect.

Syrians are extremely polite and will go out of their way to be helpful. Often when a stranger asks for directions, a Syrian will stop his work to accompany the stranger to his destination, whether it is a few blocks or several miles. Syrians are very formal in their greetings. It is considered polite to accept a small cup of Arabic coffee or *gazoz* (a local carbonated drink) when visiting friends or business houses. *Shookran* is "thank you." It is customary to take a gift when visiting someone's home. Syrians are particularly generous, and it can be embarrassing to admire some object in a home only to have your host present it to you. Many Moslem rules are followed to the letter, particularly with regard to home life and women.

COMMUNICATIONS . . . A 3-minute phone call to the States costs L.S. 57.50 ($15) plus L.S. 2.60 to place the call. Day-rate cablegram to the U.S. is L.S. 2.15 per word for a 7-word minimum. Airmail postage for letters to the U.S. costs L.S. 1.05, postcards 90 piasters. The main post office is located between the

Semiramis Hotel and the Railway Station on al Jabri Street and is open 24 hours daily. There is a branch post office in front of the Omayad Hotel, open daily except Friday.

Almost all towns and cities in Syria have automatic dialing. Long-distance calls to foreign countries can be made daily between 12 noon and 3 P.M. and should be booked in advance. The Central Telegraph and Telephone Office, Nasr Street, is open 24 hours daily.

CURRENCY . . . The unit of currency is the Syrian pound (called *lira*), which is equivalent to 100 Syrian piasters (called *erish*). One Syrian pound equals $.25, or one U.S. dollar equals 4.00 Syrian pounds (L.S.). The rate is based on the free-market rate and may fluctuate from day to day. Variation in size of coins and different colors for banknotes are aids to identification; in addition, banknotes are printed in French on the reverse side. Coins, however, are written in Arabic only. Be sure to keep a stock of small coins on hand; taxi drivers, porters, etc., never have change.

A tourist can bring in any amount of foreign currencies in the form of banknotes or travelers checks and can take out any amount up to the quantity he brought in. Banks and first-class hotels are authorized to change money. The bank at the airport is not always open. If you are entering by car on the Damascus road from Beirut, you can buy Syrian money at the exchange office in the security headquarters at the frontier.

CUSTOMS REGULATIONS AND DOCUMENTS REQUIRED FOR UNITED STATES CITIZENS . . . Passport and visa required. An entry or *transit* visa allows a maximum stay of 15 days without reporting to police authorities. The visa is given to tourists who arrive at the frontier without a visa. Fee is L.S. 8, and the visa is good for several entries within one month at the frontiers of Lebanon, Jordan, Iraq and Turkey. At the Lebanese border you can also obtain a multi-entry visa valid for six months. Fee is L.S. 21. Collective visas for tourist groups are issued when applied for by a representative of the group, a tourist company organizing the tour, or through a steamship or airlines company. Tourist groups of not less than ten persons can obtain a free visa at any Syrian border provided they hold a passenger manifest in duplicate giving full name, number of passport with date and place of issue, and nationality.

A traveler from the United States should hold an International Vaccination Certificate against smallpox. Typhus, typhoid, tetanus and polio inoculations are required if coming from infected area.

A tourist is allowed to bring in his personal belongings duty-free, provided that they are carried by him or included in his luggage and that they accompany him on his departure. Personal belongings include all clothes and other effects, whether new or used, which suit a tourist's reasonable needs for his visit. Tourists are also allowed free of duty: one camera with five rolls of films, a pair of binoculars, one portable radio and record player with 20 records, sporting articles, one tent and camping accessories, 200 cigarettes or cigars, or 250 grams of tobacco, one bottle of wine and one opened quart or liter of alcoholic beverages. Firearms must have prior clearance by local police.

DRUGSTORES . . . Drugstores follow the French and English rather than American system of filling prescriptions. Most all medical supplies and medicine can be obtained in Damascus. Prices are reasonable and many medicines can be purchased without prescription. Leading American and European cosmetics and toiletries are sold at pharmacies and specialty shops.

ELECTRIC CURRENT . . . 110 volts, A.C., 50 cycles. Adapter plugs for round prongs are necessary and can be purchased locally.

FAUNA . . . Of interest to tourists are the camel, the ever-present patient donkey, the Arabian horse, and the gazelle. Goats, sheep and fine cattle also.

FLORA . . . Interesting herbs are tarragon, thyme and caraway. Trees include pistachio, apricot, poplar, platanus orientalis, apple and cactus fruit. Several varieties of grapes also grown locally. In spring the mountains and river beds are covered with beautiful wild flowers.

FOOD . . . Both European and Syrian foods are offered in restaurants. If you keep to reliable places, you should not have any difficulty. Syrian cuisine is excellent, though more highly seasoned than American food, and it can sometimes upset your system. Eat lightly. As a precaution, until you become accustomed to the new foods, avoid eating fruits and raw vegetables which cannot be peeled. Pasteurized milk is available.

GAMBLING . . . There is gambling in some clubs and resort hotels.

LANGUAGE . . . Arabic is the official language of the country and French the major European one. On the tourist track, English is widely used.

LAUNDRIES AND DRY CLEANING . . . Laundries, including those with dry-cleaning facilities, can be found throughout the country. Hotels can also take care of your laundry.

LIQUOR . . . The better hotels and restaurants have bars where familiar brands of whisky, usually Scotch, are available, in addition to wine, cognac and beer. Try *araq,* an aperitif made from grapes and flavored with anise.

MEDICAL FACILITIES . . . There are many Government hospitals in both Damascus and Aleppo with English-speaking doctors. Inquire at your hotel or from Pan American.

MOTION PICTURES . . . Damascus theaters show mostly

films in English and French with Arabic subtitles. Shows at 3, 6:15 and 9:15 P.M. Seats should be reserved in advance.

MUSIC . . . The prevailing music is Arabic. Some chamber music in the "Club of the Friends of Art" and other clubs.

NIGHT CLUBS . . . Night life in Damascus centers on restaurants with orchestras for dancing, stereo clubs and a few night clubs with shows. The *Orient Club* on Najmeh Square, and the *Casino International* have dancing and drinks while the Orient Club also has gambling. Others which also have restaurants include the *Airport Restaurant, Caravan* and *Semiramis. Ashbilia* in Doummar near Damascus is open only in summer. The most popular stereo clubs are the new *Elysse,* Abu Roumaneh; *Cave du Roy,* near the Omayad Hotel, which also serves good food; the *400,* Salhieh Avenue; and *L'Aiglon,* Orient Club.

PHOTOGRAPHY . . . Photographic equipment and supplies, including color film for movie cameras and developing service for black-and-white film, are available in Damascus and Aleppo, but it's wise to bring film with you. Photographing military installations is prohibited. You should use tact and discretion in photographing "picturesque scenes of local color." Ask permission first in a friendly way, and you will usually find the Syrians cooperative. *Dunia,* Port Said Street, is the Kodak agent.

RELIGION . . . 85% of the people are Moslems. Christian sects include Catholic, Protestant, Syriac, Greek Orthodox.

RESTAURANTS . . . Most restaurants are open from noon to 3 P.M. for lunch and from 7 to 11 P.M. for dinner. An average meal costs $1 plus 10% service charge. Hotel dining rooms usually serve Continental cuisine, while restaurants tend to specialize in either European food or Syrian dishes. The leading restaurants in Damascus are *Romanoff, Candles, Caves du Roy, Alcazar, Oasis, Abu Kamal, Gondola, Morocco, Airport Restaurant* and *Orient Restaurant.*

SHOPS AND STORES . . . Shopping hours are normally from 9 A.M. to 7 P.M. (many close from 1 to 4 P.M. for lunch). Prices are moderate. Some shops close on Friday, others on Sunday.

SPECTATOR SPORTS . . . Spectator sports are held regularly at the National Stadium in Damascus. Soccer, basketball, volleyball, boxing and bicycle races are popular.

SPORTS . . . The best swimming is along the Mediterranean coast, where several developed beaches in the Latakia area have basic amenities. The Mediterranean is also excellent for fishing, but you need to bring equipment. In summer there are several swimming pools in and around Damascus open to the public. You can ride horseback at the Damascus Riding Club located 10 miles outside the city on the Dera'a Road. Aleppo has long been famous as a center for the breeding of the finest Arabian horses.

TIME . . . Greenwich Mean Time plus 2 (in summer, plus 3). When it's noon in New York, it's 7 P.M. in Syria.

TRANSPORTATION . . . Buses, taxis and cars for hire (with driver) are plentiful at moderate prices. See Chapters VI and VII.

TIPPING . . . Most hotels and restaurants add a 10% service charge. If not, a 10% tip is adequate. Taxi drivers do not expect tips, but agree on the price *beforehand*.

WATER . . . Syria boasts the purest water in the Middle East. In the cities of Aleppo and Damascus tap water is safe to drink. In the smaller villages and at sites of antiquity, soft drinks or beer are available. On long trips to out-of-way places, it is wise to take water with you.

WHAT TO BUY . . . Damascus has been famous throughout history for its craftsmen. Today, *damask* is a household word for the finest textured silk, and *Damascene* is an adjective denoting quality in craftsmanship.

The bazaars of Damascus and Aleppo are highlights in a visit to Syria. The variety of people and wares will fascinate even the most casual shopper. Crowds and scents mingle and meander through miles of narrow lanes covered by arched roofs. Here time has no meaning. And, fortunately, *time* has left these historic bazaars for a modern traveler to enjoy. The ancient caravanserais with exquisitely carved doors and archways no longer serve as lodging quarters, and their stables have now been converted into modern shops and storehouses. But even with such modern intrusions, they will evoke scenes of a time in the past when Damascus and Aleppo were the great centers of trade along the major caravan route between East and West.

In the bazaars bargaining is a way of life. Don't be afraid to try it. On the other hand you need not be disappointed if you do not get a purchase at half the original asking price. Syrians are not only skilled craftsmen; they are crafty merchants! One-third off is good. If your time allows, remember, it pays to shop around before you buy. When you have an idea about prices and selections, your bargaining becomes more effective.

In Damascus, the main bazaars are *Souq Hamadiyeh* and the Biblical *Street called Straight*. Souq Hamadiyeh runs from El Nasr Street and Post Gate to the Umayyad Mosque. It was built in the late 19th century during the reign of Sultan Abdel Hamid and bears his name. Along the way you will see a vast display of oriental goods such as silk brocades which run from $1.25 to $2 per yard for a coarse weave to $5 to $10 for the finest. (Comparable ones are about $25 per yard in the States.) An unusual gift is an *abaya* (Kaftan) woven with gold or silver. These are copies of the flowing Arab robe, popular as house robes for men and ladies. They are light, easy to pack and inexpensive. Rayon, $2.50 to $4; pure silk, $7.

Embroidered table linens are wonderful buys. For $2.25 you can purchase an organdy embroidered bridge cloth and four napkins. Rayon ones are $1.25. The dinner size with eight napkins in soft cotton and rayon start at $4 and they come in many colors.

The selection of silver work includes filigree jewelry, cigarette cases, perfume bottles and Bedouin jewelry. A piece of silver flatware with a filigree handle is a nice gift. A demitasse or iced-tea spoon, for example, costs $1 and up.

The most delicate work for which Damascus is famous is mosaic wood inlaid with mother-of-pearl. A jewelry box or backgammon board might take six months to be completed, for every tiny piece in the design is placed by hand. A cigarette box costs $1.25 and up.

Leather slippers, ottomans and novelty handbags are readily available in Oriental shops, as are suitcases and carry-alls for $4 and up. Old or new brass and copper trays, candlesticks, pots, vases, lamps and samovars are plentiful.

Book shops with the best selection of books, magazines and newspapers in English are Atlas, Mutanabbi Street, Avicenne Libraire International, near the Omayad Hotel; Sayegh, Parliament Street; and Universale, Port Said Street, near the Semiramis Hotel.

WHAT TO WEAR . . . In general, dress as you would in any large American or European city. In winter be prepared for cool days, especially in the north of Syria. A warm coat is necessary, especially for evenings in the desert. From November through February in Aleppo and Latakia you will need a raincoat. From June through September cottons are preferable to synthetic fabrics.

In winter, for ladies, daytime dresses with sleeves and suits with changeable blouses or sweaters are recommended. In the evening, silk or wool cocktail outfits are appropriate, and be sure to take along a stole or sweater, as many places do not have central heating. In summer, cool (but conservative) cotton dresses are best, and a light jacket or sweater is practical for evenings, especially in the desert.

For men, a lightweight conservative business suit for summer and medium weight or tweeds for touring the rest of the year. In the hottest months, men often wear sport shirts and slacks for touring. In the evening, dark and conservative clothes are appropriate. Formal attire is seldom worn and is not available for rent.

Comfortable walking shoes are a *must* for sightseeing, at sites of antiquity and shopping in the *souqs* in all seasons. Sunglasses are *vital* the year around. If you plan to do much traveling around the country, carry a supply of Kleenex, a collapsible drinking cup and disposable premoistened face cloths.

WHERE TO GO SIGHTSEEING . . . The main organization to facilitate tourism is the Tourism Bureau of the Syrian Government, 29 May Street (Tel. 17060), Damascus. Travel agencies in Damascus offer regular tours of the city and can arrange special tours for the surrounding area. Also, a guide can be obtained through the Guide Office (Tel. 17060). Guide fees are set at L.S. 7 for a half day (4 hours) for one to four persons and L.S. 12 for a full day (8 hours). For a party of five to 20, the fees are L.S. 12 for a half day and L.S. 20 for a full day. Fees are doubled for visits outside the city. In Aleppo there are no regular sightseeing tours, but an agent can arrange one for you upon request.

On a first trip to Syria visitors usually make Damascus their headquarters and tour the southern and central area from there. For sightseeing in the north, a stay of one or two nights in Aleppo is necessary. Trips to out-of-the-way places such as Palmyra or the Krak des Chevaliers are best made from Damascus, where tours with guides are available.

Travel in Syria is normally unrestricted except in certain areas in the south where permits are needed. **Hours at archaeological sites:** SUMMER (May 1–Sept. 30), 8 A.M.–1 P.M. daily, 4–7 P.M. (Fri. till 12:30 P.M.); WINTER (Oct. 1–Apr. 30), 8 A.M.–1 P.M. and 2 P.M.– 4 P.M. daily (Fri. till 11:30 A.M.). CLOSED Tuesdays.

SOURCES OF FURTHER INFORMATION . . . Pan Am's representative is Khoury Bros., al Nasr Street (Tel. 12500). Arab Information Center, 757 Third Avenue, New York, N. Y. 10017. For complete details on practical information and sightseeing, read *Travel Syria* by Kay Showker (Librairie du Liban, Beirut, 1966). For historical background, *Syria, an Historical Appreciation* by Robin Fedden (Robert Hall, London, 1955) is excellent.

St. Paul's Chapel, Damascus.

Umayyad Mosque, Damascus, which dates from the eighth century.

CHAPTER VI

SYRIA: THE COUNTRY AS A WHOLE

TYPES OF ACCOMMODATIONS

HOTELS

There are first-class hotels in Damascus and tourist-class ones in Aleppo, Latakia, Homs, Hama, Palmyra and Tartous. You should plan your sightseeing so as to arrive at one of these centers by evening, as hotel facilities are not available in smaller villages en route.

YOUTH HOSTELS

The headquarters of the Youth Hostel Association is located at 66 Al-Ali Street, Damascus (Tel. 21426). In winter the hostel can sleep 50 persons; in summer, 100 persons. The fee for members of the YHA is L.S. 1 per person per night. Guests must have their own linens, otherwise the rental fee for linens is an additional L.S. 1 for the full stay. Use of the kitchen and gas is 25 piasters per person per day; for hot shower or bath, 50 piasters. The hostel is open from 7–10 A.M. and from 4 to 10 P.M. Other YHA centers are in Aleppo, Boy Scout Building, Baghdad Railway Station Sq. (Tel.

14774), 10 beds; in Homs, Boy Scout Building, 10 beds; in Dera'a Youth Sport Center, 40 beds; in Bosra, at the ancient theater, 10 beds; in Idlib (halfway between Aleppo and Latakia), Sport Center, 10 beds.

CAMPSITES

The only organized camping site in Syria is near Harasta, four miles north of Damascus near the Aleppo highway. If you have the proper equipment, there are many good camping sites throughout the country.

TOURING

AUTOMOBILES AND MOTORCYCLES

A tourist can enter Syria with his car, provided he holds an international car license, a triptych and an international driving license. The car may remain in Syria for six months, and the authorization can be extended for a longer period. Insurance is not compulsory, but it is strongly recommended and is available locally at reasonable fees. Self-drive cars are not available, but you can hire a car with driver for a reasonable fee. For example, the one-way price from Damascus to Beirut is $6.25.

There are no special security regulations except in military zones. The speed limit in Syrian cities is 30 kilometers (18 miles) per hour. Traffic moves on the right. Roads between major cities are two-lane highways and are generally in good condition. The names of towns and villages are posted in French and Arabic at the entrance and exit of main roads. There are very few caution signs. City traffic and parking signs follow European designations.

Gasoline costs 40 piasters per liter, or about $.45 per gallon. In major towns service stations are plentiful, but on the open highway and off the beaten track they are scarce. Since distances are long between major cities where there are hotels and gasoline stations, you should plan your driving so as to arrive at your destination by sundown. Spare parts for most leading make automobiles are available. The Automobile Club of Syria is located on Al-Azmi Square, Damascus.

BICYCLES

These can be rented by the hour from shops at the entrance to Souq Hamidiyeh.

AFOOT

Recommended only in towns. Distances between towns and villages are too great to attempt excursions on foot. Damascus is a very pleasant city for walking. The modern sections have broad, tree-lined streets, and the old sections are made colorful by the milling crowds. There are no detailed maps of the city, but it is easy to learn even with a sketchy map and by remembering a few landmarks.

TRAINS

Syria is served by three railways. The Northern Railway is part of the old Berlin-to-Baghdad Railroad and runs from Turkey through Aleppo to Iraq. The Damas–Homs Railway operates from Aleppo through Hama and Homs to Tripoli, Lebanon. The Hejaz Railway runs from Damascus to Amman and is being reconstructed to Medina, Saudi Arabia. None of these trains carries many passengers. Since good and inexpensive transportation is available by other means, train travel is not recommended for tourists.

AIRPLANES

From Damascus Syrian Arab Airlines has daily air service to Aleppo and twice-weekly service to Palmyra. Latakia, Deir ez-Zor and Qameshli are also served by air. Domestic air fares are very low.

TRANSPORTATION TO
NEIGHBORING COUNTRIES

The cheapest means of transportation from Damascus to other cities in Syria and neighboring countries is by taxi-service (shared taxi). Prices are from the taxi garage in one city to the garage in another. For an extra charge of L.S. 1.50 you will be picked up or dropped off at a specific address. Damascus is 2 hours from Beirut by car, 4 hours driving time from Amman, and another hour to Jerusalem. Convenient transportation is also available by plane.

MAJOR EVENTS

Flower Day in Latakia, April 20: A traditional feast of the Alawite community. Townspeople and merchants decorate their houses and shops with beautiful spring flowers.

Grape harvest in Sueida, July 31: Prizes are given to the best exhibits of grapes. There is an election of a Queen and folklore dancing.

Damascus International Fair, August 25–September 30: This is the main fair held annually in the Middle East. Most of the major countries of the world along with well-known manufacturers from East and West have exhibits. The fair is also the main event in Syria during the year.

MENU TRANSLATOR — See Chapter XXII.

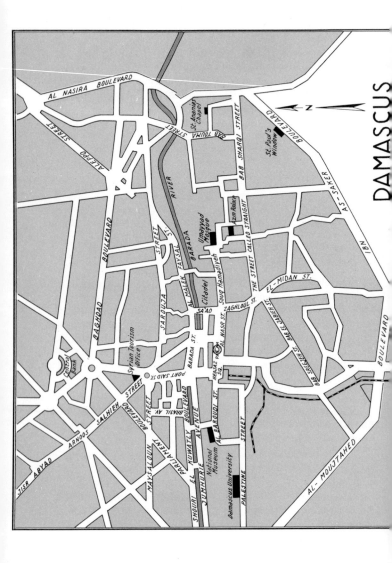

CHAPTER VII

DAMASCUS

DAMASCUS INTERNATIONAL AIRPORT

A new streamlined airport for Damascus is expected to open in late 1967. The present one is located at Mezzah about 15 minutes from town. Taxis and airline buses are available to transport passengers and their luggage into town. The taxi ride to a downtown hotel costs L.S. 5. (You should settle the price with the driver in advance.)

HOTELS

All hotels are subject to government control, and prices are fixed by the government. Advanced reservations are recommended. A 10% service charge is added to the bill. From June 15 to September 30 there might be an extra charge of $1.25 for air-conditioning and from November 15 until April 15 $.15 for central heating.

Hotel (Tel.)	Single	Double	Rooms
WITH BATH AND HALF BOARD			
Semiramis (13813) Jumhurie Ave.	$ 6.63	$12.26	125
New Omayad (17700) Brazil Ave.	$ 6.63	$12.26	66
Orient Palace (11510) Baroudi Sq.	$ 6.63	$12.26	71
Cattan (12513) Jumhurie Ave.	$ 6.37	$11.76	66
WITH BATH AND BREAKFAST			
Grand Hotel (11666) Shouhada Sq.	$ 2.75	$ 5.00	43
Samir Palace (19509) Shouhada Sq.	$ 2.75	$ 5.00	80
Rami Palace (19971) Rami St.	$ 2.75	$ 5.00	41
Ramsis (16702) Shouhada Sq.	$ 2.75	$ 5.00	37
Al Siyaha (14772) Shouhada Sq.	$ 2.75	$ 5.00	47
Kassioun (18200) Brazil Ave.	$ 2.75	$ 5.00	33
Ambassador (11328) Brazil Ave.	$ 2.75	$ 5.00	37

YOUTH HOSTELS
See Chapter VI.

CITY TRANSPORTATION

Bus service is available along major streets. The fare is 7½ piastres for most routes, 10 piastres on longer ones. Most bus routes begin and end along the main avenue leading to Souq Hamidiyeh. No. 4 bus is very useful for visitors. It passes near the American Embassy in Abou Roumaneh and continues to the Omayad Hotel and National Museum, goes near the university and ends at Souq Hamidiyeh.

Shared taxis, called *service* (pronounced *sirveece*), operate along the same routes as the buses. The charge is 25 piastres per person, with a maximum of five passengers. All Damascus taxis have red license plates and are usually available at the main intersections of the principal streets. You may also phone for a taxi. Taxis do not have meters, so it is important to settle the fare before you start out. L.S. 1.50 to 2 is the average fare for most trips within the city, and you need not tip the driver. A higher fare will be charged for longer trips or if extra stops are made. You should have the exact change to avoid any argument over the fare. Taxis may be hired for sightseeing at about L.S. 5 per hour. Arrangements can be made with a taxi company for trips to historic sites in Syria, Jordan and Lebanon. The charge depends upon the distance, but in general taxis are not expensive.

CITY SIGHTS

The capital of Syria is built at the foot of Mt. Qassioun, 2,275 feet above sea level, on the edge of the fertile Ghouta Oasis. It is watered by the Barada and the Awwaj rivers, the Biblical "rivers of Damascus." From the dawn of history the oasis of Damascus has been the "Paradise of Earth" to the tribes of the surrounding desert.

Damascus claims to be the oldest continuously inhabited city in the world. While its exact origins are lost in history, it was known as a city before the time of Abraham. The Ghouta Oasis, according to some legends, was the Garden of Eden. In the 10th century B.C. Damascus became the capital of the Aramaic kingdom and was called "the Great Holy Damascus." Its altar to the Syrian god Hadad was the most magnificent of all Syrian sanctuaries.

About 733 B.C. Damascus became part of Assyrian territory and later was conquered by the Babylonians. Under the Persians it was a provincial capital until it passed without struggle to Alexander the Great in 332 B.C. After Alexander's death Damascus was one of the prizes over which his successors—the Ptolemys and Seleucids—fought bitterly. In the 1st century B.C. Damascus came under Roman rule and remained part of the Roman province of Syria until the breakup of the empire.

Damascus was one of the first cities of the East to adopt Christianity. It was on the road to Damascus that Paul experienced his dramatic conversion. Emperor Theodosius I had a church built about A.D. 375 on the foundation of the Roman Temple of Jupiter.

When the Arabs took the city in A.D. 635, Damascus became the capital of the great Umayyad Empire, which stretched from the Atlantic Ocean to the Indus Valley. The Great Mosque built by the Umayyads on the site of the Roman temple remains today one of the principal sights of the city.

In 1516 Damascus along with all of Syria passed to the Ottoman Turks and for more than 300 years remained part of their Empire. The city's caravan trade on which it had long thrived was greatly cut after completion of the Suez Canal in the 19th century. After World War I Damascus was the capital of the "Kingdom of the Arabs," proclaimed in 1920 by Emir Faisal, but in the end it had to yield to the establishment of the French Mandate.

Damascus has a decidedly Oriental atmosphere with a Western overtone. The old town, enclosed by the ancient city wall, is characterized by miles of narrow, winding streets lined with bazaars and crowded with people. You will see Bedouins in flowing robes, peasants in their bright village costumes and dodge a few donkeys on the way. These bazaars and the stately minarets of 250 mosques give Damascus its Eastern aspect. The broad avenues of the new city and residential quarters are flanked by modern houses and office buildings and surrounded by trees and flowering gardens. Here both dress and ideas from Europe show their influence.

As a religious center Damascus was second only to Jerusalem. Its Biblical significance is indicated by such vestiges as St. Paul's Window, St. Ananias' Chapel and the Mausoleum of St. John the Baptist, while its Moslem heritage is reflected in the Umayyad Mosque and the graceful Tekieh Suleimaniah of the Ottoman period. Further, the city's museums are some of the best in the Middle East.

In the hills behind Damascus history speaks in many small villages, which still preserve their ancient way of life and colorful dress. In Maloula, for example, Aramaic, the language of Christ, is still spoken.

The heart of Damascus is Hedjaz Square in front of the railway station. From it the main boulevard of the town, Shoukri El-Kuwatly Street, bordering the Barada River, leads west to Beirut. On the east the large Nasr Boulevard leads to the Souq Hamidiyah. Along the street and those branching north and south are the principal shopping areas and historic sites. About a mile from the main square a road on the right leads up a hill to Abou Roumaneh, the most modern and beautiful residential section of town.

National Museum: Unquestionably, this is one of the most beautifully arranged museums in the world. Its valuable contents attract scientists and tourists alike. A famous archaeologist has paid it tribute with the following description: "It would be sufficient for measuring the importance of archaeological research in Syria to visit the Syrian Museum, which has neglected nothing in order to appeal to the imagination; they have done so not only by exhibiting the products of excavation in Syria which have revealed the cultures that have flourished in the country since four thousand years but also by successful monumental restorations. No museum in the world can show as spectacular restorations as those in the Damascus Museum."

Exhibits are divided into four departments: I. Syro-Oriental Antiquities; II. Syrian Antiquities in the Greek, Roman and Byzantine periods; III. Arab and Muslim Art; IV. Modern and Contemporary Art. The most important objects in the first department are the collections from Mari (3000–2000 B.C.), Ras Shamra/Ugarit (1500–1300 B.C.), and the stone on which the oldest known alphabet in the world was inscribed. One of the most outstanding exhibits of the museum is the famous Synagogue of Dura-Europos, built in A.D. 244. It was moved here from its original site on the Euphrates River after its discovery in the early 1930s by a group of archaeologists from Yale University. Hours: 8 A.M.–1 P.M. and 4–7 P.M. daily. Closed Tuesday. Entrance: 50 piasters.

The Temple of Jupiter: In about the 3rd century A.D. the Romans replaced the Temple of Hadad, which had been built in the 9th century B.C., with the Temple of Jupiter. Parts of it were used in the construction of the Umayyad Mosque. Today the center gates of the Roman temple are the eastern gates of the mosque.

Roman Arch: What has been called the "Triumphal Arch" was in fact part of the western propylaea of the Temple of Jupiter. It stands in front of the entrance to the Umayyad Mosque. Its pediment rests on six columns, 52 feet in height, crowned with Corinthian capitals.

The Ancient Walls and Gates: The great Roman wall which extended around the city was repaired many times over the centuries so that very little remains of the original structure. The lower level of big stones dates prior to the 12th century, while the upper courses belong to the era of Nur ed-Din, the Ayyoubids and the Mameluks. The East Gate (Bab Sharqi) is the only one of the seven gates built during the Roman era which has survived. It was built at the end of the 2nd century A.D. and opened onto the Street Called Straight. The Gate of Chagour (the Little Gate), located on the south side, was built under Nur ed-Din in the mid-12th century.

The Umayyad Mosque: On the site 3,000 years ago stood a pagan temple dedicated to Hadad, built by the Aramites. Centuries later the Romans built a temple to Jupiter of Damascus, a Roman version of the Syrian god Hadad. Emperor Theodosius (379–395) destroyed part of the Roman temple to build a church dedicated to St. John the Baptist. According to tradition, the site is the burial place of the head of St. John.

After the Arabs conquered Damascus they built the greatest monument of the empire on the site. The Umayyad Mosque came to symbolize the splendor of Damascus and the Umayyad era throughout the Moslem world. The mosque was decorated with fine mosaics of colored glass, gold and mother of pearl, which were designed in the form of nature scenes, decorative plants and symbolic pictures of Damascene buildings during the Umayyad period. Entrance fee, 1.50 piasters

Near the mosque is the elaborately decorated Mausoleum of Salah ed-Din (Saladin). The cupola was presented by the German Emperor William II during his visit in the late 19th century.

Northwest of the Umayyad Mosque on Zahiriah Street is the 13th-century Adlia School, in which one hall has a cross vault topped with a corbelled cupola. The frame of the door in basalt and limestone is decorated over the lintel with black stucco. The building now houses the Arab Academy. Across from Adlia School is Zahirieh School, dating from the late 13th century. It contains the mausoleum of the Mameluk Sultan Baybars. Its walls are faced with colored marble and mosaics.

El Azm Palace: The best example of an old Arab house in Damascus is the palace built about 1750 by Asad el Azm, a governor of Damascus under the Turks. The wood decorations of the walls and ceilings were made by skilled Damascene craftsmen, who developed the art to such a degree that today this type of woodcraft is called "Damascene" the world over.

The palace consists of two groups of halls: Salamlek (visitors' room) and the Haramlek (women's and children's quarters). The halls, walls and ceilings are engraved with marble, painted wood and inlaid with ivory in the shapes of plants and geometrical forms and calligraphy. Marble fountains with fresh water cool the interior. Trees and flowers around the two pools decorate the spacious court of the Haramlek. The rooms of the Haramlek now house a folklore museum. Entrance fee: 50 piasters.

The Citadel and the Bazaars: Halfway through the Souq el Khouja, one of the roofed bazaars, is the entrance to the Citadel (El Qalaa), built in the 13th century on the site of earlier Roman and Byzantine fortresses. Today it is the headquarters of the Syrian mounted police and part of it is a state prison. A special permit is needed for a visit.

From the Citadel, Souq el Khouja leads to the Souq Hamidiyeh, the most important bazaar in the city. Nearby is the famous Street

Called Straight. The New Testament records that after St. Paul's miraculous recovery of his sight during his visit to the house of Ananias, the apostle walked on the "Street Called Straight." In Roman times it was one of the main thoroughfares of the empire. The street crossed the old city from east to west and divided it into its northern and southern sections. Nothing is left of its ancient splendor except the remains of the monumental arch. Yet it is still one of the main streets of old Damascus and bustles with people in much the same manner as St. Paul must have seen.

The Church of Saint Ananias: Located at the end of the Street Called Straight, the Church rests on the traditional site of the house in which St. Paul recovered his eyesight. In an underground chapel constructed by Franciscan monks the walls are inscribed with the Biblical account of St. Paul's dramatic conversion. During his visit to Damascus the apostle came to the house of St. Ananias to discuss and learn the Christian faith. From the house St. Paul walked to the city wall, where his fellow Christians lowered him in a basket over the fortification. This part of the town wall has been restored and is called St. Paul's Cathedral, or St. Paul's Window.

El Tekieh Suleimaniah: A hostelry, built by Sultan Suleiman the Magnificent in 1554, was a shelter for pilgrims en route to Mecca. Its slim minarets and large cupola are favorite subjects for picture-taking. The Tekieh is located next to the National Museum.

EXCURSIONS

Two of Syria's main summer resorts Zabadany (28 miles, altitude 3,900 feet) and Bloudan (30 miles, 4,500 feet), are located in the mountains near Damascus. The scenery, the fresh air, mild climate and the mineral waters have made them popular summer retreats. Both resorts have good hotels and tourist facilities. The source of the Barada River at the foot of Mt. Gharbi lies five miles southwest of Zabadany; while a nearby mineral spring, Ain Bokain, is well known as a place for the treatment of kidney diseases.

Hotel (Tel.)	Single	Double	Rooms/Baths
	WITH FULL BOARD		
Bludan Al Kabir (011) Bludan	$ 7.50	$13.76	110

SEIDNAYA: 22 miles northeast of Damascus, altitude 4,640 feet, population 2,500 . . . According to legend, the Monastery of Seidnaya was built as a result of a miracle experienced by Justinian in A.D. 547, when the Emperor, en route to fight the Persians, camped in the Syrian desert near Damascus. While Justinian was searching for water for his men, he caught sight of a deer. The Emperor aimed his shot, but was stopped by a brilliant light. The deer, transformed into a lady dressed in white, pointed to the Emperor, saying, "You will not kill me, Justinian, but will establish for me a monastery on this rock." Then the light faded and the lady vanished. Traditions say that the Virgin appeared once more to Justinian and showed him a magnificent design for the monastery.

The Monastery of Seidnaya is one of the most important religious places in the East and is visited annually by pilgrims and tourists. The first senior nun of the monastery was Justinian's sister. Moslems share with Christians the respect of this shrine. Saladin's sister often visited it. A small room called the "Shaghoura" contains a number of old silver and gold icons and oil chandeliers. Its most important treasure is the Icon of the Virgin, said to have been painted by Saint Luke. Tradition recalls that during the Crusades, the Knights Templars sent oil, which oozed from the icon's face, to churches of France and Europe as a holy relic.

The monastery is built on a rock overlooking the village of Seidnaya. At the foot of the monastery stands a square building in yellow stone, known as Mar Peters. Its history and purpose are unknown. The area surrounding the village has many chapels and churches named after Orthodox saints. On the neighboring hill there are grottos cut in the rocks which were used as tombs.

MALOULA: 36 miles northeast of Damascus, altitude 5,200 feet, population 1,500 . . . After passing through a mountain pass in the eastern slopes of the Anti-Lebanon Mountains, you come to a village built on the craggy terraces of a steep mountain. Its houses, some in grottoes and caves, are accentuated by pale-blue paint around the windows.

Above the village a path through the rock cliffs leads to the top of the mountain. According to tradition the split, called Al-Fajj, was caused by a miracle. When St. Takla, one of the pupils of St. Paul, was escaping from her pagan father, she reached Maloula, where she found the high mountain standing in her way. She raised her hands and prayed. The mountain split at once and she passed safely.

The monastery which St. Takla built here is one of the earliest Orthodox settlements in the world. Near the tomb of the saint water drips from the rocky ceiling. Many pilgrims believe that the water has miraculous powers.

The Convent of St. Sarkis stands at the top of the village. Its dome was built in the Byzantine period. From here there is an excellent view of Maloula and the surrounding countryside.

What adds to the fascination and distinction of Maloula is that the inhabitants still speak Aramaic—the language of Jesus. Spoken Aramaic has vanished from the world except in three small Syrian villages, the largest of which is Maloula.

CHAPTER VIII

SYRIA: TOWNS AND SITES

ALEPPO: 216 miles north of Damascus, 116 miles northeast of Latakia, population 750,000 . . . Situated near the Turkish border between the Orontes and the Euphrates rivers, Aleppo has held a strategic commercial position along the caravan routes since ancient times. Today, with a population larger than Damascus, it is the second most important city in Syria.

Over the 4,000 years of its history Aleppo has kept its Hittite name, Halap, in the Arabic form of *Halab*. Before 1000 B.C. it was the center of the prosperous Hittite Kingdom of Yamhud. From the middle of the 2nd millennium B.C., it was a point of rivalry between the Hittites and the Egyptians and, later, between the Assyrians and the Egyptians. The city was controlled by the Assyrians from the beginning of the 1st millennium until the fall of Nineveh (612 B.C.), by the Persians until Alexander the Great and by the Seleucids until the Roman conquest in 65 B.C. Throughout these periods Aleppo never ceased to be prosperous. It gained further in commercial importance after the fall of Palmyra in A.D. 272, and later it flourished under the Byzantine Empire.

After its conquest by the Arabs in 637, Aleppo lost ground to Damascus, the capital of the Umayyad Empire. For the next four centuries it was held intermittently by the Byzantines and various Arab dynasties, until it was taken in 1070 by the Seljuk Turks. In 1183 the famous Saladin united the Moslems of Syria and Egypt by capturing the emirate of Aleppo. Under his son, El Zaher Ghazi, the great citadel was built in its present form. After a brief invasion in the 13th century by Hulagu Khan, the grandson of Genghis Khan, Aleppo passed to the Egyptian Mameluks, who made it the chief town of the province. From 1516 to World War I it was part of the Ottoman Empire and became the main European trading center in Syria. After the war Aleppo fell under the French Mandate until 1945, when it was united with other parts of the country into the Republic of Syria.

Aleppo is the major commercial and industrial center of Syria, particularly for the textile industry. Almost half of the city's population is Christian, and there is a large Armenian community.

There is daily air service from Damascus (1 hr., 20 min.) and thrice weekly from Beirut (1 hr., 20 minutes) to Aleppo. Latakia is about 4 hours by car. There is also rail connection for Turkey, Iraq and Lebanon.

The U.S. Consulate is located in the Sebil Quarter (Tel. 17600).

Hotel (Tel.)	Single	Double	Rooms
BARON (10880) Baron Ave.	$ 3.75	$ 6.26	60
Ramsis (16701) Baron Ave.	$ 3.25	$ 5.50	34
New Omayad (14104) Central Bank St.	$ 3.25	$ 5.50	30

CITY SIGHTS: Aleppo has developed into a modern city without disturbing its ancient center. In the old quarters, the khans, bazaars, baths, houses, schools and mosques of the once great caravan city can be visited. The souqs of Aleppo are famous through the Middle East. Unquestionably, they are the best. The narrow lanes covered by high walls and arched stone roofs run for miles. Their atmosphere is authentic, as they are still used in much the same way as in olden days.

A tour of the old city can begin at the 13th-century *Gate of Antioch*, which leads into the *Souq el Atarin*, once the main thoroughfare of the medieval town. Nearby is the *Madresseh Mukaddamiye*, formerly a church converted into a Moslem school in the 12th century. It is the oldest *madresseh* (church school) in Aleppo. Near the souq of the dyer's shops is the *Bahramiye Mosque* in Turkish style and the *Khan el Gumrok*, which housed the banking houses and consuls of France, Britain and the Netherlands in the 17th century. Opposite the khan is the *Great Mosque*, originally built in the 8th century by the Umayyad Caliph El Walid. Most of the present building dates from the 12th century. The mosque was erected on a square in front of a Byzantine cathedral, now the *Madresseh Halawiye*. The cathedral is said to have been built by Empress Helena on the site of a pagan temple.

North of the Great Mosque is the *Madresseh Sharafiye*, the doorway of which has a honeycombed arch dating from the 13th century. Its library contains valuable ancient manuscripts. East of the Great Mosque is the 17th-century *Khan al Wazir*, the largest and most handsome caravanseria in Aleppo. *Khan al Saboon*, north of the Khan Wasir, was built by the governor of Aleppo in the early 16th century.

On the south side of the old city near Bab Qinnesrin is the *Maristan Arghun*, a 14th-century hospital and insane asylum. The inner courtyard has a pool which reflects the east and west iwans (salons), creating a restful setting for the inmates in olden times. *Bab Qinnesrin*, 13th century, is the best-preserved gateway of the ancient city wall.

In the Jedeidah quarter on the north side of the old city there are many old houses with richly decorated interiors which are typically Oriental in design. Basically, the houses were built around an open courtyard with a pool and a garden of fruit and citrus trees. The best examples are *Dallal House*, 17th century, and *Sayegh House*, 18th century, which are now occupied by Armenian schools, and *Basil House*, early 18th century.

West of the old city and dominating all the town is the *Citadel of Aleppo* on a rocky spur 1,440 feet at the summit. The site was occupied as early as 1000 B.C. and possibly even earlier. Assyrian, Hittite and Byzantine remnants have been found. It had a temple to the Syrian god Hadad, and as late as the 4th century A.D. the Romans offered sacrifices to Zeus on the temple site. At that time it was probably the acropolis of the city. Eventually the hill came to be a fortress. In the 12th century A.D. its huge walls and the gates were added, and in 1292 it served as a royal residence. Today the citadel is considered one of the purest examples of Moslem military architecture remaining.

The steep, smooth fortress walls rise from a moat 72 feet deep and 98 feet wide. The walls are over half a mile around and follow the oval shape of the hill. In some places the walls are 39 feet high.

The entrance of the citadel, on the south side, is in excellent condition. The gate is connected to the fortress by a bridge on which there are two towers dating from the early 16th century. These towers lead to a larger tower which dates from the 12th century. The passageway inside the tower has five bends and three gates intended to resist every possible attack from an enemy. Each gate is named after its decoration—the gate of serpents with two interlocking dragons, and the gate of the weeping lion and the smiling lion. These gates (13th century) still have finely executed ironwork.

At the top of the big tower there is a throne hall, which was built in the 15th century under the Mameluks. The façade is beautifully ornamented with engravings and decorations, and its door is decorated with moldings. (The hall is being completely restored.)

Inside the citadel there is a wall that is said to date from the Seleucid period. There are passages, wide underground halls cut out of rock, tunnels with secret passages, the ruins of a bath and palace that was once decorated with marble mosaics, and a pool. On the tell stand the small mosque of Ibrahim built by Nur-ed-Din in 1167 and the Great Mosque built by El Zaher Ghazi in 1214. Nearby are the ruins of a Hittite temple. The square minaret of the Great Mosque, 68 feet in height, served as a watch tower. The view from the minaret overlooks the city and its suburbs to the edge of the desert.

War and earthquakes destroyed many parts of the huge fortress, and over the centuries it was rebuilt many times. Entrance fee: 50 piasters.

In front of the citadel is the imposing *Khosrafiye Mosque,* 16th century, and the *Madresseh Zahimiye,* 13th century, which contains the tomb of El Zaher Ghazi, the son of Saladin. Southwest of the citadel is the *El Otrush Mosque,* 15th century. Farther south is the 13th-century *Madresseh el Firdows,* the most beautiful religious monument in Aleppo. Especially to be noted are the graceful doorway, courtyard and pool, and the *mihrab* of inlaid marble.

The *Aleppo Museum* has an outstanding display of archaeological monuments from the Sumerian, Hittite, Assyrian, Phoenician and other ancient civilizations which flourished on Syrian soil. From the important city of *Mari* the collection includes a statue of the goddess of Fertility, another of Ishtup Ilum (King of Mari in the late 3rd millennium B.C.), god of the sun Shamash, and statues of the kings and princes. Exhibits from *Ugarit* include a stele of the Baal of Ugarit and a bronze harp with an iron edge said to be the oldest-known iron in the world (15th century B.C.). Entrance fee: 50 piasters.

Aleppo College was founded by American missionaries in 1860 as a Seminary for girls in Aintab, Turkey. Later with the North Syria School for Boys it merged into Aleppo College. Today it accommodates about 700 students ranging from ages 12 to 20 and offers a wide range of subjects. The campus is located on the south side of the new city.

EXCURSIONS

Monastery of St. Simeon Stylite (Qalaat Seman and Deir Seman): 41 miles via Tell Aqibrin, or 28 miles by a track from Aleppo . . . In the 4th century A.D. lived one of the strangest men in Christian history. The stories of his extreme endurance sound unbelievable. Simeon, born about A.D. 390, lived for 27 years on top of a pillar 88 feet high. From here he preached to his disciples and pilgrims, who came great distances to hear him.

After the death of Simeon a large cathedral was built around the pillar. There is still a small piece of the pillar inside the church ruins. The cathedral was built in the shape of a cross which intersected in an octagonal court. It was considered one of the greatest Christian monuments in the East for its architecture, decorations, arches and façade.

Another building southeast of the cathedral was used for housing pilgrims. About 200 yards south of the basilica lies the baptistery, considered one of the finest remnants of Christian architecture in Syria. The group of buildings are known as Qalaat Seman (the Fortress of Simeon). In later years the buildings were used as a fortress by both the Crusaders and the Arabs.

The Monastery or Deir Seman, situated about 1/3 mile from the cathedral, is a ten-minute walk down a steep slope. Many Western churches in the Middle Ages were patterned on the style of this monastery.

BANIYAS: 35 miles south of Latakia on the Mediterranean, population 1,500 . . . The ancient town of Baniyas dates back to Phoenician times and was apparently important under the Romans and Byzantines. The Crusaders settled here in 1098 and called it *Valenia*. The Mansur family who owned it at that time ceded it to the Knights Hospitalers in 1186. After its fall to the Mameluk Sultan Qalawan, it was never more than a village. Today, it is important as an oil terminal. The large oil pipeline from Kirkuk, Iraq, is located north of the village.

Sixteen miles north of Baniyas (2 miles west of the Latakia road) is *Jeble*, the *Gabala* of the Phoenicians. The town was important in ancient times, judging from its large Roman theater. It is about 300 feet in diameter and could accommodate 7,000 spectators. Next to the theater is a mosque containing the tomb of a famous Moslem saint. The mosque was built on the site of an ancient church. From Jeble a mountain track leads to the Ismaili *Fortress of Beni Israel*.

A mile south of Baniyas a road east into the mountains leads to the *Castle of Marqab,* the Margat Castle of the Crusaders. (From the coastal highway the castle is in view for five miles south of Baniyas.) Authorities say that the castle was originally built in 1062. In 1186 it was ceded to the Knights Hospitalers, who held it until 1285, when it was captured by the Mameluk Sultan Qalawan. The fortress crowns the summit of a mountain overlooking the Mediterranean Sea. To the north and south the Syrian mountains and coast stretch for miles. The fortress was built of basalt rock, which gives it a formidable appearance.

BOSRA (Busra Eski Sham): 85 miles southeast of Damascus, 26 miles east of Deraa, altitude 2,625 feet., population 3,000 . . . The history of Bosra goes back 6,000 years. It is mentioned in the Old Testament in connection with the Amalekites. Bosra came under Greek rule in the late 4th century B.C. Three hundred years later it was the capital of the Nabataean Arabs, who embellished it with palaces and temples. After the Roman conquest it became the capital of the province of Arabia and had a population of 80,000. The city prospered as the meeting place of commercial caravans, and its markets were full of goods from all over the world. Under the Byzantines Bosra was the seat of a bishopric and later of an archbishopric and had a magnificent cathedral. After the Arab conquest the city became a halting place for pilgrims en route to Mecca.

The most important remains in Bosra are from the Roman period. The theater, dating from the early 2nd century, is said to be the largest and

Hotel (Tel.)	Single	Double	Rooms

the most complete Roman theater in the world. It could hold 15,000 spectators and was built in three tiers. The Byzantines left the great cathedral and house of the Monk Bohaira, while the Islamic era left the Umayyad Mosque of Omar and the Mosque of Fatima.

DERAA: 65 miles south of Damascus, population 8,000 . . . Chief town of the Hauran district and turn-off point for the ancient site of Bosra. It is located near the Jordanian frontier. Deraa is ancient *Edrei,* mentioned in the Bible in connection with Og, King of Bashan. Thirteen miles northwest of Deraa are the waterfalls of *Tell Shehab,* from where there is a good view of the Yarmuk Valley and the Mezeirib River, which flows into the Yarmuk. With the necessary equipment it is a good area for camping.

HAMA: 125 miles north of Damascus, population 65,500 . . . Hama clings to the banks of the winding Orontes and is surrounded by gardens irrigated by ancient Roman water wheels. Excavations of a tell north of Hama reveal that the site was occupied as early as the Neolithic period. As *Hamath,* it is mentioned often in the Bible. Its builder is said to be Arados, King of the island of Arwad. The city was invaded by the Hittites about 1,000 years before Christ. Around 1100 B.C. it became the north capital of the Aramaic kingdom. In 720 B.C. it was taken by the Assyrians under Sargon II. Later, it passed to the Persians, then to Alexander the Great in 332 B.C. and afterwards to the Seleucids.

Hama fell under Roman rule after Pompey's conquest of the East. With the breakup of the empire, Hama came under Byzantine rule. In the 7th century it was taken by the Arabs. The Crusaders held it briefly in the 12th century, until it was regained by Saladin in 1178. Afterward it was governed by one of his nephews. In the 16th century it passed to the Turks.

The historic monuments in Hama include the *Great Mosque,* built on the foundations of a pagan temple that had been converted into a church; the 13th-century *Mausoleum of el Malek el Muzaffar;* and the *Mosque of el-Hayyat,* with the tomb of Abu el Fida, a famous Arab historian and descendant of Saladin. The *House of Al Azm,* governor of Hama in the 18th century, is a miniature of the Azm Palace in Damascus. It houses a museum, and the view of the Orontes from its terrace is charming.

At Hama nine water wheels (naoura), 90 feet in diameter, elevate the water of the Orontes River (Nahr el Assi) to irrigate the farmlands and gardens and to carry water to the houses and baths of the town. These ancient wheels produce a melancholy sound, which gives the town and its gardens a romantic aspect.

Hama is a conservative town, less touched by Western influence than any other large town in Syria. Its souqs are unspoiled and colorful with local costumes.

Hotel (Tel.)	Single	Double	Rooms
Abu El Fida (1770) Hurrieh Square	$ 2.00	$ 3.26	20
Basman (2838) Kuwatly St.	$ 1.75	$ 2.76	18

EXCURSIONS

In the vicinity of Hama and along the road to Aleppo you can see picturesque villages that are characteristic of the northern Syrian plains. The village houses are cubical in form and topped by a dome. They are built with unbaked bricks and shaped like sugar loaves.

Castle of Shaizar, 16 miles northwest of Hama on the site of ancient *Cesara* . . . The castle belonged to the princes of the Beni Munqis, who had seized it from the Byzantines in the 11th century. It was captured two centuries later by the Mameluks under Baybers and later was destroyed by the Mongols. The castle was built on a bend in the Orontes which commanded a strategic passage on the river.

Qalaat el Mudiq, 40 miles northwest of Hama . . . The castle stands on the site of *Apamea,* once one of the great cities of Syria. Apamea, together with Antioch and Seleucia on the Tigris, were the most important centers in the Seleucid kingdom and prospered also under Roman rule. The Persians occupied Apamea in A.D. 540. It was seized by the Crusaders in 1106 and regained by Nur ed-Din in 1139. Archaeological excavations of Apamea have revealed ancient temples and remnants of the gates and pillars. The city walls once covered an area of four miles. The main street, 1,600 yards long and 113 feet wide, crossed the town from north to south. At each end stood monumental gates. The Gate of Antioch (2nd century A.D.) was in two sections, about 19 feet high, and joined by an arch. North of the gate are the remains of a basilica. Beautiful mosaics from the 4th and 6th centuries were found near the Roman theater.

At **Maarat el Numan,** 32 miles north of Hama, stands the Tomb of Abul 'ala al Ma'ari, the most famous philosopher and poet of Islam, who lived in the early 11th century. There is also a mosque with a minaret dating from the 12th century, a school of the same period, a 16th-century khan and the remains of a citadel.

HOMS: 97 miles north of Damascus, altitude 1,625 feet, population 129,500 . . . The third largest city in Syria lies in the fertile Orontes Valley. Homs is situated in the center of the country halfway between the coast to the west, Palmyra to the east, Aleppo in the north and Damascus in the south. It is the communication center of the Damascus–Aleppo road and railroad. Since World War II it has become an important center for industry, among which is the Petroleum Company refinery.

Homs is ancient *Emesa,* the site of a great temple to the sun god. It became important after the marriage of Septimus Severus to a Homs citizen and the election of Elagabalus (Heliogabalus), the high priest of the temple of Homs, as Roman Emperor in A.D. 218.

The Arabs conquered Homs in the 7th century. The town's *Great Mosque* is dedicated to the famous Arab leader Khaled Ibn el Walid, who headed the Moslem army. The mosque rests on the traditional site of his burial place. The Crusaders captured Homs in 1099, and in the 16th century it passed to the Turks. Homs joined forces with Ibrahim Pasha of Egypt in 1832 in his unsuccessful attempt to dislodge the Turks from Syria.

Other historic sites include a citadel and the underground ruins of a chapel and monastery. In the Syrian Aramean Church of Homs a holy relic, said to be the sash of the Virgin Mary, was discovered under the altar in 1953. Near Homs stands the famous Krak des Chevaliers, the best preserved Crusader Castle in the world. *Tell Nebi Mind,* 11 miles from Homs

Hotel (Tel.)	Single	Double

near the village of Qattineh, is identified as Qadesh, the site of the famous battle between Ramses II and the Hittites. The battle is described on the temple walls at Luxor, Abydos and Abu Simbel in Egypt.

Raghdan (2211)	$ 2.50	$ 4.50
Shoukri Kuwatly St.		
Basman (2009)	$ 2.00	$ 2.50
Abul-Alaa Street		

KRAK DES CHEVALIERS (Qalaat el Hosn): 36 miles west of Homs, 11 miles north of Tell Kalakh, 78 miles north of Beirut . . . For a trip into the Middle Ages, none could be as dramatic as the Crusader Castle of Krak des Chevaliers. Qalaat el Hosn, as it is known in Arabic, is the best preserved and most magnificent Crusader castle in the world. Over its thirty towers and high keeps the Knights Hospitalers kept the great banner of St. John of Jerusalem flying for almost two centuries.

The castle was originally built in 1031 as an Arab fortress. It was enlarged by the Crusaders and later by the Mameluks, which explains the variety of its architecture and decoration. The Crusaders occupied the fortress in 1110. Raymond, Count of Tripoli, gave it to the Hospitalers in 1142. Finally, in 1271, after four years of siege, the Crusaders were expelled by the Mameluk Sultan Baybers.

The Krak is situated on the summit of Jebel Khalil, 2,460 feet above sea level. Its location was carefully chosen to enable the Crusaders to observe any movement on the mountain pass between Tripoli and Homs, or between the Bekaa Valley and the Plains of Homs.

The Krak once held a garrison of 5,000 men. It is surrounded by two great walls, one inside the other. The walls are separated by a moat which was filled with water and encircled by another trench on the outside. The southern side of the fortress lies against a hill from which the enemy could attack. To ensure its defense, this side was reinforced with a solid wall and three towers. The palace itself was guarded by huge towers with gigantic angles. Inside the fortress there was a chapel in one hall. The massive walls, towers, bastions, arches, cross-vaulting, halls, porches, underground stables, huge kitchen, dining halls and sleeping quarters are on a scale so enormous it staggers the imagination. How did they do it!

The castle is situated amid beautiful scenery stretching as far as the eye can see. The view of the Bekaa Valley on the south is spectacular. Lake Homs near Qattineh can be seen in the distance on the east, beyond lies the Syrian desert. To the north stretch the Plains of Homs and the Nosairi mountains. On the western horizon lies the Mediterranean Sea. As one looks over the panorama, the highways and byways of the past suddenly come to life out of the dusty pages of our history books. The castle has had extensive and excellent restoration by the Syrian Department of Antiquities. Entrance fee: L.S. 1. Closed Tuesdays.

Monastery of St. George: 2 miles north of Krak des Chevaliers . . . The Greek Orthodox Monastery of St. George was founded during the time of Justinian. The ancient chapel, probably dating from the 13th century, contains some old icons relating episodes in the life of St. George and beautiful wood paneling. The new church, built in 1857, contains a large collection of icons, crucifixes and silver lamps.

Hotel (Tel.)	Single	Double

By returning to Tell Kalakh, you can continue to the village of Safita (the Crusader Castle of Chastel-Blanc) and to Tartous. (See page 00.)

LATAKIA: 116 miles west of Aleppo on the Mediterranean, 214 miles from Damascus, 149 miles north of Beirut, population 50,000 . . . Syria's major seaport is one of the oldest sites on the Mediterranean. During the 2nd millennium B.C. it formed part of the territory of Ugarit (7 miles north of the present city). Later it fell under Assyrian, Babylonian and Persian rule, but it seems to have been unimportant until the Seleucid era. Laodicea, as the Seleucids called it, along with Antioch, Apamea and Seleucia, were the main cities of the Empire. Latakia apparently continued to flourish under the Romans, Byzantines and Arabs. After several attempts the Crusaders captured the city in 1102 and named it *La Liche*. It became the seat of a Latin bishopric and a commandery of the Hospitalers. A century after the Crusaders had departed, a Cypriot expedition sacked the city. For the following two centuries Latakia was a dependency of the viceroys of Hama. In 1516 it passed to the Ottomans. After Syria's loss of its port, Alexandretta (Iskenderun), Latakia was developed and has served as the country's major seaport since World War II.

Despite its ancient origins, Latakia has few historic sites. On the south side of the city is a colonnade with fine Corinthian capitals, thought to be part of a Temple of Adonis. Nearby is a Roman tetrapylon. North of the town is an important necropolis.

	ROOM WITH BATH	
Al Siaha (2001)	$ 2.75	$ 5.00
Rashid Ave.		
Semiramis (1158)	$ 1.63	$ 2.76
Shouhada Sq.		
Blue Beach Motel (1144)	Bungalows	$ 5.00
5 miles north of Latakia		

EXCURSIONS

Latakia is the starting point for excursions to several important historic sites.

Ras Shamra (7 miles north of Latakia) is one of the oldest sites in the world. It was one of the main city-states of the Phoenicians. As *Ugarit* it is mentioned in Hittite inscriptions and in the tablets of Tell el Amarna (14th century B.C.) in Egypt. Yet excavations indicate that occupation of the site goes back to 6000 B.C. Five levels in all have been discovered, and excavations are continuing to uncover extremely valuable information for archaeologists and historians. Among the most important was a tablet on which was inscribed the oldest alphabet ever discovered (now in the National Museum). The language of Ugarit has been invaluable to scholars in refining their knowledge of ancient Semitic languages and cultures—to the extent that many of the traditionally accepted meanings of words in the Bible are now being revised with the new knowledge.

The site of Ugarit was discovered by accident in 1928. Systematic excavations have continued on the first and most important level—that of the

Hotel (Tel.)	Single	Double	Rooms

Phoenician era. They have revealed a fortified town, palace, houses, shops, underground burial chambers and a temple.

The impressive *Castle of Sayhoun* (the Saône of the Crusaders) stands on the peak of a mountain east of Latakia. From the main coastal highway (2 miles south of the city) a road east into the mountain leads to Hafeh (19 miles). Here a secondary road turns south for 3 miles from where the castle in all its splendor is in view, you must leave your car here and walk (one hour) up very steep terrain. (A new road leading to the castle is under construction.) The castle site is known to have been used as early as Phoenician times, though it was not important until Crusader days. The castle is built on a ridge surrounded by two deep ravines. To complete its isolation, the Crusaders made a ditch 49 feet wide, cut entirely from rock.

Farther up the mountains above Hafeh is *Slenfeh* (34 miles, altitude 4,000 feet), the leading summer resort of the Latakia area.

	ROOM/BATH/FULL BOARD		
Al Siaha and Al Istiaf (6)	$ 5.38	$10.26	50

Another popular summer resort, *Kassab* (altitude 3,445 feet), lies 33 miles north of Latakia on the Turkish border. Kassab is ancient *Casembelle* of the Crusaders. It rests on Jebel Aqra, the Mount Casius of antiquity.

Al Rawda (8)	$ 1.38	$ 2.50	31

PALMYRA: 144 miles northeast of Damascus, 99 miles east of Homs . . . Palmyra was an oasis city on the northern edge of the Syrian Desert, lying in a privileged position about 125 miles equidistant from the Mediterranean and the Euphrates. Tradition claims that it is the Biblical *Tadmor*, the city of Palms, founded by Solomon. Yet references to it have been found in Assyrian and Akkadian tablets from Mari dating about 2000 B.C.

Palmyra's rise came with the development of trade between Syria and Babylon in the 1st century B.C. After the Roman conquest the city reached its peak in the 2nd and 3rd centuries A.D. by serving as a trade center for caravans moving between Asia and the Mediterranean. Previously this trade had been in the hands of the Nabataeans in Petra.

Under Roman rule early in the 3rd century A.D. Palmyra was made a Roman colony and its citizens exempted from taxes. The Romans allowed a local leader, Septimus Odenathus (Odainat), to build Palmyra into a strong autonomous state as a buffer to Persia on its eastern flank. Odainat's territory embraced most of the Eastern Roman Empire. After his death his proud and daring widow, Zenobia, increased the territory by conquering Egypt and most of Asia Minor.

Zenobia, called the Queen of the Desert, has been described in literature as "far more beautiful than Cleopatra. Her eyes glimmered with an extraordinary charm." Zenobia was a learned woman, and history claims that she surpassed her clansmen with unusual wisdom and ability.

In 271 Zenobia and her son assumed the titles of Augusta and Augustus and had coins struck bearing their image. This, in effect, meant open rebellion against Rome. After several attempts to come to terms with her, Emperor Aurelian at the head of his army met Zenobia's forces at Homs. The Romans were victorious and pursued Zenobia's army to

Palmyra. Zenobia, as a last-minute maneuver, rushed east to seek the help of the Persians. Just as she reached the banks of the Euphrates, the Romans caught her. Palmyra then surrendered and Zenobia was taken prisoner to Rome. The story goes that the victorious Aurelian placed her at the head of his triumphal procession to walk with her hands bound in chains of gold.

The year following Zenobia's defeat, Palmyra rebelled. Aurelian returned to put down the rebellion. He sacked the town and thereafter it ceased to be important. Except for a brief period under the Byzantines, Palmyra, like Zenobia, sank into oblivion. Even the ruins were forgotten until the 17th century, when British tradesmen in Aleppo reported tales with a legendary sound about an oasis trade stop in the middle of the burning Syrian desert. Finally, in 1853, the explorers Robert Woods and H. Dawkins published *The Ruins of Palmyra*, in which the inscriptions they had laboriously copied gave the key to the deciphering of the alphabet used by the Palmyrenes. From that time on archaeologists and tourists have eagerly crossed the empty, hot desert to feast their eyes on Palmyra's great temples and tower tombs.

Palmyra surpasses Baalbeck in beauty. The gigantic temples and colonnades seem strange in the middle of an enormous desert. Yet this unnaturalness is part of Palmyra's appeal. Added to this is its extraordinary color. Temples of apricot-tinted stone rise out of the tawny sand and stand against a clear blue sky, forming a scene of unrivaled beauty, unduplicated in the world.

Palmyra is reputedly the largest area of ancient ruins in the world. At its height the city held a population of 30,000 and was the headquarters of world trade reaching as far away as France and India.

The Ruins

The immense Temple of Bel was erected in the 1st and 2nd centuries A.D. It consisted of two parts: an elevated esplanade and the temple (cella) with sacrificial altars and pools. Along each side there was a portico with a roof supported by a double row of Corinthian columns, on which once stood the statues of famous men. In the middle there was an altar and a temple with Roman-style decorations. At the entrance a monumental stairway led to an outer portico with eight columns flanked by a tower on each side. The inner court was reached through three large bronze doors. The columns of the portico numbered 390, of which only 7 survive.

The northern niche of the temple was the Holy of Holies and contained the statues of the Palmyrene triad: Bel, Yarihibol and Aghbol. Its monolithic ceiling is a cupola decorated with the seven planets, Jupiter (Bel) in the center, encircled by the 12 signs of the Zodiac. Left of the niche, a staircase leads to the top, from where you get a magnificent view of the ruins of Palmyra and the surrounding oasis.

The *Ancient Town* of Palmyra had long streets leading to various buildings. The impressive Triumphal Arch with its three gates was the entrance to the marketplace and was followed by a Street of Columns lined with 375 pillars, 31 feet in height, of which 150 columns remain. These connected the Temple of Bel, theater, forum, senate and banquet hall.

The colonnaded street crossed the city from west to east. In the middle a tetrapyle marked the main crossroad. The street westward ended near the public square (Agora), closed by four porticos which were adorned with statues of Roman and Palmyrene officials and senators. Next is the theater (A.D. 200) and Senate. Right of the Triumphal Arch are the public baths, restored under Diocletian. West of the Agora is a temple, believed to be the Banquet Hall used by the religious brotherhood for sacred meals.

East of the tetrapyle there are eight columns higher than the others. The second supported a statue of Zenobia and the third that of her husband. West of the tetrapyle along the main colonnade stands a house tomb of the 3rd century.

The Temple of Bel (Baal) Shameen: In the northeast corner of the ruins (near the hotel) stands the most complete temple in Palmyra, built in A.D. 130 and dedicated to the god of fertility and growth. It has an oblong hall and porch, and the ceiling is supported by six pillars. This temple was made a basilica in the Byzantine era.

The Tombs: Most of the tombs are situated in the southern and western valley of the town, outside the city wall. Those known as the *Tombs of the Towers* are 150 in number. They are square in form and built in three or four tiers. The walls of the rooms were designed to hold the coffins of the dead. The tower tombs represent an architectural creation peculiar to the Palmyrenes. The most important one, *Jamblichos Tower*, dating from A.D. 83, stands on a hill known as Umm Belqis. Here archaeologists found mummies wrapped in silk from China. Westward along the Homs road in the bed of the valley stands the *Elahbel Tomb*, completed in A.D. 103. The recesses for the dead were closed with limestone slabs on which the figures of the deceased were carved in high relief. The track to the southwestern cemetery runs by an ancient gate, through which ran the Roman road from Damascus to the Euphrates.

The *Underground Tombs* are rich in statues and decorations. The most important of these is the *Tomb of the Three Brothers*, built in A.D. 140. It included 65 bays each with 6 recesses for the dead, or 390 in all. The reliefs and frescoes are outstanding and show the Oriental influence in Greco-Roman art of the period.

On the Homs road about one mile from the oasis are the *Sulphur Baths*. The Roman steps leading into the water are still in good condition.

The Museum: Entrance fee is 50 piasters. A modern building near the antiquity site houses some of the important finds at Palmyra; others are on display at the National Museum in Damascus.

The Fortress of Fakhr ed-Din al Maani is located on the northwest side of Palmyra on the summit of a hill overlooking the ruins and oasis. Its construction is characteristic of castles built after the Turkish conquest. The upper terrace is enclosed between seven towers. It is well worth the steep climb for the view.

The ruins of Palmyra are considered among the most important not only in Syria but in the whole Middle East.

How to get there: From Homs a good asphalt road runs through the desert parallel to the I.P.C. pipeline. At the pumping station (T 4, 61 miles) there is a shop where you can obtain food and drinks. The drive takes about three hours. By air, Syrian Arab Airlines leaves Damascus at 8:30 A.M. on Friday and Sunday and arrives in Palmyra at 9:30 A.M. en route to Deir-ez-Zor. The plane returns to take passengers back to Damascus at 4:30 P.M. The time allows you to see the most important sites. Round trip fare: L.S. 27.50.

The famous Krak
des Chevaliers
Crusader Castle.

The ancient village
of Maloula.

Palmyra ruins which date from
the third century A.D.

Hotel (Tel.)	Single/Bed and Breakfast
Hotel Zenobia	$ 2.00
New Tourist Hotel	$ 2.00

SAFITA: 22 miles east of Tartous, altitude 1,300 feet, population 6,000 . . . On the site of the Byzantine *Argyrokastron,* the Crusaders built a fortress known as *Chastel Blanc.* Located just north of the Lebanese border on the southern range of the Alawite mountains, the castle was one of the most important communication links for the Crusaders on the northern Syrian coast. From the mountaintop fortress they could transmit messages inland to the famed Krak des Chevaliers and westward to the Castle of Marqab above Baniyas. Today, all that remains of the fortress are the tower and the church, which still serves as the Greek Orthodox Church of Safita. The modern town, built on the slopes of the mountain, encircles the ancient tower. The hillsides around are covered with olive groves, from which the village derives most of its income.

SUEIDA (Sweida): 78 miles south of Damascus, 16 miles east of Bosra . . . Sueida is the largest city in the Hauran district and center of the Jebel Druze. In ancient times it was known as *Dionisius* and was inhabited by the Nabataean Arabs. The ruins of a temple dedicated to the Nabataean god Dosares (or Dionisos) remain. There is also a basilica with mosaics in geometrical designs, dating from the 4th or 5th century. A Roman cistern north of the city is called "The Roman Pool." The Sueida Museum includes rare mosaics from Shahba and other places in southern Syria. These mosaics depict pagan rites and ancient legends. Museum entrance fee: 50 piasters.

EXCURSIONS

Qanawat, 4 miles beyond Sueida, was one of the ten cities of the Decapolis, mentioned in the Old Testament as *Kantha* or *Qanat.* The road to Qanawat passes through low basalt hills covered with dwarf oaks. At the edge of the village a rocky road leads to the ruins of a church and a triumphal arch. Farther up the hill are a few columns and a vaulted cistern-temple. In Qanawat stand seven columns of a Roman temple dedicated to the sun god. There are also remains of a Roman wall and a paved road, a palace and a church. On the south stand the remains of a triumphal arch and a small temple. On a hill north of Qanawat an ancient temple was converted into a church early in the Christian era. To the west there is a rock-carved amphitheater, 15 feet in diameter, with nine rows of seats, the remains of nympheum, a round tower and an aqueduct. All were built during the time of Hadrian.

Shahba (6 miles beyond Sueida, altitude 3,445 feet) is ancient *Philippopolis,* the birthplace of the Roman Emperor Philip the Arab (who ruled A.D. 232–237). It still retains part of its ancient rectangular walls with four gates and two paved roads. At the intersection are relics of a tetrapylon and nearby are the ruins of the baths with halls and decorations. Shahba also has an amphitheater 130 feet in diameter and the remains of a small temple dedicated to the father of Emperor Philip. Theater entrance fee: 50 piasters.

At **Salkhad** (19 miles east of Sueida) on the summit of a volcanic mountain stands a 12th-century fortress. In bygone days Salkhad was im-

Hotel (Tel.)	Single	Double	Rooms

portant as a site for guarding Damascus. Cars cannot make the climb to the castle, and it is a steep ten-minute walk, but the impressive fortress can be seen from the main road. The fortress is sometimes used by military authorities and special permission may be necessary to visit it.

TARTOUS: 59 miles south of Latakia, 37 miles north of Tripoli, population 12,000 . . . The ancient city of *Antaradus,* which derived its name from its position opposite the island of Arwad (Aradus), was a colony of the island in Phoenician times. After its conversion to Christianity it played an important role in the annals of Christian history. As Tortosa of the Crusaders it was held by the Knights Templars until 1291.

Remnants of Crusader days are abundant in the old part of the city, most of which is still contained in the *Fortress of the Templars.* In the new town stands the *Cathedral of Our Lady of Tortosa,* which is now a museum. Most of the structure dates from the 13th century, yet it preserves elements of the Byzantine chapel on which it was built. This chapel was one of the main shrines in Syria in the early Christian period.

The modern town of Tartous has undergone extensive changes in the past five years. At the cost of $9 million a new deep-water harbor has been constructed to serve central and southern Syria, especially the newly developing industrial center of Homs.

	BUNGALOWS WITH HALF BOARD		
Island Beach Motel (604)	$3.75–$7.75	$8–$10	30

The **Island of Arwad,** 3 miles off the coast, can be reached by motor-boat in 45 minutes from Tartous harbor. (Boat fee: $2.50 for up to ten passengers.) Arwad was once the capital of an important Phoenician city-state with commercial interests reaching deep into the Syrian hinterland. It fell successively under Assyrian, Babylonian, Persian, Greek, Roman and Byzantine domination. History records that St. Paul on his way to Rome stopped at the island to admire its famous pagan statues. Centuries later when the Crusaders lost Tartous, they escaped to Arwad, from where they sailed to Cyprus. Thus, a chapter in Christian history was closed forever.

Today the island's population numbers about 3,000. Most of the islanders are fishermen who supply the leading restaurants of Beirut and Damascus. Arwad sponges are also sold throughout the area. For visitors, the most interesting craft of the island is the hand-carved and painted model boats. (A sailboat, one foot in length, sells for about $8.)

The island is quaint and picturesque. Its streets are narrow alleyways only wide enough for two or three persons. There isn't a single car on the whole island! One can easily imagine it as the perfect setting for a writers' or artists' colony. Of its antiquities there are remnants of the ancient fortress walls and a castle which dates from the 13th century.

At *Amrit,* 7 miles south of Tartous, on the ancient site of Marathus, stand the most curious ruins on the Syrian coast. Two funeral monuments, called the *Spindles,* date from about 500 B.C. Nearby is another funeral monument, *Borj al Bezzaq.* About one mile west of the site are the ruins of a sanctuary, known as *El Maared,* in the center of which stands a tall altar. It also dates from about the 5th century. According to historical records Amrit was a large, prosperous city up to the Greek period.

Ugarit: see Ras Shamra.

Dome of the Rock, Jerusalem.

CHAPTER IX

JORDAN

TRAVEL FACTS

WEATHER IN JERUSALEM—Lat. N31°46'

Temp.	JAN.	FEB.	MAR.	APR.	MAY	JUNE	JULY	AUG.	SEPT.	OCT.	NOV.	DEC.
Low	38°	41°	45°	51°	56°	62°	65°	64°	62°	59°	50°	43°
High	51°	55°	62°	70°	78°	84°	87°	88°	85°	80°	66°	56°
Average	45°	48°	54°	61°	67°	73°	76°	76°	74°	70°	58°	50°
Sunny days	19	16	23	26	29	30	31	31	30	29	24	22

LOCATION . . . The Hashemite Kingdom of Jordan is an Arab country situated in the heart of the Middle East. On the north it is bounded by Syria, on the northeast by Iraq, on the east and south by Saudi Arabia.

CHARACTERISTICS . . . Jordan is the Holy Land. Within its boundaries are the places which witnessed the start of our civilization and the origins of our spiritual heritage. You will drive on modern highways and sleep in new hotels. Yet, a trip ten miles in any direction in Jordan is a journey into the past. Bethlehem, the birthplace of Jesus; Jericho, the oldest walled city in the world; Hebron, where Abraham was buried; the River Jordan; the Dead Sea; the Mount of Olives; Jerusalem, the holiest city in Christendom —these are only a few of the many places which will be familiar to you from the Bible. Jordanians are generous and friendly, and you will quickly feel at home in the warmth of their hospitality.

POPULATION . . . The population, estimated at 2,000,000, is predominantly Arab. In addition, there are fair Circassians, swarthy Copts, Persian Bahais, Syriacs, Turcomans, White Russians and 300 Samaritans who are descendants of the Biblical tribe. About one third of the population are natives of the territory west of the Jordan River; one-third are residents of what was formerly Trans-jordan; and the remaining third are Palestinian Arab refugees. Less than 10% of the population are semi-nomadic Bedouins.

SIZE . . . 37,301 square miles; 236 miles long, 87 miles wide, about the size of Indiana.

CAPITAL . . . Amman, ancient Philadelphia, is the busy and growing capital of Jordan, with a population of over 300,000.

GOVERNMENT . . . A constitutional monarchy, with a bicameral legislature.

HOW TO GET THERE . . . By Pan American Jet Clipper to Beirut, Lebanon, 13½ hours from New York; then 55 minutes by connection to Jerusalem via Middle East Airlines or ALIA (Royal Jordanian Airlines); or 40 minutes to Amman via ALIA. The overland route by car from Europe through the ancient lands of Turkey and Syria, or the scenic drive from Beirut via Damascus enters Jordan at Ramtha, about 70 miles north of Amman. Driving time from Damascus to Amman is about 4 hours and from Beirut 6 hours. (Allow one to two additional hours for border crossings.) Amman is about an hour's drive from Jerusalem.

ACCOMMODATIONS . . . There are good hotels in major cities. Some provide picturesque settings in renovated monasteries and old Arab houses. Others are new and gleaming intrusions on the timeless land of the Bible. In Jerusalem, the new *Jerusalem Inter-Continental* is completely air-conditioned and has a superb view of the Old City; the new *St. George* and *Mount Scopus* are also good. All from $8 single, $11.50 double, European plan (without meals). Other leading hotels are the *Ambassador, American Colony, Holy Land* and the *National Palace*. Rates from $6 single with bath and full board. In Amman the luxurious *Jordan Inter-Continental* has rates from about $10 single, $17 double, European plan. The *Amman Club* and the *Philadelphia* are about $8.45 single, including meals. The modern *Dead Sea Hotel* stands on the shores of the Dead Sea, 1,250 feet below sea level. It is located about 25 miles midway between Amman and Jerusalem near Jericho. You should reserve hotel space well in advance, especially at Christmas and Easter. Hotels add 10% service charge the year round and an additional 25% charge during peak seasons. Throughout the country new resthouses near historic sites have been built by the Government. They provide meals and accommodations at reasonable prices in out-of-way places.

ARTS . . . The antiquities of Jordan and its religious treasures are among the world's masterpieces. Collections in the museums and churches throughout the country are outstanding. The Jordan-American Society and the British Cultural Centre in Amman hold regular lectures, art exhibits and concerts throughout the year. The Jordan Painting and Sculpturing Society in Jerusalem has a permanent display of Jordanian artists and sculptors.

The Friends of Archaeology was started in 1962 by two American women living in Jordan to promote study and visits to archaeological sites and to enable members to participate in archaeological excavations. Lectures in English by prominent archaeologists are sponsored for members and are open to the public. These are usually held in Amman.

BANKS . . . In Amman, the Arab Land Bank, Arab Bank, Jordan National Bank, and Ottoman Bank have U.S. affiliations.

CALENDAR OF HOLIDAYS . . . Museums are closed but stores are usually open on national holidays: *Arbor Day,* January 15; *Birthday of Prince Abdullah* (King Hussein's first son), January 30; *Commemoration of the accession of King Faisal I to the throne in Syria,* March 8; *Arab League Day,* March 22; *Independence Day,* May 25; and *King Hussein's Birthday,* November 14.

Moslem feasts are based on the lunar calendar; *Muharram 1* (New Year); *Moulid al-Nebi* (birth of the Prophet Muhammad); *Feast of Al-Miraj* (commemorating Muhammad's nocturnal visit to heaven); *Arab Renaissance Day* (commemorating the Arab Revolt against Ottoman Rule); *Feast of Al-Fitr* (breaking the fast at the end of Ramadan)—3 days; *Feast of Al-Adha* (feast of Sacrifice at the end of the pilgrimage to Mecca, commemorating Abraham's offering of his son)—3 days.

For Christians, *Christmas* and *Easter* are the most impressive and moving services during the year. Celebrations of the Western and Eastern churches usually fall about one week apart. Christmas is observed as an official holiday only in Jerusalem. The Roman Catholic and Protestant churches celebrate December 25; Orthodox, January 6; and the Coptic and Abyssinian churches, mid-January.

CIGARETTES AND TOBACCO . . . Local cigarettes such as *Reem, 28¢, Petra, Philadelphia,* 33¢, are good. American brands are 51¢ per pack.

CLIMATE . . . Jordan's climate and scenery range from the temperate heights of the rugged, purple-hued mountains of Moab to the gently rolling hills of Judea, the deep tropical depression of the Jordan Valley and the Dead Sea to the dry, arid desert of the eastern plateau. Daytime summer temperatures are hot, but nights are cool. Winter often brings light snow on the mountains. Spring carpets the hills with wild flowers and the valleys with pink oleander. Rain falls in winter and spring from November to April, but the rest of the year the sun shines every day. Ramallah, Qubeibeh and Beit Jala are pleasant summer resorts. In winter you may swim in the Dead Sea when perhaps it is snowing in Jerusalem 20 miles away. Aqaba on the Gulf is also a popular winter resort.

CLUBS ... YMCA, Lions Club, Rotary Club, Masonic Lodge, Orthodox Club, Sporting Club. A tourist should be a member or accompanied by a member to use these clubs.

COMMON COURTESIES AND LOCAL CUSTOMS ... Jordanians are extremely friendly and hospitable. A guest is considered a sacred trust, and you'll have many occasions to say, *"Shookran"* (Thank you). Local residents of Amman and Jerusalem are accustomed to foreigners and are helpful to them. While people in smaller towns are courteous, they appear more curious and certainly more conservative. Jordanians of all stations are formal in their greetings to friends and strangers. If you respect their customs and formality and are polite and smiling in your manner, the treatment will be reciprocated. The Jordanians manifest the finest qualities of their Arab heritage. As a people, they are proud, hospitable and very kind.

COMMUNICATIONS ... A 3-minute call to the States costs $10.50 (J.D. 3.750); day-rate cablegram to the U.S. is 108 fils per word, with a 10-word minimum. Airmail postage to the U.S. is 40 fils for a postcard or airletter, 80 fils for a 5-gram letter. Local phone calls cost 10 fils. Amman and Jerusalem have automatic dialing systems. All main towns in Jordan are connected by telephone service. Jordan is also connected by phone to all the Arab countries, Europe and the Americas. Phone calls *cannot* be made from Jordan to Israel. The main post office in Amman is located on Wadi es-Seer Street; in Jerusalem, on Salah ed-Din Street. You may buy stamps between 8 A.M. and 8 P.M. at either post office.

CURRENCY ... The monetary unit in Jordan is the Jordanian Dinar (J.D.), which is divided into 1,000 fils. One dinar equals $2.80 (i.e., one pound sterling). Each 10 fils is also called a *piaster*; therefore, $1 equals 35 piasters (pt.). You are allowed to bring J.D. 100 into Jordan and an unlimited amount of foreign banknotes, travelers checks and gold. Foreign currency, drafts, travelers checks should be cashed at banks and at authorized money changers.

CUSTOMS REGULATIONS AND DOCUMENTS REQUIRED FOR UNITED STATES CITIZENS ... Smallpox vaccination certificate. Tourists may get visas at Jordanian consulates or at frontier posts, if they arrive via a neighboring Arab country or hold a visa to an Arab country. A gratis visa is granted to American tourists staying in Jordan for a week or more. As for travel between Jordan and Israel, only a one-way crossing is permitted. American visitors in Jordan wishing to cross over into Israel must contact their consulate or travel agent three days in advance for arrangements to be made. After crossing over to Israel they cannot thereafter return to an Arab country. You may bring into Jordan duty free your personal effects, a pair of binoculars, one camera, typewriter, transformer, projector, 200 cigarettes, 25 cigars or ½ lb. of tobacco, one liter each of wine and spirits. Radios, phonographs and records are subject to duty.

DRUGSTORES . . . Amman and Jerusalem pharmacies are well stocked with U.S. and European products. At least one in each city is open 24 hours. Most well-known European and American cosmetics and toiletries are available at pharmacies and specialty stores.

ELECTRIC CURRENT . . . 220 volts A.C., 50 cycles. Wall plugs are the round, two-prong European type. Adapters for American products are available locally. Transformers are required for American products but not for British ones.

FAUNA . . . Mules, camels, Arabian horses, sheep, goats, and cattle as well as poultry, migratory and local birds. Among wild animals Jordan has the jackal, hedgehog, gazelle, mole, field mouse and fox.

FLORA . . . Jordanian flora is similar to that of southern Europe. The country is rich in flowers, and olive trees grace the Biblical hills of Judea and Samaria.

FOOD . . . Hotels serve a good variety of Continental food. You should try some of the delicious Arab dishes, such as roast lamb and chicken. Jordanian fruits and vegetables are excellent. Pasteurized milk is available. See MENU TRANSLATOR in Chapter XXII.

GAMBLING . . . Horse racing is a weekly event at Marka in Amman in summer and at the Dead Sea track in winter. At the same tracks you can have the unusual experience of seeing camel races which are held occasionally.

LANGUAGE . . . Arabic is the official and principal language of the country. English is the second language and is widely used, especially in hotels, shops and at tourist facilities.

LAUNDRY AND DRY CLEANING . . . Good and inexpensive. Hotels have facilities for their clients.

LIQUOR . . . *Araq,* the native drink, is an aperitif flavored with anise. Bourbon is rare, but Scotch whisky and American cocktails are available in leading hotels and bars. Prices are reasonable. Minimum legal age to be served a drink is 18. Red or white wine, brandy and Triple Sec, made by the Trappist monks at their monastery in Latroun, are available at restaurants and groceries and range in price from 250 fils to 1 J.D. *Cremisan,* another local wine, is made by the Salesian Fathers in Bethlehem. Local beer is good too.

MEDICAL FACILITIES . . . Most doctors are graduates of American or British universities and speak English fluently. Good medical and surgical care, including obstetrics and pediatrics, is available. Mouasher Memorial Hospital and Palestine Hospital are new, well-equipped hospitals in Amman. In Jerusalem, St. Joseph and St. John Opthalmic Hospital can be recommended.

MOTION PICTURES . . . Movie houses show American, English and Arabic films. Consult the newspapers for showtime. Features change each week or so.

MUSIC . . . Familiar dance music in night clubs. Jordan's own Arabic music is hauntingly unforgettable, particularly when heard on a moonlit night in Amman's 2,000-year-old Roman Theatre.

NIGHT CLUBS . . . Leading night clubs are in the Jordan Inter-Continental, the Philadelphia, and the Continental hotels (in Amman), and in the Grand Hotel (in Ramallah). Typical of Jordan are the attractive garden cafés that have orchestras for dancing. While there are several nice, small bars around the cities, the best ones are in hotels. Bar drinks cost 300 fils and up. In Amman, the bars of the Jordan Inter-Continental and the Philadelphia hotels are popular. In Jerusalem, the Seven Arches Lounge (Jerusalem Inter-Continental) serves drinks—with a magnificent view of the city thrown in.

PHOTOGRAPHY . . . Color and black-and-white films are available for still cameras, Kodachrome for movie cameras. Ektachrome and Kodacolor can be processed locally. Jordan is a photographer's paradise. The weird shapes and color-rich rocks of Petra and Wadi Rum, architectural details in the Old City of Jerusalem, the drama of the Jordan Valley, the sunset at Jerash, the panorama from Kerak are only a few of the delightful subjects. Except for military installations along the truce frontier, there are no restrictions on taking pictures in Jordan. But if you want to photograph "picturesque local color," ask permission first to avoid embarrassing a Jordanian or yourself.

RELIGION . . . Most Jordanians are Moslems. Approximately 15% are Christians and there are churches and missions of all denominations in Jerusalem.

RESTAURANTS . . . Lunch is usually served from 1 to 3 P.M. and dinner after 8 P.M. Jordanians eat a light breakfast, their main meal at lunch and a light supper. The best restaurants in

Amman are at the hotels. Others which can be recommended are *Ali Baba,* specializing in Arabic food; *Gardenia,* an outdoor restaurant serving local food; *Le Cesar,* an ultramodern restaurant, bar and lounge serving European and Middle Eastern food; *Orient,* small, pleasant and specializing in *musakhan; Roy's Barbecue,* featuring roast chicken and Arabic food.

In the Old City of Jerusalem, *Al-Salam* is a typical local restaurant serving good Arabic food; *Arz* has European and Arabic food; *Casa Nova* is the dining room of an Italian monastery; and *Dom Polski,* a small dining room in a convent run by Polish nuns. The *Benedictine Monastery, Golden Chicken, National* are popular eating places in new Jerusalem. The *Oriental Jerusalem* specializes in *mansaf, musakhan* and many other Arabic dishes.

SHOPS AND STORES . . . Generally open from 9 A.M. to 1 P.M. and 3 to 7 P.M. Most but not all shops close on Sunday, others on Friday. You should bargain in the bazaars. The handicrafts of Jordan are varied and tempting. You will want to allow yourself time to wander through the narrow lanes of Old Jerusalem stopping at tiny shops along the way to admire the wares over a cup of coffee, and to chat with shopkeepers.

In addition to local handicrafts, modern shops are full of American and European products.

SPORTS . . . Football, basketball, boxing, swimming, tennis and horse racing are popular. Horse and camel races on Sunday by the Dead Sea shore, 1,250 feet below sea level. Fishing is a year-round sport at Aqaba, where there is a wide variety of colorful and exotic fish. A glass-bottom boat and fishing equipment can be rented through the Aqaba Hotel.

You can swim in pools at the Philadelphia and Jordan Inter-Continental hotels in Amman and at the St. George Hotel in Jerusalem. The Dead Sea is less than an hour's drive from either Amman or Jerusalem. Swimming here is an experience not to be missed. The water contains so much salt that you float more than swim. For sandy beaches the Gulf of Aqaba is 4½ hours by car from Amman over a good highway. Hotel facilities are available there for a weekend visit. You can also enjoy superb skin diving, snorkeling and sailing.

TIME . . . 7 hours later than U. S. Eastern Standard Time. Greenwich Mean Time plus two hours.

TIPPING . . . Tip luggage porters 100 fils for 2 or 3 bags, 50 fils for any small services, 50 fils for shoeshine boy. For waiters, 10% of the bill before the service charge is added is generous. Taxi drivers do not expect tips, but be sure to agree on the price before taking a taxi.

TRANSPORTATION . . . Taxi fare from the airports in either Amman or Jerusalem is 500 fils (about $1.60). All the major historic and religious sites are easily accessible by car. Although a network of buses connects major towns, tourists usually use taxis, which are comfortable and inexpensive. You can take a taxi for 10 miles for about $1.50. Taxi-service, which are 5-passenger cars, operate regularly between major towns. This way you can hire a seat in a car and thus travel comfortably and cheaply indeed.

TOURIST TAXES . . . An airport tax of 600 fils has to be paid in Jordanian currency on departure from Jordanian airports.

WATER . . . Water is safe to drink in cities. Bottled water and soft drinks are available too. On trips to the desert and to small villages, take along water or bottled soft drinks. You will find it handy to include a collapsible drinking cup in your hand luggage on such occasions.

WHAT TO BUY . . . Jordan's heritage is reflected in its handicrafts through the designs which were once created by the Greeks, Romans, Byzantines, Crusaders and Arabs. Tourists love the delicate bronze and silver work, the fascinating Oriental jewelry, the exquisite mother-of-pearl products, the rich embroidered linens, the attractive Crusader jackets, the famous olivewood products, the colorful Palestine pottery, and religious art. Prices for these goods are very reasonable.

The most characteristic silver jewelry is the Crusader's cross— five crosses grouped as one, symbolizing the five nations of the Crusading armies. These crosses are made as brooches, necklaces, earrings, bracelets and cuff links. Bedouin jewelry such as bracelets, earrings, necklaces and forehead ornaments might include the hand of Fatima worn as a good-luck symbol, or blue stones to ward off the evil eye.

Bethlehem is known for its skilled olivewood craftsmen who carve rosaries, Bible covers, crucifixes, creches and camel caravans. Inlaid mother-of-pearl, also a specialty of Bethlehem, is worked into intricate designs on crucifixes, picture frames, jewelry boxes and Bible covers.

Delicate skill is employed in cross-stitch embroidery to reproduce the patterns and colors from designs on dresses of peasant women. The towns best known for their handwork are Ramallah, Bethlehem and Jerusalem. In recent years this handwork has been adapted to useful products, such as table linens, dolls, aprons, guest towels, bookmarkers, children's dresses, neckties, baby bibs and skirts.

Jerusalem's pottery factories, founded in 1919 by two potters brought from Turkey to restore the ancient tiles of the Dome of the Rock, are located in front of the American Consulate and in the Old City. Here the pottery is shaped by hand and painted with traditional Islamic designs and decorative Arabic script. Other pieces show designs of Christian significance, such as the cross, the fish, and scenes from the life of Christ.

The small glass-blowing industry in Hebron is a tradition of one family handed down for many generations. The factory uses ancient techniques to produce jugs, bowls, plates, vases, glasses and mugs which are charming for their primitive qualities. There is also a new glass blowing factory in Jerusalem.

On Christian Street in the Old City of Jerusalem candlemakers produce tapers unique to the Holy Land. They are shaped like flat, elongated bells with a gold tracery design on one side and religious symbols on the other. Huge encrusted candles and bunches of votive tapers are also on sale. You may have candles (and rosaries) blessed in the Church of the Holy Sepulchre.

Jerusalem is one of the best places in the world to buy gold because it is sold by weight, and the price is based on the world-market rate. The price of any item will be the cost of the gold plus the workmanship.

Several stores in Jerusalem have antiquities such as old coins, Roman glass, pottery and statuary found in Jordan. These shops also sell old brass, copper and silver trays, candlesticks, pots and jewelry.

WHAT TO WEAR . . . Jordan has four well-defined seasons; each requires a different wardrobe. In spring and autumn, a gentleman should have medium-weight suits and warm sweaters, but a topcoat is unnecessary. Women will be comfortable in medium-weight suits with blouses and sweaters, light woolen dresses and a wrap or lightweight coat. For summer, only summer clothing is necessary. While drip-dry clothes are practical, cotton is definitely more comfortable in the hottest months. Winter can be cold and sometimes rainy. You will need warm suits, dresses, coat and rain apparel. Warm house slippers are practical because floors in hotels are tiled. From late spring through early autumn a hat for protection against the sun is recommended. Be sure to bring comfortable walking shoes for summer or winter.

WHERE TO GO—SIGHTSEEING . . .

The main organization to facilitate tourism is the Tourism Authority of the Jordan Government, Salt Road, P. O. Box 224, Amman (Tel.: 41462), and Salah ed-Din St., P.O. Box 184, Jerusalem (Tel.: 344/914). English-speaking guides are available through travel agencies and the Tourism Authority for J.D. 2.000 per day. During heavy tourist seasons, book a guide in advance. Jordan's Tourist Police are extremely pleasant and cooperative and are also trained to act as guides.

What to see depends on the amount of time you have available and your personal interests. Many people come to see the Holy Land and to spend their time in Jerusalem and other places connected with the life of Christ. Others discover that Jordan is an open museum. With enough time you can do both. At every step along the way archaeology and Biblical history overlap.

The Jerusalem Inter-Continental Hotel.

SOURCES OF FURTHER INFORMATION . . . Jordan Tourist Bureau, 530 Fifth Avenue, New York, N. Y. 10036. Jordan Tourist Bureau, Halaby Building, 2nd floor (next to the Alcazar Hotel), Beirut, Lebanon. Tel. 247642. For complete details and practical information on Jordan, read *Travel Jordan* by Kay Showker (Librairie du Liban, Beirut, 1965). Other suggested reading: *The Antiquities of Jordan* by G. Lankester Harding (Lutterworth Press, London, 1965) and the *Bible*.

A Shepherd in the Jordean Hills, Jerusalem.

CHAPTER X

JORDAN: THE COUNTRY AS A WHOLE

TYPES OF ACCOMMODATIONS

HOTELS

Outside of the major towns there are only a few good hotels plus the new resthouses recently built by the government. So, it is preferable to use Jerusalem or Amman as your base and plan your sightseeing as daytime excursions from there.

YOUTH HOSTELS

While there is no Youth Hostel Association in Jordan, there are many hostels run by church organizations, such as the YMCA, YWCA, the Lutheran Hostel and St. George Close. Most of these are located in or near Jerusalem.

CAMPSITES

If you have your own equipment, you can enjoy camping in the desert and near antiquity sites such as Petra and Jerash. There is one organized campsite in Jerusalem, next to the Cliff Hotel.

TOURING

AUTOMOBILES AND MOTORCYCLES

You may bring your automobile duty-free into Jordan for a maximum period of one year upon the presentation of triptych issued by a recognized automobile club. You must have a license for the vehicle and an international driver's license. Automobile insurance is not compulsory but is strongly recommended.

In recent years Jordan, with U.S. aid, has built a network of excellent roads between major cities and towns of the country. On new roads distances are well marked, but on secondary roads they are not. Good maps are available from the Ministry of Public Works in Amman and from the Jordan Distribution Agency in

Jerusalem. Traffic moves on the right. Gas and service stations are ample in main towns and scarce on the open road. Gasoline costs 1.050 J.D. for 30 liters. Servicing is adequate for most American and European cars.

There are no security regulations banning motoring in any part of Jordan except for military areas along the truce frontier, where motorists and pedestrians *must* observe warning signs. For desert driving, be cautious, as you could get lost. The Bedouin Desert Patrol is cooperative in arranging an escort for desert trips.

BICYCLES

Not recommended.

AFOOT

Neither Amman nor Jerusalem has many name signs for streets, but if you learn a few landmarks you will be able to know your way around quickly. In the Old City you must walk, as most lanes are too narrow for cars. Here a good map is especially helpful. Maps are available from the Tourism Authority, bookshops and travel agents.

TRAINS

Available to Damascus and to Ma'an but seldom used by tourists, as good and cheap transportation is available by other means.

BUSES

Available but rarely used by tourists, as taxis are cheap, and more comfortable.

TRANSPORTATION TO NEARBY COUNTRIES

Daily air service is available to Beirut and Cairo. The easiest and cheapest overland travel is the 5-passenger taxi service, which leaves hourly from downtown stations in Amman and Jerusalem for Damascus with onward connecting service to Beirut and Aleppo.

MAJOR EVENTS

CHRISTMAS IN BETHLEHEM

Christmas has three dates in Jordan. Western Christmas is celebrated on December 25, the Orthodox one on January 6, and the Armenian Christmas on January 19.

On Christmas Eve, December 24, in the little town of Bethlehem the Latin Patriarch makes his ceremonial entrance into the town square at 1 P.M. He is followed by a colorful procession of churchmen, choir boys, scouts, and by a large crowd of townspeople and visitors. At dusk the YMCA holds a service in English and Arabic at Shepherd's Field where the angels appeared to the shepherds as they sat watching their flocks. The congregation joins the choir in singing well-known Christmas carols. At nine o'clock in the evening, community carol singing is held in the courtyard of the Church of the Nativity. Bethlehem is gaily lighted and a festive spirit is in the air.

At midnight the Pontifical High Mass is celebrated in the Franciscan Church of St. Catherine, adjacent to the Church of the Nativity. At the moment the choir sings the *Gloria,* a huge star over the altar is set aglow and the bells of Bethlehem are rung. The little town's special message of "Glory to God in the highest, and on earth, peace and good will toward men" is carried throughout the world.

Christmas-morning services are held in churches throughout Jordan. Before noon on Christmas Day at Manger Square in Bethlehem the Jordanian Army gives a colorful performance of ceremonial dances.

EASTER IN JERUSALEM

Few ceremonies rival in pomp, pageantry and piety the Easter services in Jerusalem. Holy Week starts on Palm Sunday with the Anglican procession from Bethany to the Mount of Olives and Gethsemane, and then to the Cathedral of St. George in Jerusalem.

Among the most splendid rituals of Holy Week are those of the Roman Catholic Church. They begin at 6:30 A.M. on Palm Sunday with the ceremonial entry of the Latin Patriarch into the Church of the Holy Sepulchre, followed by his Blessing of the Palms, and concluding with the Pontifical Mass before the Holy Tomb. At 1:45 P.M. on Maundy Thursday in front of the Holy Tomb the patriarch performs the Washing of the Feet, as did Jesus before his last Passover. The next day, Good Friday, at 11 A.M. the Franciscan Fathers lead a procession along the Via Dolorosa, pausing for a brief service at each of the fourteen Stations of the Cross. In the Burial Service later in the day, a procession visits the Stations of the Cross within the Church of the Holy Sepulchre. When the procession reaches the Cross, an effigy of Christ is taken down and wrapped in a winding sheet. It is then carried to the Stone of Unction, where it is anointed, spiced and scented with incense. The effigy of Christ is laid to rest in the Holy Tomb, and the Good Friday services are concluded with a memorial sermon.

The Abyssinian Orthodox Church, established in Ethiopia sixteen centuries ago and having rights to the sanctuary of the Holy Sepulchre, does not have an altar inside the church. Its tiny altar is located on the roof of St. Helena's Chapel near the entrance to the Church of the Holy Sepulchre. Here on the night of Easter Saturday the church celebrates a colorful procession known as the Abyssinian Search, a symbolic search for the risen body of Christ.

The Ceremony of the Holy Fire is the major Easter service in Jerusalem and one of the most ancient. It symbolizes the Resurrection when Christ, the Light of the World, rose from the Tomb. The ceremony is conducted by the Greek Orthodox Patriarch.

At 11 o'clock on Holy Saturday, the door to the empty tomb of Christ in the rotunda of the Church of the Holy Sepulchre is closed and sealed. Exactly at noon on Easter the Patriarch enters the crowded rotunda, the seal is removed, and the unlit silver Holy Lamp is placed in the tomb. At 12:30 the service begins with the Patriarch leading a solemn procession three times around the rotunda. Then, the Patriarch enters the Holy Sepulchre and prays before the Holy Tomb. The Holy Lamp is lighted, and from it torches are set aflame by the Patriarch. The flaming torches are raised to small openings above the Holy Sepulchre, where they are received by the congregation. The instant the fire is seen the crowd rushes frantically with their candles and torches to receive the fire. Lasting honor is bestowed on the one whose candle is lit first. As the light of the Holy Fire appears, the massive bells of the church are rung, and the fire passes rapidly from candle to candle until the entire church is aglow.

MENU TRANSLATOR — See Chapter XXII.

CHAPTER XI

AMMAN

AMMAN INTERNATIONAL AIRPORT

The airport is located about 7 miles west of the city. The drive over an excellent road takes about 15 minutes and costs 500 fils by taxi. Remember, there is an airport tax of 600 fils upon departure.

HOTELS

Amman has only a small selection of hotels, as the city is fairly new. The best by far is the *Jordan Inter-Continental*—deluxe in every sense, with air conditioning, swimming pool, bar and beautifully appointed rooms. A 10% service charge is added to the bill.

Hotel (Tel.)	Single	Double	Rooms/	Baths
Jordan Inter-Continental (41361) Jebel Amman, 3rd Circle	$10–$11	$17–$18	105	105
	WITH TWO MEALS			
Philadelphia (25191) Facing Roman theater	$ 5.88	$10.08	76	72
	WITH TWO MEALS			
Amman Club (24321) King Faisal St.	$ 5.88	$10.08	38	38
	WITH BREAKFAST			
Select (27101) Jebel Luwebdieh	$ 4.62	$ 8.12	20	20
	WITH BREAKFAST			
Continental (23161) King Faisal St.	$ 3.50	$ 5.88	38	15

CITY TRANSPORTATION

Buses operate in Amman and Jerusalem and between cities and villages throughout Jordan. An average bus ride costs 10 fils. You will probably prefer to use taxis, which are reasonably priced, or the inexpensive taxi-service. Taxi-service (pronounced *serveece*) are 5-passenger cars which run along set routes in town, to outlying areas between Amman and Jerusalem and to towns north and south. The price is based on distance. In Amman, the taxi-service leaves from the main square on King Faisal Street. (In Jerusalem, most buses and taxi service leave from Damascus Gate.) There are no metered taxis, but a taxi ride to most sections of Amman or Jerusalem is 150 to 200 fils.

As there are no regularly scheduled sightseeing buses in Jordan, taxis are used unless a group is large enough to charter a bus. Hertz and Avis car rental services have offices in Amman and Jerusalem. Also you may hire a car and driver for the day from any taxi company.

CITY SIGHTS

Amman (population 275,000, altitude 3,000 ft.) is a modern city spread across seven hills. It was only a village when King Abdullah moved the seat of his newly formed government there in the 1920s. Now, broad streets lined with modern shops and buildings have replaced the simple little town, and hilltops abound with spacious villas, gardens, government ministries, schools and hospitals.

The Bible mentions "Rabboth of Ammon" as the capital of the Ammonites about 1200 B.C. Two hundred years later David stormed the town and sent Uriah the Hittite to his certain death in order to have Uriah's beautiful wife, Bathsheba. The city gained a reputation for pride, wealth and wickedness, and the prophets foretold its destruction. When the Ptolemic general Philadelphus (285–247 B.C.) seized the site he named it Philadelphia. After the Roman conquest it joined the Decapolis and flourished because of its location along the caravan trail. Amman's great Roman theater is still used today. After a brief prominence under the Umayyads during the 8th century, the city sank into obscurity.

Today Amman is the seat of government and the hub of the country's commercial activity. It is also the center of a network of new roads which greatly facilitate travel. Northward a new highway runs through the hills of Gilead to Jerash, called the "Pompeii of the East"; westward, another highway swings down through the Hills of Moab to the Dead Sea, Jericho and on to Jerusalem. Southward, the new desert road leads to Aqaba on the Gulf and branches west at Ma'an to the rose-rock city of Petra.

You can visit the important sites in Amman in a half day. The main antiquities are from the Roman period.

The *Roman Theater* (facing the Philadelphia Hotel) is built against the slope of a hill and has a seating capacity of 6,000 spectators. It dates from the 2nd or 3rd century A.D. Nearby are columns which probably once surrounded the Forum. East of the Philadelphia Hotel are the ruins of a smaller theater, commonly named the *Odeum*. On the west was the *Nymphaeum*. No inscriptions have been found on the monuments, but authorities believe they were built in the 2nd century A.D.

The Citadel was built on a plateau (now Jebel Hussein) surrounded by valleys on all sides except the north, where an escarpment was cut to isolate the site completely. The fortress was enclosed by a stone wall and fortified by towers at each corner. The entrance leads into a spacious court in the middle of which stand the ruins of a temple dedicated to Hercules, built in the 2nd century A.D. The Byzantine gate of the Citadel is still standing, and outside the Roman walls is a rock-carved cistern which supplied water to the fortress in times of siege. North of the Citadel lies *El-Qasr* (the castle), dating probably from the Umayyad period.

The *Amman Archaeological Museum* is located at the Citadel. Exhibits are arranged chronologically and include artifacts from prehistoric times (180,000 B.C.) to the Roman Age. The museum also houses a collection of Nabatean pottery, unique for its fineness and decoration; exhibits from the early Moslem and Crusader periods; and a display of the Dead Sea Scrolls. Admission is free. Hours: winter, 8 A.M. to 3:30 P.M. Closed Fridays. Summer, 7:30 A.M. to 1:30 P.M. Closed Fridays.

The *Basman Palace*, the residence of King Hussein, is located on a hilltop facing the Citadel. The palace is guarded by Circassian soldiers wearing colorful black and red uniforms.

EXCURSIONS

Jerash: 30 miles north of Amman . . . After a 45-minute drive over an excellent highway through the hills of Gilead, you arrive at Jerash—the best and most complete ruins of a provincial Roman city in the world. Jerash (Gerasa) was founded by the soldiers of Alexander the Great about 332 B.C. After the Roman conquest in 63 B.C. it joined the Decapolis and established trade with the Nabateans of Petra. Finally, in A.D. 90, Jerash was absorbed into the Roman province of Arabia and in the following two centuries reached its zenith. Afterward, the rise of Palmyra and a shift in trade routes caused its steady decline.

After the 12th century it was abandoned until 1878, when the Turks settled the east side of the ancient site with Circassians, Moslems from the Caucasus.

Southeast of the road immediately before Jerash stands the *Triumphal Arch* to the city, built to celebrate Hadrian's visit in A.D. 129. Beyond the arch is the ancient *Hippodrome*. The present entrance to ancient Jerash is by the *South Gate*. Here a path leads to the *Temple of Zeus,* built in the 2nd century A.D. on the site of an earlier sanctuary, and a large theater which accommodated 6,000 spectators.

Proceeding north, you reach the enormous oval-shaped *Forum*, encircled by 56 columns standing in their original positions. It is the only oval-shaped Roman forum ever uncovered. The forum leads to the *Street of Columns,* the main thoroughfare of Jerash. Crossing the main street at right angles were two other streets running east to west. Beyond the first crossroads is the elaborately carved *Nymphaeum,* which was a fountain and a temple of the nymphs. Immediately next to it stands the *Temple of Artemis,* built in the 2nd century A.D. for the patron goddess of Jerash. It is the most imposing building in Jerash. Facing the temple are the remains of a *Viaduct Church,* built over the forecourt of the temple.

A few steps farther along the Street of Columns on the west side are the *Baths,* dating from the 2nd century A.D. The dome is the oldest known example of one built on pendentives. Across the street from the baths is the *North Theater,* with a seating capacity of 1,200 spectators. Two hundred yards farther along the same street is the *North Gate,* hence the north limit of the city.

Thirteen churches have been uncovered in Jerash. North of the city walls lie the ancient cemetery, a spring and a small theater. According to an inscription on the theater, the licentious water festival of Maiumas was held here as late as the 6th century A.D.

Jesus is believed to have passed through Jerash on a trip to Jerusalem, using the eastern highlands route through the Decapolis.

Jerash Resthouse: Facilities and refreshments. No sleeping accommodations.

MADABA: 20 miles south of Amman . . . Madaba, the city of mosaics, dates from the Middle Bronze Age. It is first mentioned in the Bible at the time of the Exodus. Later, in the mid-9th century B.C., the Hebrews were driven out by the Moab king Mesha.

Under Roman and Byzantine rule Madaba was one of the main cities in the Middle East. In 747 the town was badly destroyed by earthquake and finally abandoned. And so it remained until the early 19th century, when 2,000 Christians from Kerak settled on the ancient site.

Several houses and churches in Madaba rest on foundations of Byzantine churches, which were paved with fine mosaics. The best example is the Byzantine mosaic floor of a modern Greek church. The mosaics picture maps of Palestine and Jerusalem at the time of Justinian.

Madaba Resthouse: Food and refreshments but no sleeping accommodations.

Mount Nebo: 27 miles south of Amman (3 miles northwest of Madaba) . . . The mountain is one of the alleged sites of the tomb of Moses. The principal ruins are at *Syagha* and include a church and an adjacent monastery. From here—a remarkable panorama across the Jordan Valley to Palestine—Moses saw the Promised Land. From Mount Nebo a road runs southwest to the mineral springs of *Zerka Ma'in* (the *Callirhoe* of classical times) and the famous springs of Herod the Great.

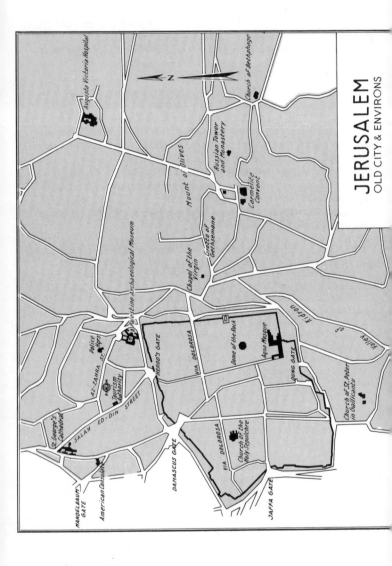

CHAPTER XII

JERUSALEM

JERUSALEM AIRPORT

The airport serving Jerusalem is about 10 miles north of the city. At the present time it cannot receive jets, but plans are under way to extend the runways and modernize it. A taxi ride into town costs 500 fils and takes about 15 minutes over an excellent highway.

HOTELS

Jerusalem has some charming old hotels and a wide variety of new ones. Reservations should be made in advance, especially for the Christmas and Easter seasons. The best first class hotel in the city is the *Jerusalem Inter-Continental*. The leading second-class hotel is the *American Colony*, situated in three century-old houses and surrounded by pleasant gardens. There are many new and modern tourist-class hotels conveniently located for touring the city's religious and historical sights and for shopping.

Hotel (Tel.)	Single	Double	Rooms/	Baths
NEW CITY				
Mount Scopus (4891) Sheikh Jarrah	$ 6.50	$ 9.00	50	50
Saint George (510) Salah ed Din	$ 7.85	$ 9.00	150	150
Jerusalem Inter-Continental (1494) Mount of Olives	$ 7–$12	$10.50–$15.50	204	204
Ambassador (493) Sheikh Jarrah	$ 4.30	$ 7.00 WITH BREAKFAST	108	108
Holy Land (1571) Rashid St.	$ 4.90	$8.40 WITH BREAKFAST	80	80
National (316) As-Zahra St.	$ 4.20	$ 7.00 WITH BREAKFAST	106	106
American Colony (116) Sheikh Jarrah	$ 3.50	$ 5.88 WITH BREAKFAST	44	39
Aeolia Capitolina (79) YMCA, Damascus Gate	$ 4.20	— WITH BREAKFAST	—	—
Capital (683) Salah ed-Din St.	$ 3.50	$ 5.88 WITH BREAKFAST	25	25
Christmas House (2588) P.O. Box 491, Jerusalem	$ 5.88	$10.08 WITH HALF BOARD	20	20
New Victoria (1299) Commercial Centre	$ 6.00	$10.30 WITH HALF BOARD	29	29

Hotel (Tel.)	Single	Double	Rooms/Baths	
Pilgrims Palace (1558) Herod's Gate	$ 5.04 WITH BREAKFAST	$10.08	37	37
Ritz (1063) Salah ed-Din St.	$ 3.50 WITH BREAKFAST	$ 5.88	50	50
Az-Zahra (140)	$ 2.66 WITH BREAKFAST	$ 4.20	22	8
Jordan House Pension	$ 2.24 WITH BREAKFAST	$ 3.64	7	7
St. George Close	$ 2.24 WITH BREAKFAST	$ 3.64	12	—
OLD CITY				
Gloria (120) Jaffa Gate	$ 3.50 WITH BREAKFAST	$ 5.88	64	64
Knights Palace (534) New Gate	$ 2.66 WITH BREAKFAST	$ 4.20	36	16
Christ Church (82) Jaffa Gate	$ 2.66 WITH BREAKFAST	$ 3.08	27	12
Imperial	$ 2.66 WITH BREAKFAST	$ 4.20	60	15

CITY SIGHTS

Few places in the world have commanded the devotion of men for so long a period as has Jerusalem (population 90,000, altitude 2,466 feet). From your first day in the Holy City you will be awed by a sense of history, the presence of Christ, the city's spiritual significance. Jerusalem is a city with a special destiny. Its effect on visitors is unique.

According to archaeologists, Jerusalem dates from the 15th century B.C. In ancient Egyptian and Babylonian records it is called Urusalimu (hence, Jerusalem). In the Bible it is first mentioned under the name of Salem, and afterward it is called Jebus. When David captured the Jebusite fortress of Zion he made the city his capital and there placed the ark. Solomon built the first great temple on Mount Moriah.

After Nebuchadnezzar overran the city in 586 B.C., the Jews were taken captives to Babylon. A half century later Cyrus, King of Persia, allowed the Jews to return. The temple and city were rebuilt on a modest scale. Subsequently the city was conquered by Alexander the Great in 332 B.C. and Antiochus Epiphanes in 168 B.C. Under the Maccabeans and later the Herods, Jerusalem enjoyed a certain independence. Herod the Great rebuilt the temple on a more grandiose scale than the previous ones and enlarged and beautified Jerusalem. In the 36th year of his reign Jesus Christus was born in Bethlehem.

During a Jewish revolt in A.D. 70 the temple and city were destroyed by the Romans under Titus. After a second revolt in A.D. 132 the Jews were expelled. On the ruins a pagan city was built by Emperor Hadrian and named Aelia Capitolina.

In the 3rd century under the reign of Constantine, Jerusalem became a Christian shrine. The Emperor's mother, Helena, ordered the construction of the Church of the Holy Sepulchre and established the "official" sites connected with the life of Christ.

In the 7th century the city was sacked by the Persians and later fell to the Arabs. The Crusaders under Godfrey de Bouillon entered Jerusalem in 1099 and established the Latin Kingdom of Jerusalem. Less than a century later they were driven out by the Arabs under Saladin.

In 1517 the Ottoman Turks occupied Jerusalem and governed it until World War I, when it surrendered to the Allied troops. After World War I Jerusalem and Palestine were placed under British Mandate. When the British withdrew in 1948, hostilities broke out between the Zionists and the Arabs. The United Nations Armistice Line, drawn in 1949 as a result of this conflict, divided Jerusalem. "No man's land"—a narrow strip about 100 feet wide—separates the two parts.

The ancient walled city of Jerusalem, Bethany, Bethphage, the Mount of Olives and Gethsemane are in Jordan.

Within an area of about one square mile in Old Jerusalem are concentrated some of the most important historic and religious shrines of the world's three great monotheistic religions—Judaism, Christianity and Islam.

Ancient Walls and Gates: The 16th-century wall which encloses the Old City contains eight gates: Jaffa (west), New (north), Damascus (north), Herod's (north), Zion (south), Dung (south), St. Stephen (east), Golden (east). Jaffa, New and Zion Gates are closed because they border "no man's land." The Golden Gate was closed by a Turkish governor in 1530. Legends say that the governor hoped to postpone the final judgment and the end of the world by closing the gate, which, according to tradition, would be the place of the first trumpet call and the resurrection of the dead.

Within the walls on the east side are the Moslem quarters, containing the Haram esh-Sharif and the Islamic Museum. On the northwest side are the Christian quarters, where the Church of the Holy Sepulchre and the Via Dolorosa are located.

Southeast of the walled city is the city of David, ancient Ophel. It is bounded by the Valleys of Kidron and Hinnom, which meet at the Pool of Siloam. Opposite the east wall of the Old City is the Garden of Gethsemane, and across the Kidron Valley is the Mount of Olives.

In the great wall overlooking Gethsemane and the Mount of Olives stands the stately Gate of St. Stephen, the legendary site of the stoning of St. Stephen. (Entering the Old City from this gate will orient you best, as the road leads directly into the Via Dolorosa and passes the main shrines.)

Al-Haram Esh-Sharif: On your left after entering St. Stephen's Gate is the sacred enclosure holding the Dome of the Rock and the Aqsa Mosque on the summit of Mount Moriah. The site is associated with the Prophet Muhammad's nocturnal journey to Jerusalem and his visit to heaven. During his lifetime Muhammad faced Jerusalem while he prayed. Hence, the city was the first *qiblah* (the direction toward which Moslems face to pray) in Islam. The Rock acquired early sanctity in Moslem eyes and became second only to Mecca and Medina as a Moslem shrine.

Tradition holds that Mount Moriah is the site where Abraham prepared to sacrifice his son. Here at a later date Ornan the Jebusite had his threshing floor, which David bought and upon which he erected an altar. David's altar was superseded by Solomon's Temple, which was later destroyed by Nebuchadnezzar. On the same site Herod the Great built an enormous and splendid temple—the one Jesus knew. His prophecy of its destruction was fulfilled in A.D. 70 at the hands of the Romans. After the second Jewish revolt a temple dedicated to Jupiter was erected on the site of the previous temples.

When Queen Helena came to Jerusalem in the early 4th century, she had all pagan shrines, including the Roman temple on Mount Moriah, destroyed. The area was then abandoned because Christians believed it was defiled, and eventually it became the city's rubbish heap.

Early in the 7th century after the Arabs conquered Jerusalem, Caliph Umar Ibn Al-Khattab helped clear with his own hands the accumulated refuse of centuries and had a simple mosque of wood built on the site. A half century later the Umayyad Caliph Abdul Malik Ibn Marwan built the Dome of the Rock. To this day it remains a magnificent example of Moslem architecture and one of the most beautiful monuments to be found anywhere.

Next to the Dome of the Rock is the *Mosque of al-Aqsa,* built by Walid, son of Abdul Malik ibn Marwan. The Haram area also holds smaller domes, minarets, fountains, shrines, a library, the Islamic Museum and underground vaults known as *Solomon's Stables.* Part of the lower courses of the Haram is the *Wailing Wall,* a section of the wall remaining from the temple built by Herod.

Visiting hours for al-Haram ash-Sherif: Apr. 1–Sept. 30, 7:30–11 A.M., 12:30–3 and 4–6 P.M. Oct. 1–Mar. 31, 7:30–11 A.M., 12:30–2:30 and 3:30–4:30 P.M. Entrance fee: 250 fils.

At the entrance of St. Stephen's Gate across from the Haram

Bethlehem, Jordan.

edouin tribesmen of Jordan.

Garden of Gethsemane.

esh-Sharif is the *Church of St. Anne.* It stands on the traditional site of the house of Anne and Joachim, parents of Mary, at the time of the Virgin's birth. Within the church grounds is the Pool of Bethesda, where Jesus healed the sick man who had waited faithfully for 30 years to be cured by its waters. St. Anne's Church was built during Crusader days on the remains of an earlier 5th-century shrine.

The Via Dolorosa (Way of the Cross, or Way of Sorrows) . . . is the road Jesus walked carrying his cross from the Praetorium to Calvary. The street winds through the cobblestone alleys of Old Jerusalem, past churches, chapels, bazaars and ancient archways. Every Friday at 3 P.M. the Franciscan Fathers, accompanied by pilgrims of all denominations, retrace the steps of Jesus, stopping at the 14 Stations of the Cross.

The first station is located in the Umariyyah School on the site of Pilate's Praetorium (200 yards beyond the Church of St. Anne). The Franciscan Convent of Flagellation stands on part of the site of the Praetorium.

The second station is fixed outside on the street, opposite the Chapel of the Condemnation. The chapel stands on the Gabbatha, or Lithostrotas (the street by which Christ went out of the Praetorium to Calvary). Part of the original pavement is visible in the Chapel of Condemnation and in the Convent of the Sisters of Zion. The third station is marked by a small chapel which was once the main entrance to the Baths. Back of the third station is a small museum. The fourth station is an altar outside of the Armenian Catholic Church. On the altar rests a marble statue of Jesus meeting his mother.

Stations four to nine are marked by small chapels along the Via Dolorosa. Stations ten to fourteen are located inside the Church of the Holy Sepulchre. The tenth station indicates the summit of Calvary, and the fourteenth station marks the burial place of Christ.

The *Church of the Holy Sepulchre* is the holiest church in Christendom, erected upon the traditional site of the crucifixion, burial and resurrection of Jesus Christ. The site on which the church stands was outside the city walls during the time of Jesus and included Calvary and the garden of Joseph of Arimathea where Jesus was buried.

Even after the destruction of Jerusalem in A.D. 70, Christians continued to worship at Calvary and the Tomb. In an attempt to distract Christians from their faith and holy places, Hadrian built a temple dedicated to Venus on the site of Calvary. Ironically, his deed marked the spot forever. Upon Constantine's conversion to Christianity, he ordered the erection of a magnificent basilica on the site. Over the centuries the church was destroyed and rebuilt several times. Today, the church is approximately the same as the one restored by the Crusaders in the 12th century.

The *Church of Alexandros Nephki,* southwest of the Church of the Holy Sepulchre, is known as the Russian Excavations. Its position helps you understand the orientation of the original Church of the Holy Sepulchre, as it contains the ruins of the Triumphal Arch at the time of Hadrian and part of the enclosure walls of the temple.

Near Jaffa Gate the *Citadel,* also known as David's Tower, was built during the 14th century on the base of a 12th-century Crusader castle, which in turn had been built on an ancient foundation. The oldest part is said to date back to the time of Herod the Great.

The Armenian Orthodox *Cathedral of St. James,* located in the Armenian quarters near the Citadel, was erected in the 12th century on the traditional site where St. James was beheaded by Herod Agrippa. Architecturally, the church is beautiful. Nearby stands the *Church of St. Mark.*

The road along the old walls from Zion Gate leads out of the city through *Dung Gate.* In the southeast corner of the city wall foundation stones of Solomon's walls have recently been uncovered. South of Dung Gate is the *Church of St. Peter's in Gallicantu,* built by the Assumptionist Fathers to commemorate St. Peter's denial of Jesus and the former's repentance. It is believed to be on the site of Caiphas' Palace, where Jesus was taken on the night of his arrest. From Dung Gate the road drops down and crosses the *Valley of Kidron.* Below lie many tombs, including Absolom's Pillar and the Tombs of St. James, Zachariah and Josephat. In the city wall overlooking the valley is the Golden Gate. According to tradition, this is the gate through which Jesus rode into Jerusalem on Palm Sunday.

Gethsemane and the Mount of Olives: Across the Valley of Kidron and facing the Golden Gate is Gethsemane and the Mount of Olives. North of the road before climbing the hill stands the Tomb of the Virgin, or the *Church of the Assumption.* According to tradition, this is the site of the Virgin's resting place before her ascension into heaven. The present church was built by the Crusaders in 1130 to replace an earlier Byzantine basilica.

Farther up the hill is the Garden of Gethsemane, a peaceful grove of ancient olive trees, where customarily Jesus spent the night with his disciples when he visited Jerusalem. The *Grotto of Gethsemane* is traditionally believed to be the place where Jesus was betrayed by Judas and arrested by the soldiers. The Basilica of the Agony, or the *Church of All Nations,* is built over the Rock of Agony where Christ prayed and wept before his arrest.

On the road up the Mount of Olives you come to the *Church of Ascension,* which is believed to mark the spot from which Jesus ascended into heaven. The chapel dates back to Crusader times and stands on the site of an earlier 4th-century church. After Saladin recaptured Jerusalem in 1187, the church was made into a mosque. Inside the mosque is a rock bearing a footprint which tradition holds is the footprint of Christ. Nearby, the *Church of the Pater Noster* marks the traditional site where Christ taught his disciples the Lord's Prayer. In the church the glazed tiles, on which the Lord's Prayer is written in 44 different languages, were donated by Christians around the world.

At the summit of the Mount of Olives the Church of the *Dominus Flevit* rests on the traditional site where Jesus wept over Jerusalem before his entry into the city on Palm Sunday.

The Garden Tomb: Outside the old walls of Jerusalem north of Damascus Gate is an ancient tomb in a garden. Some Protestant groups believe it is the place of Jesus' crucifixion and burial, as it more accurately fits the description in the Bible. The site was located and excavated by General Gordon (of Sudan fame) in 1883. A nearby hill, still used as a graveyard, is believed to be the site of Calvary. It was known that Christ was crucified at "the place of a skull." Immediately in front of the Garden Tomb is a rock formation resembling a skull, which Gordon believed to be an obvious identification of the original site.

Palestine Archaeological Museum near Herod's Gate: The museum, built and maintained by a gift of John D. Rockefeller, Jr., houses many treasures from years of excavation in the Holy Land. Among the most interesting ones are a collection of jewelry dating from 1700 B.C. to A.D. 700; a coin collection dating from 500 B.C. to A.D. 1600; and a group of oil lamps from the early Bronze Age to the Islamic period. Exhibits from the Stone Age include objects 200,000 years old. In a corner of one exhibit room you can see a copy of a tomb with skeletons and artifacts exactly as they were found in Jericho. Samples of the Dead Sea Scrolls are displayed in a separate room.

Hours: 9 A.M. to 2 P.M. daily, except holidays. Entrance fee: 100 fils.

EXCURSIONS

Bethany: 1¼ miles south of Jerusalem . . . Bethany was the home of Lazarus and his sisters, Mary and Martha, and Simon the Leper. On the site where Jesus called forth Lazarus from the tomb stands a Franciscan church built on the foundations of earlier Byzantine and Crusader churches.

Jesus sent two disciples from Bethany to Bethphage on the Mount of Olives to fetch a donkey, which he rode into Jerusalem on Palm Sunday. Today the exact site of Bethphage is no longer known, but the name is given to the enclosure of the Franciscans.

Valley near Ram, northeast of Jerusalem.

On Palm Sunday, following a tradition set in the 4th century, Bethphage is the starting point for the procession which ends at the Church of St. Anne in the Old City.

Rachel's Tomb: 10 miles south of Jerusalem . . . On the west side of the road before Bethlehem, a small building marks the traditional site of the tomb of Rachel, wife of Jacob. The structure was originally built by the Crusaders but was altered many times.

Jerash called the Pompeii of the East.

CHAPTER XIII

JORDAN: TOWNS AND SITES

PART I: WEST OF THE JORDAN RIVER

BETHLEHEM: 11 miles south of Jerusalem, population 40,000, altitude 2,550 feet . . . Bethlehem is first mentioned in the Bible in connection with the death of Rachel. It was also the scene of the idyll of Ruth, the Moabite, and Boaz. In Bethlehem, Samuel anointed David King of Israel.

The *Church of the Nativity,* facing Manger Square in the center of Bethlehem, stands above the traditional site of Jesus' birth. The first Church of the Nativity was built at the time of Constantine about A.D. 326. It was destroyed two centuries later but rebuilt in the 6th century by Justinian. The present-day structure is basically the same as the 6th-century one. Beneath the protective floor boards of the church are fragments of the beautiful mosaics of the church built by Justinian. Fragments of other mosaics dating from the 12th century decorate the inside walls of the church.

On each side of the altar steps descend to the *Grotto of the Nativity,* where a silver star marks the birthplace of Christ. All the outside entrances to the basilica are closed except one called the *Door of Humility.* North of the basilica is the *Church of St. Catherine.* Here on Christmas Eve the church bells are rung during the midnight Mass, announcing the dawn of Christmas around the world.

The *Milk Grotto* is near the Church of the Nativity. Tradition holds that while Mary was nursing Jesus, drops of her milk fell on the rock and turned it white. The original church is said to have been built in the 4th century.

EXCURSIONS

A road to the east just before Manger Square in Bethlehem leads down to *Beit Sahour* and *Shepherd's Field.* On Christmas Eve before sunset, services are held in the field next to the YMCA hostel. Services at the nearby Shepherd's Field of the Catholic and Orthodox churches are held earlier in the day. (The YMCA hostel has sleeping accommodations for about 20 people.)

Qala'at El Burak (Castle of the Pools), 2 miles beyond Bethlehem on the Hebron road, is a fortress built in the 17th century for the protection of *Solomon's Pools,* three ancient reservoirs set in a grove of pine and cyprus trees. These enormous pools collect rainwater from the surrounding hills and the water of the nearby springs. According to scholars, the pools are misnamed. Solomon probably came to the spot to enjoy the gardens and springs, yet history records that Pilate, not Solomon, built the great aqueduct which supplied water to Jerusalem.

HEBRON: 28 miles south of Jerusalem, population 55,600 . . . *Al-Khalil,* as Hebron is called in Arabic, means "the Friend" (of God—i.e., Abraham). It lies in a valley identified with the Biblical *Valley of Eshed.* The Bible relates that "Abraham moved his tent and came and dwelt in the plain of Mamre, which is in Hebron, and built there an altar unto the Lord." After the death of Sarah, Abraham bought the *Cave of Machphelah* from a Hittite and buried her there. Later, Abraham was buried beside her. In the years which followed, Isaac and Rebecca, Jacob and Leah were also buried there.

Hebron was captured by Joshua and later was David's capital. In Herod's time a temple was built on the site. After the Moslem conquest of Palestine in the 7th century, Hebron, because of its association with Abraham, became one of the four sacred cities of Islam. To Moslems, Abraham was the first Moslem.

In 1100 the Crusaders took Hebron, but later it was recaptured by Saladin. It has remained predominantly Moslem since that time. Today it is the seat of government for the southern district of the West Bank.

Al-Haram al Ibrahimi al Khalil (the Sanctuary of Abraham, the Friend) is a mosque built on the traditional site of the Caves of Machphelah. The lower part dates from the time of Herod. The main part of the building was formerly a Crusader church which was an enlargement of the original Byzantine basilica used by Christian pilgrims en route to Abraham's Oak at Mamre. The upper part and minarets were added by the Mameluks. In the mosque are the stately cenotaphs of Abraham and Sarah, Isaac and Rebecca, and Jacob and Leah. Their bodies lie in the cave below. The cave itself cannot be visited, but you can look through an opening in the floor by the dim light of a suspended oil lamp into the eerie chambers below.

Plan to be in Hebron between 8 and 11 A.M. to obtain tickets to visit the Haram and to sightsee before noonday prayers. Entrance fee: 250 fils.

On a side street north of the mosque is a small glass factory which has been making hand-blown glass since Crusader times. You may watch the men at work around the ancient furnace turning and blowing the green, blue, amethyst glass into vases, pitchers, candlesticks and beads. The factory is open only from November to May.

Hebron Resthouse: Food and non-alcoholic refreshments, no sleeping accommodations.

Hebron is a conservative town. There are no cinemas. Some of the women wear a veil of flowered material which, when viewed from afar, is weird and startling. You should be careful about photographing in Hebron, especially in the area of the Haram or in the bazaars.

Mambre (Mamre), one mile north of Hebron, is the traditional site of the Oak of Mamre, where Abraham received the three angels of God. Ruins from the Abrahamic period have been excavated, although only those from the time of Herod, Hadrian and Constantine are now visible.

NABLUS: 35 miles north of Jerusalem, population 90,000 . . . Between Mount Garizim and Mount Ebal lies Nablus, one of the largest towns in

Jordan. It is located in an area which has an abundant water supply. Its gardens and fields are irrigated from sixteen springs. The Nablus area is known for its olive crop and the production of oil and soap. Prior to the partition of Palestine, Nablus was more important as a commercial center than Jerusalem.

Nablus was founded in A.D. 72 by Roman legionaries under Titus. In 636 the town was taken by the Arabs and, except for a brief period during the Crusades, has remained Moslem to the present day. The town's main ancient building is the *Great Mosque,* originally a Byzantine basilica, rebuilt as a church by the Crusaders.

In addition to its small Christian minority, Nablus is the home of 300 Samaritans, whose high priests are the direct descendants of Levy, the descendants of Aaron, the son of Jacob. In their new synagogue, built to replace the ancient one destroyed by an earthquake in 1927, you are shown an ancient Pentateuch Scroll or Torah written on sheepskins. The Samaritans claim it is the original copy of the words of Moses. Scholars say the oldest part of it is no older than the 10th or 11th century A.D.

EXCURSIONS

Mount Garizim, the holy mountain of the Samaritans, is located southwest of Nablus. Here the Samaritans celebrate the feasts of the Passover, Pentecost and Tabernacle. Also on the summit are the ruins of a mosque and an octagonal church, the earliest known one dedicated to Mary. (The panoramic view of the Holy Land from the summit of Mount Garizim is magnificent.)

In the valley between Mount Garizim and Mount Ebal, the twelve tribes of Israel assembled. By Joshua's orders, the six nobler tribes stood for blessings on the side of Mount Garizim, while lesser nobility stood on Mount Ebal. The priests, judges and elders gathered around the Ark of the Covenant placed in the valley between the two mountains.

Jacob's Well, where Jesus met the Samaritan woman, is located one mile south of Nablus. In the early 4th century a church was built over the well. The church, apparently destroyed during the Samaritan revolts of the 5th century, was restored under Justinian. The Crusaders built a new church over the old one. The area containing the Crusader church ruins was acquired by the Greek Orthodox Church in 1860. The monk in attendance will lower a bucket into the well and bring up clear, fresh water for you to drink.

Joseph's Tomb . . . Before his death Joseph had requested that his body be buried in the Land of Canaan. Four centuries later Moses brought Joseph's mummy up from Egypt and Joshua buried him near the site of Jacob's well. Northeast of the tomb is *Askar* (Sichar), the village home of the Samaritan woman.

East of the road immediately before Nablus, the small town of *Balata* is the site of ancient *Shechem* (Sichem), the first capital of ancient Samaria. Excavations reveal the ruins of two city gates and a large temple built about 1600 B.C. Shechem was probably first settled by the Canaanites in the 4th millennium B.C. It is mentioned in the Bible in connection with Abraham and Jacob.

Hotel (Tel.)	Open	Single	Double	Rooms/Baths

RAMALLAH: 15 miles north of Jerusalem, population 35,000, altitude 2,850 feet . . . In the year Columbus discovered America, a small Christian community in Shobak in southern Jordan fled north to avoid the marriage between one of their daughters and the son of the chief of the Moslem tribe. The little community settled near *Bireh*, a Moslem village north of Jerusalem. Today the Christian town of Ramallah and the Moslem town of Bireh form a single adjacent community.

Ramallah is Jordan's leading summer resort. It is connected with Jerusalem by a four-lane highway. The 20-minute drive through rolling hills and green valleys is a lovely glimpse at life in the Holy Land. Ramallah has several good hotels and restaurants which are open in summer (and move to Jericho in winter). The town is well known for the chocolates and ice cream made there. Here in 1866 the American Friends (Quakers) opened their first school, which is still one of the best schools in the country.

Hotel (Tel.)	Open	Single	Double	Rooms	Baths
Carlton (392)	all year	$ 3.50	$ 5.88	21	21
Grand (232)	all year	$ 3.50	$ 5.88	23	14

EXCURSIONS

While Ramallah itself does not have historic sites, the town is surrounded by places familiar to us from the Bible.

Bireh, mentioned above, was the first stopping place for caravans from Jerusalem to Galilee and is believed to be the place where Mary and Joseph missed the 12-year-old Jesus. Afterward they returned to Jerusalem to find him in the temple. *Rentis*, east of Ramallah, near *Bir Zeit*, was the home and burial place of Samuel.

East of the Jerusalem–Ramallah road, *Tel el-Ful* is the site of Gibeah or *Gabaath*, the birthplace and residence of King Saul. At *Er-Ram*, ancient Rama, the prophet Jeremiah was freed from the convoy of captives on its way to Babylon. At *Tel en-Nasbeh*, the site of *Mizpah*, Saul was elected the first King of Israel.

West of the Jerusalem–Ramallah highway, 10 miles north of Jerusalem and 5 miles south of Ramallah, a road leads to the village of *El-Jib*, identified as *Gibeon*, "where the sun stood still." Excavations of the ancient site are located south of the village. About three miles farther along this road is *Qubeibeh*, the traditional site of ancient *Emmaus*, where Jesus appeared to the two disciples Cleophas and Simon on the third day after his burial. A Franciscan church, reconstructed on the foundation of an earlier Crusader church, stands on the traditional site of Cleophas' house.

		WITH HALF BOARD			
German Hostel	all year	$ 2.80	$ 3.08	14	9

On the same road one mile before *Latroun* is the small village of *Amwas*, believed by many Biblical scholars to be the correct site of Emmaus, as the name of the present village is almost identical to the ancient one. Further on at *Latroun* the Abbey of the Trappist monks stands on the ruins of a 12th-century Crusader castle.

North of Ramallah en route to Nablus the road passes through the fertile *Wadi el-Haramiyeh* (Valley of the Robbers). The police· post and ruins of a khan at Ain al-Haramiyeh (the Robbers' Spring) mark the major pass through the hills on the route from Jerusalem to Nablus.

About halfway to Nablus a road on the right leads to Kirbet Seilun, the site of ancient Shiloh (Silo). After the conquest of Palestine, the Tabernacle and the Ark of the Covenant were placed in Shiloh, where they remained for two centuries until the Ark was captured by the Philistines about 1050 B.C. Farther along the Nablus road *Ain Berkit,* near Khan al-Lubban, marks the traditional frontier between Judaea and Samaria.

SEBASTIA (Sebaste): 48 miles north of Jerusalem . . . History tells us that Omri, the sixth King of Israel, bought an isolated and defensible hill for two talents of silver from Shemer. On the hill he built a city called *Samaria* and made it his capital. The city was embellished by his successors, one of whom was Ahab. Under the influence of his Phoenician wife, Jezebel, Ahab built a temple in honor of Baal. For Ahab's blasphemy the prophets foretold that Samaria would be "a heap of stones in the field." After Israel's defeat by the Assyrians and, later, the Babylon captivity, the prophecy came to pass. The area was subsequently settled by the Chaldeans but destroyed again by Alexander the Great in 331 B.C.

After the Roman conquest the town was rebuilt by Pompey. Later Augustus bestowed it on Herod the Great, who called it Sebaste. According to legend, here Salome danced for the head of John the Baptist. Ruins of a 5th-century church, built on the traditional site of the first finding of the head of St. John, contain frescoes representing the beheading.

In the present-day village of Sebastia, ruins of the Crusader Church of St. John the Baptist may be visited. The church was built on the remains of a Byzantine basilica in the crypt of which were found the relics of several prophets. The presbytery and the apse of the church were made into a mosque called Nebi Yaha (i.e., Prophet John). On the hill above the village the site of ancient Sebaste includes the ruins of a Roman forum, a colonnaded street, a theater and a temple to Augustus. South of the temple are ruins of the palace of Omri. The walls of the town, many times enlarged by successive conquerors, are also visible in the excavations.

About 14 miles north of Nablus is the town of Jenin, ancient *Engannin.* There, according to tradition, Christ cured the ten lepers. At Jenin you get an excellent view of the Plain of Esdraelon and a glimpse of Nazareth across the plains. Nearby is the site of ancient *Dothain,* where Joseph was sold by his brothers and taken to Egypt.

PART II: THE JORDAN VALLEY

The Jordan Valley has an almost central position between Amman and Jerusalem. The drive from either city is a delightful ride through hills at 2,500 feet above sea level and dropping down to the lowest spot on the earth's surface. As the road winds out of the Biblical wilderness into the valley you see the lush green oasis of Jericho stretching to the north and the silvery waters of the Dead Sea sprawling to the south. Here, in an area of ten square miles, some of the world's most important sites of antiquity and Biblical history are concentrated.

JERICHO: 22 miles northeast of Jerusalem, population 85,000, 853 feet below sea level . . . Jericho (*Ariha* in Arabic) is one of the oldest, continuously inhabited sites in the world. On a mount overlooking the Jericho oasis excavations have uncovered settlements dating back to 8000 B.C. and the oldest walled town (7000 B.C.) yet discovered.

In Roman times Jericho was a garden of fruit and palm trees. So bountiful was its crop that Anthony presented the town as a gift to Cleopatra. Jericho reached its peak under Herod the Great. His winter palace was located south of present-day Jericho along *Wadi al Qilt* (the Valley of the Shadow of Death in the 23rd Psalm). On the old road from Jericho to Jerusalem, 3 miles after the Good Samaritan Inn, a road on the left leads down the ancient Roman road into the Wadi.

On a street in Jericho, Jesus healed the blind beggar. Later he was entertained at the house of Zaccheus, the publican. Byzantines, Arabs and Crusaders also came to Jericho and left their mark.

EXCURSIONS

In the excavations at *Tell es-Sultan* you can see layer upon layer of ancient civilizations. Joshua's attack when he blew his horn and the "walls came tumbling down" was Canaanite Jericho (probably about 1250 B.C.). In the center of the site a massive Neolithic defense tower dating before 7000 B.C. has been cleared to bedrock. The original entrance of the stairway, the oldest known stairs in the world, is exposed.

At the foot of Tell es-Sultan is *Elisha's Fountain,* the main water spring of the oasis. Tradition says it is the fountain which Prophet Elisha sweetened by casting a handful of salt into it. At sunset you can see a colorful procession of village women in native dress, water jugs balanced on their heads, come to the spring.

West of Jericho and overlooking the Jordan Valley is the famous *Mount of Temptation* in the Wilderness, where Jesus spent forty days and nights. The path to the top of the mountain passes by a Greek Orthodox monastery perched on one of the cliffs.

The *Jordan River* is only 200 miles long. It has no cities on its shores, and its value to the agriculture of the valley is insignificant. Yet, as the place of Jesus' baptism, the river has an immeasurable significance to Christians throughout the world. The main source of the river springs from a grove on Mount Hermon, long considered sacred by the ancients. After leaving the little grove, the stream drops through a basalt gorge and plunges to Lake Huleh. The descent continues another six miles until the waters enter the Sea of Galilee (600 feet below sea level). From Galilee, the waters flow south through the Ghor region and finally empty into the Dead Sea.

While today there are no important settlements on the river, archaeologists believe its banks were the site of the earliest community life of man.

Hotel (Tel.)	Open	Single	Double	Rooms/Baths

The Cities of the Plain were in the Jordan Valley, possibly at the mouth of the river.

For the Christian world, the most important site on the Jordan is *Makhad al-Hajla* (the Ford of the Partridge), 8 miles from Jericho, where John baptized Jesus.

The Dead Sea, 10 miles from Jericho, 1,290 feet below sea level, is the lowest spot on the earth's surface. In Arabic it is called *Bahr Lut,* Sea of Lot. The sea, 46 miles long and 3 to 10 miles wide, has no outlet. The heavy salt content of the water makes animal life impossible and makes swimming an unusual experience. The buoyancy is such that it is almost impossible to sink. You can lie on your back in the water and read a magazine.

		WITH HALF BOARD			
Dead Sea Hotel	all year	$ 5.88	$10.08	24	24

KIRBET QUMRAN AND THE DEAD SEA SCROLLS: 14 miles from Jericho . . . The story of the Dead Sea Scrolls began in 1947 when, by accident, a Bedouin discovered several scrolls in clay jars hidden in a cave on a rocky cliff high above the Dead Sea. Since then Bedouins and archaeologists have searched these desolate hills and have turned up one of the most exciting discoveries of modern times. Biblical manuscripts, 2,000 years old, predate by some 1,000 years the earliest known Hebrew text of the Old Testament. Also among the finds have been books of an unknown religious community, now identified as the Essenes, a pre-Christian, mystical Jewish sect mentioned in ancient writings. The discoveries are important as verification of Biblical text and for the study of Biblical history. The writings of these scrolls covered a period of 300 years, including the birth of Christ. Thus they have unveiled part of the background on which the teachings of Christ and the early Church were based.

The Essene community lived in caves and dwellings at a site known as Kirbet Qumran. Under strict rules of obedience and high ethical standards set down in their Manual of Disciplines, the "brothers" spent their lives studying the Holy Writ and praying for the coming of the Messiah.

At Kirbet Qumran the oldest ruins date from the 8th century B.C. During this period the site was probably a fortress. Apparently it was deserted for a long period until the Essenes came in the late 2nd century B.C. Experts believe the Essenes fled the area during an earthquake in 31 B.C. After about thirty years they returned to repair their buildings and to settle again into the secluded life of prayer and study.

In A.D. 68 the settlement came to an abrupt end. A Roman legion en route to Jerusalem to put down the first Jewish revolt destroyed the settlement, and the members of the community fled after placing their precious manuscripts in the nearby caves for safekeeping. The site was not inhabited again, and the settlement and its people were lost to history until a few years ago.

HISHAM PALACE: 3 miles north of Jericho at Khirbet al-Mafjar . . . The Umayyad Palace of Hisham Ibn Abdul Malik (A.D. 724–743) was built as a country residence. Hisham, like most of the early Arab rulers, preferred the freedom of the desert to city life. The palace is a complex of buildings, baths, mosques and colonnaded courts. Its mosaics and stucco ornaments are fine examples of Umayyad art and architecture. Experts say an earthquake destroyed the buildings before they were completed. Thus the accumulated sand and debris helped to preserve the palace's lovely mosaics. The Tree of Life is one of the most beautiful mosaics in the world.

BOYSTOWN . . . The model farm of the Arab Development Society is located in the Jordan Valley near Jericho. Its creation is the story of the courage and determination of its founder, Oxford-educated Musa al-Alami. The major problem in setting up the farm was finding enough water. Experts said there was no water between Jericho and the Jordan River. Musa Bey, in spite of their advice, dug for water and proved them wrong. The farm is now fed from underground wells. It is one of the best-equipped and operated farms in the Middle East, and its high-quality products are sold throughout the area. More important, many boys left orphaned by the war in Palestine have been given life, hope and education through the work of the society.

PART III: EAST OF THE JORDAN RIVER

AJLUN: 41 miles north of Amman . . . *Qala'at al-Rabad*, a mountaintop medieval fortress at 4,068 feet overlooking Ajlun, is one of the best examples of Arab military architecture in Jordan. The castle was built in 1184 by one of the generals of Saladin. It was destroyed in 1260 by the Mongols and later rebuilt by the Mameluks. The view from the castle dominates the Jordan River and the Biblical land of Gilead. On a clear day you can see from Mt. Hermon in the north to Hebron in the south.

AQABA: 209 miles south of Amman . . . Jordan's only seaport lies at the southernmost tip of the country on the Red Sea. Aqaba is probably Biblical *Elath*. Excavations at *Tell al-Khalifa*, west of the present town, uncovered what archaeologists believe are King Solomon's copper smelters of *Ezion Geber*. In ancient times Aqaba was engaged in extensive trade with South Arabia and flourished up to the time of the Arab conquest. The great Roman road from Damascus via Amman and Petra extended south to Aqaba, where it turned west to Egypt. The Crusaders occupied the site about A.D. 1116 and built a fortress near the present town. After their retreat little was known about the area until its sudden prominence in World War I during the famous Arab Revolt under the leadership of Amir Faisal of Hejaz and Lawrence of Arabia. The ancient port, set against a background of rugged, stark mountains, is quickly changing from a tiny fishing village into a modern resort. The sandy beaches along the shore are ideal for swimming, and the clear blue waters of the Gulf are excellent for water skiing, boating and skindiving.

Hotel (Tel.)	Open	Single	Double	Rooms/Baths	
		WITH HALF BOARD			
Aqaba Motel (158)	all year	$ 5.88	$10.08	36	36
Aqaba Resthouse	all year				

EXCURSIONS

WADI RUM: 41 miles east of Aqaba . . . The desert valley of Wadi Rum was the setting for the film *Lawrence of Arabia.* Its magnificent scenery of weirdly shaped and richly colored rocks has a strange and haunting beauty, unsurpassed elsewhere in the Middle East. Recent excavations in the south have uncovered a small village dating from 4500 B.C. The area was apparently one of the earliest inhabited sites in Jordan and a holy site during Nabatean times.

The trip to Wadi Rum should be made in a landrover or jeep from Aqaba through the desert to the police post at Wadi Rum. It is a full day's excursion and is best made from early fall through spring.

KERAK: 78 miles south of Amman . . . The road from Madaba passes through *Dibon* (Biblical Dhiban) and winds down into and across the spectacular *Wadi Mujib.* The drive from Amman to Kerak takes about two and a half hours. You should take a picnic lunch, as the trip is a full day's excursion. Kerak was a walled Crusader city, built for defense, not beauty. In the castle, masterful cross-vaulting leads into long galleries, stables, chambers and lookouts. The present town of Kerak, still enclosed in the ancient Crusader walls, has about 10,000 inhabitants. Many Christian families here trace their origins to the Byzantine period.

MA'AN: 134 miles south of Amman . . . The major town of south Jordan, Ma'an, is located on the desert road between Amman and Aqaba. It is the terminal of the railroad line and turn-off point for the road to Petra.

Ma'an Resthouse: Facilities and refreshments but no sleeping accommodations.

PETRA: 166 miles south of Amman . . . Decades ago travelers rode camel and horse over mountains, through valleys, across streams, into desert to reach a site hidden in the mountain fastness of southern Jordan. After its rediscovery in the early 19th century, ancient Petra, capital of the Nabatean Arabs, became the goal of adventurers, globe-trotters, explorers, historian and archaeologists. Today a new road from Amman enables you to drive to Petra in 3 hours. The fact that the trip can now be made with ease and comfort does not lessen Petra's wondrousness in the slightest. It is still mysterious and magnificent.

Petra was a fortress city set in a canyon whose only entrance was a long, narrow passage, the *Siq.* Inside the canyon the Nabateans created a city by carving their houses and temples out of the variegated rock of the canyon walls. The sunlight plays on the canyon and the changing light casts a mood over Petra which words cannot describe.

Petra was probably the land of the Biblical Horites around 2000 B.C.

and later the land of Edomites, who controlled southern Jordan at the time of the Exodus. It is sometimes identified with Sela in the Bible. The Nabateans, a Semitic tribe from North Arabia, settled in Petra about 800 B.C. By the 4th century B.C. they had occupied the territory astride the main trade route from Arabia to the Fertile Crescent and were able to extract enormous tolls from the merchants for protection of the caravans which passed through their lands.

After defeating the Seleucids in 312 B.C. the Nabateans for the next two centuries maintained their independence and carved out an empire which extended as far north as Damascus. With the wealth they acquired from the caravans and their expert engineering skills, the Nabateans enlarged their rose-colored city and embellished it with high temples, houses, and tombs.

After Pompey's conquest of Syria and Palestine in 63 B.C. the Romans gradually extended their control into south Jordan. Finally in A.D. 106 Nabatean power gave way, and their lands, along with most of Palestine and Jordan, were incorporated into the Roman province of Arabia. Under the Romans Petra reached its zenith.

Early in the Christian era Petra became part of the Byzantine Empire. Later, when the Moslem armies marched north from Arabia, they seized Petra, but by this period the main trade routes of the east had shifted and Petra's source of wealth had vanished. With time, Petra's glories were forgotten, and after hundreds of years even its location was lost to the world. Early in the 19th century the Swiss explorer John Burckhadt stumbled upon it by chance during a Middle Eastern expedition he had undertaken for an English learned society.

The track into Petra leads down a hill past the ancient dam of the Nabateans. In olden times the dam dispersed the dangerous flood waters of the wadi (valley) into terra-cotta pipes which ran along the walls of the Siq into Petra and eventually connected with the water system of the town.

Beyond the dam one enters the Siq. From here the dreamlike world of Petra begins. The Siq, barely wide enough for a car, hides between sheer rocks towering 200 to 300 feet. In some places the walls are so close they appear to be meeting overhead. In ancient days the Siq was Petra's protection from surprise attack, as only a few men were needed to hold the passage against invaders. In Roman times a stone-paved road led through the passage and into the main thoroughfare of the city.

Upon emerging from the path you are dazzled by the sight of an imposing tomb in classic Greek style, carved out of rose-colored rock on the side of a cliff. This is the *Treasury*, or Khaznat Faron, one of the best-preserved monuments in Petra. The Treasury gets its name from an old belief that pirates hid their stolen treasures here.

Beyond the Treasury the path turns to the right and leads past many of Petra's fine tombs and temples topped with the characteristic crow-step design, the hallmark of Nabatean architecture. Farther along, the trail runs by a 2nd-century Roman theater carved from rock at the foot of Mt. Nejr. The theater once seated 3,000 spectators. Behind it a trail leads to the High Place of Sacrifice, a mountaintop sanctuary in the center of Petra canyon. Farther ahead, on the original Roman road, stand the remains of the Roman Triumphal Arch and the Temple of Jupiter.

On the north side of the canyon a footpath leads up the mountain to the *Monastery,* or Deir, one of the largest and handsomest temples in Petra. It was carved about the 3rd century A.D. as a temple to the glory of the pagan god Dhu-shara, chief deity of Petra. Crosses carved on the temple walls probably indicate that at some later date the temple was used as a church.

The panoramic view from the hill beyond the monastery is one of the most impressive in the Middle East. In view some 4,000 feet below, are two ravines, Wadi as-Siyagh and Wadi Araba. These depressions are part of the Great Rift Valley which extend from the Jordan Valley in the north to the eastern coast of Africa in the south. Also in view are Sinai, the Negev and the Biblical lands of Canaan stretching to the horizon. Three hundred yards on the southwest side of the hill is another peak, Jebel Harun (Mt. Hor), which is said to be the site of the tomb of Aaron, the brother of Moses.

A trail on the southeast side of the canyon along the Wadi Tarasa leads up Mt. Nejr to the *High Place of Sacrifice.* Along the way much of Petra's stupendous rock formation, temples and tombs are in evidence. Especially important are the *Tomb of the Soldiers* and the inner chamber of the *Festival Hall.* At the High Place, the ancient altar with drains for the blood of the sacrifice is flanked by two obelisks of solid rock. These were probably meant to mark the limits of the sanctuary. From the summit of Mt. Nejr, one of the highest peaks in Petra, the entire canyon and surrounding area are in view. The descent from Mt. Nejr can be made by an ancient rock-cut stairway on the reverse side of the mountain. The path ends near the Roman theater and the main road of Petra.

On the east side of the canyon by way of the old Roman road is a cliffside faced with many amazing structures. These include the dramatic *Corinthian Tomb,* the *Palace Tomb* and the *Urn Tomb.* The latter has a paved and colonnaded courtyard extending over a two-story vault. A Greek inscription inside the Urn Tomb says that the building was used as a church in A.D. 447.

The best time to visit Petra is fall or spring. The fee from Amman or Jerusalem is standard: 15 J.D. for one person overnight at the hostel and including transportation to Petra by five-passenger cars, meals, horses, entrance fee and guide. Many people make the excursion in one day. The cost is about 8 J.D.

Al-Ji Resthouse: Single, bed and breakfast, J.D. 1.500.

Nazzal Hostel and Camp: Located in the center of Petra canyon. Open year round. Simple but adequate accommodations for 85 persons. The tent camp in front of the hostel and the caves behind the hostel have outdoor sleeping accommodations. Price: Single, with full board, J.D. 3.500.

At *Shobak,* 19 miles north of Petra (117 miles south of Amman), stands the Crusader castle of Montreal. A modern village has sprung up within its well-preserved walls. A good view of the fortress is obtained from outside the walls.

The Sphinx and the peak of a Pyramid of Giza.

CHAPTER XIV

EGYPT (UAR)

TRAVEL FACTS

WEATHER IN CAIRO—Lat. N30°3′

Temp.	JAN.	FEB.	MAR.	APR.	MAY	JUNE	JULY	AUG.	SEPT.	OCT.	NOV.	DEC.
Low	45°	47°	51°	56°	62°	67°	70°	71°	67°	63°	56°	49°
High	67°	70°	76°	83°	89°	94°	96°	94°	89°	86°	79°	70°
Average	56°	59°	64°	70°	76°	81°	83°	78°	78°	75°	68°	60°
Sunny days	28	26	29	30	31	30	31	31	30	31	29	29

LOCATION . . . Egypt occupies the northeastern corner of Africa, with the Mediterranean Sea on the north and the Red Sea on the east. Libya and the Sudan are border countries on the west and south. Egypt's northeastern corner, the Sinai peninsula, is separated by the Gulf of Suez and the Suez Canal. The Nile River, like an elongated oasis, cuts Egypt from Wadi Halfa on the Sudan border to Cairo. There, the river divides into two main branches which form the great Nile delta. The delta area is called Lower Egypt; the rest of the Nile Valley below Cairo, Upper Egypt.

CHARACTERISTICS . . . Egypt is a curious blend of Pharaonic, Christian and Moslem cultures represented in temples, churches and mosques. It is a unique country whose 6,000 years of history have had a singleness of purpose—the Nile River—to which it owes its very existence. Cairo, the mighty, bustling capital, stands in sharp contrast to the small, sleepy villages on the banks of the Nile resting from the bright sun under graceful palms. Along the valley green fields, made possible by the river, stretch to the edge of the solemn desert.

POPULATION . . . Only about 3.5% of the land in inhabited, cultivated land; the rest is desert. 95% of Egypt's 29,000,000 people live along the fertile banks of the Nile River. The density— over 2,000 persons per square mile in the delta—is probably the highest in the world and dramatically illustrates the meaning of the Nile to Egypt. The people fall into four categories: the *fellahin* (peasants), who form the bulk of the population; the Copts, who claim to be the direct descendants of the ancient Egyptians; the Bedouins, nomadic Arabs; and the European, Turkish and Levantine minorities.

SIZE . . . 386,101 square miles; about 660 miles long.

CAPITAL . . . Cairo, with a population of about 3,858,000.

GOVERNMENT . . . A republic, known as the United Arab Republic, with a President and Presidential Council. The National Assembly selects the President, whose nomination is submitted to public referendum.

HOW TO GET THERE . . . By Pan American Jet Clipper to Rome, about 8 hours from New York. Then by connecting airline, about 2¾ hours to Cairo. For travelers visiting the Middle East, Cairo is one hour via Middle East Airlines from Beirut and may be included at no extra cost on a ticket purchased in advance covering your full itinerary. By ship to Alexandria, 13 to 17 days from New York. Overland you can drive across North Africa from Morocco to Alexandria and Cairo. The distance is approximately 2,000 miles.

ACCOMMODATION . . . (Rates and more hotels are listed on page 00). In Cairo, the deluxe *Nile Hilton Hotel,* overlooking the river, has 400 air-conditioned rooms, swimming pool, and a floating annex on the Nile—the Isis Boat. *Shepherd's Hotel* has 285 air-conditioned rooms. The *Semiramis* is old, yet charming. The *Cleopatra* is new. *The Nile Palace* is on the Nile. The *Continental-Savoy* is downtown. *Mena House* overlooks the Pyramids of Giza. The *Omar Khayyam,* Zamalek, and *Manial Palace,* Roda Island, have rooms in converted palaces and bungalows in the surrounding gardens.

Alexandria, Egypt's second largest city and major summer resort, has new hotels such as the *Salamlek* and the *Palestine,* several first-class hotels such as the *Cecil* and *Windsor* and a selection of smaller second-class ones. Antiquity sites such as Luxor and Aswan have grand old hotels of world fame—the *Winter Palace* and *Cataract,* as well as new ones.

ARTS . . . Egypt's fabulous art treasures cover 7,000 years of history. The Egyptian Antiquities Museum has the superb Tutankhamen collection, while the Coptic Museum, Islamic Art Museum, Anderson House, Manial and Abdin Palace in Cairo and the Greco-Roman Museum in Alexandria house other masterpieces. From Alexandria to Abu Simbel, Egypt is an open-air museum of art and architecture.

In a modern vein, Egyptian art is a fusion of the country's art heritage—Pharaonic, Coptic and Islamic. Exhibits of local artists are held regularly throughout the year. *Akhenaton Gallery,* Kasr el Nil Street, displays the work of local artists weekly. *Galerie des Beaux Arts,* Bab al-Luc, and *Atelier,* Talaat Harb, also have regular showings.

BALLET . . . Foreign troupes perform occasionally from November through March. The National Ballet (Bolshoi-trained) is of recent origin. It and several folklore dance groups, such as the Reda Group, give frequent performances.

BANKS . . . Money may be exchanged only at banks and at such authorized outlets as American Express Co., 15 Kasr el Nil St.; Thomas Cook & Sons, 4 Champolion St., and branches in major hotels.

CALENDAR OF HOLIDAYS . . . National holidays include Sham en Nassim (Spring Feast) in late April, Evacuation Day (June 18), Anniversary of the Revolution Day (July 23), and Victory Day (December 23). The major festival is the Feast of the Nile (second half of July).

Religious feasts are based on the Moslem calendar and vary in date from year to year. The main ones are Bairam (at the end of Ramadan), Eid al Kabir (at the end of the Pilgrimage), Moslem New Year (Muharram I) and Moulid el-Nebi (Prophet Muhammad's birthday).

CIGARETTES AND TOBACCO . . . Egyptian cigarettes are made of the best qualities of Turkish and American tobaccos and cost 41¢ a pack. Cleopatra and Belmont are popular. American cigarettes cost 80¢ a pack. Buy a carton on the plane before arriving and carry a lighter. Matches are scarce.

CLIMATE . . . Lower Egypt has one of the most pleasant year-round climates of the Mediterranean, while Upper Egypt is famous as a winter resort. The temperature in Cairo in autumn is usually in the 60s and drops to the low 40s by winter. In spring and early summer, it ranges from the 70s to the high 80s, reaching the high 90s by late summer. At sundown the temperature drops suddenly 5 to 20 degrees the year round. Alexandria is about 10 to 15 degrees cooler than Cairo; Luxor and Aswan are correspondingly hotter. The Mediterranean coast has a short rainy season in winter. In summer, tourist facilities are available in Upper Egypt. But make no mistake: it is hot. October through May is the ideal time to visit Egypt.

CLUBS . . . The important clubs in Cairo are the Automobile Club, Cairo Yacht Club, Fishing and Shooting Club, Gezira Sporting Club, Heliopolis Sporting Club, Maadi Sporting Club, Maadi Yacht Club, National Sporting Club, Rowing Club, Touring Club and Rotary Club (meets every Tuesday at 1:30 at the Nile Hilton).

COMMON COURTESIES AND LOCAL CUSTOMS . . . Egyptians are intensely proud of their country and its progress during the last decade, made against severe problems of over-population and the legacy of ancient customs. During your visit you will be reminded frequently of the difficulties in transforming a nation whose social and cultural patterns are 7,000 years old.

The Egyptians are Moslems—pride in which is second only to their being Egyptians. A veiled woman is an unusual sight these days, and polygamy is dying fast. Egyptian women, especially the younger generation, are considered emancipated by their society and have played an active role in the development and modernization of their country.

Egyptians are good-natured, friendly and accommodating to visitors. You are greeted with *saida,* meaning "hello," and *shukran,* "thank you." The educated class is generally sophisticated and well-traveled. However, the bulk of Egyptians living along the banks of the Nile have never ventured beyond Cairo.

Under the warm African sun and the gentle Mediterranean breeze, time has little importance. The unconcern for time is often frustrating to visitors. Yet the relaxed atmosphere accounts for a great deal of Egypt's charm. Most Egyptians, except perhaps the younger generation, cannot be hurried. *Bukra* (tomorrow) is a common expression. It is the tomorrow of the future. It has no time limit.

In Cairo, Alexandria and other major cities a woman is safe traveling alone, but her first travel within Egypt will be more fun and less costly if she joins a group—especially to visit the sites in Upper Egypt. Leading travel agencies in Cairo have groups leaving daily for major sites of interest.

COMMUNICATIONS . . . Cairo and Alexandria have dial telephone systems. Public phone booths are located at main squares throughout both cities. Phone calls to the U.S. are made between 4 and 11 P.M. A three-minute call costs £.E. 3.300 (U.S. $7.55); a cablegram is 23 piasters (52¢) per word. Airmail to the United States is 8.5 piasters for postcards, 11.5 piasters for letters. Airmail letters from New York are delivered in Cairo within four to six days. Surface mail from the U.S. takes four to six weeks. Post offices are open daily except Friday. The central post office, Ataba Square, has 24-hour service daily.

CURRENCY . . . The Egyptian pound (£.E.) is divided into 100 piasters (P.T. 100) or 1,000 milliemes (1,000 mills). One U.S. dollar corresponds to 43.5 piasters. Many different coins for the same denominations are in circulation, and often their values are written in Arabic characters only. Early in your stay ask the hotel concierge to explain the different coins to you.

You are not allowed to bring in *any* amount of Egyptian currency. It must be bought in the UAR. No limit is set on the amount of foreign currency and traveler's checks you may bring in, but you must declare all of it. You may not take out more foreign currency than you brought into the country. Your declaration of currency is made on a customs form given you upon arrival at ports or airports.

Currency may be exchanged at airports on arrival. All foreign currency must be exchanged through authorized banks or their representatives in the UAR. All amounts so exchanged should be recorded on your customs form. Upon departure you may return all unused Egyptian pounds purchased at local banks for their equivalent in the currency with which the Egyptian pounds were bought.

Egypt's currency exchange regulations are stringently controlled by the government. Do not use "greenback" or any other foreign currency to purchase goods from local merchants. It is illegal. Use only Egyptian currency in Egypt.

CUSTOMS REGULATIONS AND DOCUMENTS RE-QUIRED FOR UNITED STATES CITIZENS . . . Passport and visa (which can be obtained at the airport upon arrival) required, also smallpox certificates and others if coming from Eastern, yellow-fever or cholera areas. Check with Pan American. The U.A.R. is a member of the United Nations World Health Organization and adheres strictly to its immunization requirements. You must have an international immunization card. If you arrive without proper records, you will be quarantined. If you are transiting by ship or plane and not remaining in the U.A.R., you do not need a visa. You will be given a landing permit valid for the time your ship or plane is calling at a U.A.R. port or airport. Passengers transiting the Suez Canal may obtain free transit visas valid for three days. Personal effects are admitted duty free, although some need to be declared. One hundred cigarettes or 25 cigars or ½ lb. of tobacco and one opened pint of liquor allowed. Valuable personal jewelry is exempted from duty but must be declared on arrival.

Foreigners must register at the Passport Office within 72 hours of their arrival. For those persons staying in a hotel, the formality is handled by the hotel registration clerk.

DRUGSTORES . . . Egypt's state-run pharmaceutical plant bottles and packages medicines of a leading American pharmaceutical company. Most pharmaceuticals are available, but local packaging and labeling in Arabic make it difficult for a newcomer to recognize them. Bring your required medicine and prescriptions with you. Imported American cosmetics are practically nonexistent. Some American products are packaged locally and some European stocks are available. Bring supplies sufficient for your visit.

ELECTRIC CURRENT . . . 220 A.C., 50 cycles in Cairo and Alexandria, 110 A.C. in Heliopolis. Wall plugs are the round two-prong European type. Adapter plugs for American products should be brought with you. American appliances need transformers; British ones do not.

FAUNA . . . The camel, which can be ridden around the Pyramids and the Sphinx, but not in the streets of the towns. In the Egyptian deserts, desert rabbits, gazelles and foxes. Hunting excursions can be organized through the Hunting and Fishing Club or the Touring Club of Egypt.

FLORA . . . Cairo has a year-round profusion of flowers such as geraniums and roses and a variety of tropical flowers and plants. The palm tree, eucalyptus and flamboyant are characteristic silhouettes against the Egyptian sky.

FOOD . . . Most hotels serve European meals, but visitors may enjoy a *mezzah* (assorted hors d'oeuvres) that includes *tahina* dip, stuffed grape leaves, *babaghanous* and *tamiya,* followed by shishkebab. (See Menu Translator, Chapter XXII.) These might be followed with a dessert of *muhalabiya, eish el saraya* or *kunafa* and, of course, a cup of strong Turkish coffee (*mazbut*—sugared; *sada*—without sugar). Local fruits and vegetables are good but seasonal. Milk should be boiled. (Powdered and canned milk are seldom available.)

In leading hotels and restaurants, food is usually clean and well prepared. Until one has spent some time in Egypt or other Middle Eastern countries, reasonable caution should be exercised. Eat food that has been cooked and fruits and vegetables that can be peeled. Also as a health measure always use a blanket when you sleep. Temperatures drop considerably at night, and there is quite a difference between inside and outdoor temperatures in the daytime.

GAMBLING . . . Cairo's modern casino is located at the top of the Muqattam hills from where it commands a splendid view of the city. A foreign visitor must show his passport to enter. Roulette, twenty-one, chemin de fer and baccarat are played. The night club has a European show and music for dancing. Free transportation to the casino from the company's downtown office on Adly Street is provided for patrons. In Alexandria the casino is located at Montaza Palace.

Horse races are held during the winter season at the Gezira Sporting Club in Cairo and in summer at Smouha or the Alexandria Sporting Club in Alexandria. Horses may be viewed in the paddock before each race. Betting is pari-mutuel, and the lowest sum which may be bet is 10 piasters.

LANGUAGE . . . A visitor can make himself understood in English in most of Egypt. Useful Arabic expressions are *sabah al-khair* (good morning), *ahlan wa sahlan* (welcome), *shukran* (thank you) and *baksheesh* (tip). Arabic is the official language of the country. Most educated Egyptians speak English and French.

LAUNDRY AND DRY CLEANING . . . Facilities are available at major hotels in Cairo and Alexandria and are adequate for normal needs. Rates are rather high.

LIQUOR . . . Egypt produces a good quality of beer, Stella, and several good, inexpensive table wines made from Alexandrian grapes by Chateau Gianaclis. Omar Khayyam (red), Cleopatra (red) and Cru des Ptolemees (white) are the best. Cocktails and mixed drinks are served at bars, hotels and restaurants. The cost of the average drink is 40 piasters. Spathis Lemonade, a lightly flavored lemon soda, is an excellent thirst quencher. Coca-Cola and Pepsi-Cola are also available.

Safari Bar is the lively bar of the Hilton Hotel, and the bars at Shepheard's and Semiramis hotels are also popular. All the leading sporting clubs have bars—often outdoors by a pool or on a terrace overlooking the Nile and Cairo. Cocktail time in Egypt is usually from 7 to 9 P.M.

MEDICAL FACILITIES . . . There are private and government hospitals with English-speaking doctors in attendance. A list of English-speaking doctors, general practitioners and specialists is maintained at the American Embassy. Information on doctors and medical services is available in Cairo at the Superior Medical Professions, 42 Sharia el Qasr al-Aini, and in Alexandria at Official Medical and Sanitary Centers, 97 Sharia al-Hureiya.

MOTION PICTURES . . . Many Cairo theaters show American films. The most important ones are Metro, Kasr el Nil, Radio, Rivoli, Ramses and Cairo Palace. All first-class theaters are air-conditioned. Theater seats are reserved; the more expensive ones are in the balcony (considered the best location). Check the English or French-language newspapers or ask the hotel concierge for a current schedule. Show times are 10 A.M., 3 P.M., 6 P.M. and 9 P.M.

MUSIC . . . In the winter season symphony orchestras and ballets by European and Eastern-bloc groups are performed at the Cairo Opera House. A six-week visit of an Italian opera company is an annual event. Other concerts by visiting and local musicians are held at various cultural centers throughout the city. The Cairo Symphony Orchestra gives concerts weekly during the season.

Cultural activity of a Western nature extends as deep as Western influence. The bulk of Egyptians participate in cultural activities arising from their own heritage. Unfortunately for the visitor, these require a knowledge of Arabic to appreciate and enjoy.

NIGHT CLUBS . . . Cairo has a variety of night clubs. Many have romantic settings in outdoor gardens or terraces where you dance under swaying palms against a moonlight sky. Night clubs often have both local and European floor shows; others have none. Most shows start about 10 or 11 P.M. and end with a belly dancer, of which Egypt has the best.

Some of the leading places are *Auberge des Pyramides,* big and brassy; *Dugout* at Shepheard's; the *Mena House Supper Club* for dining and dancing on an outdoor patio set in a flowering garden under the moonlit silhouette of the Pyramids of Giza; the *Omar Khayyam,* a yacht on the Nile; *Pearl of the Desert* and *Sahara City,* fancy tents in the desert near the Pyramids; the *Semiramis Roof* for Cairo habitués; the *Starlight Roof* (Hilton Hotel); the *Pyramids Stereo,* especially popular with the younger set; and *Cheops,* near the Sphinx with a magnificent view of the Pyramids.

PHOTOGRAPHY . . . Photographers will have a heyday in Egypt. But remember that the sun is deceivingly bright, especially at sites of antiquity. Inside tombs and monuments you need a flash. Bring all film and photographing needs with you. These items are expensive in Egypt. Less ambitious photographers can buy slides of all the important sites in Egypt. Tourists are requested not to take pictures of military installations, factories and public works.

RELIGION . . . The official religion is Islam. Approximately 90% of the population are Sunni Moslems. There are churches of every sect, as well as synagogues. The Coptic Church, one of the oldest in Christendom, is the monophysitic branch of Christianity which split from the general church at the Council of Chalcedon in A.D. 451.

RESTAURANTS . . . Leading restaurants serve Continental food and some local cuisine. Some of the best restaurants are in night clubs and hotels, where prices are only slightly higher. Expect to pay about $.75 for breakfast, $2 for lunch, $3.50 for dinner, and slightly more at luxury hotels and night clubs. Leading restaurants are *Aladdin,* one of the best restaurants in Cairo for European cuisine; *Ali Hassan al Hati,* one of Cairo's oldest and best known for Egyptian food; *Estoril*; *Groppi's*; *Casino des Pigeons,* specializing in charcoal-broiled pigeons; *Ibis Café,* coffee shop of the Nile Hilton, open 24 hours daily; *Jewel of the Nile,* Hilton dining room; *Khomais,* Oriental food in colorful Arabian Nights atmosphere;

Kursaal, European selections from an à la carte menu; *Le Grillon*; *Omar Khayyam,* a yacht on the Nile, pleasant for lunch.

SHOPS AND STORES . . . In Cairo's modern shopping districts stores abound with wide selections of clothing, shoes, accessories, furniture and household appliances made in Egypt. The main streets for shopping are Kasr al Nil (Cairo's Fifth Avenue), 26 July, Talaat Harb, Emad ed-Din, Adly, the Arcade, Midan Mustapha Kamel and the area encompassed by these streets. Store hours: 9 A.M. to 1 P.M., 3 or 4 to 8 P.M. Some shops close on Friday, some Saturday, others Sunday.

For tourists the biggest attractions are the old bazaars situated in or near the street called the Mouski, the original and oldest commercial street in Cairo. Its narrow, picturesque lanes are lined with tiny shops and teem with milling crowds and mingled scents. The owner of each shop will invite you to enter and will offer you coffee or tea while you browse. In the Mouski, Khan al Khalili is the best of all the bazaars.

Bargaining is an accepted pattern in Egypt; no one pays the original asking price. One-third off is the usual settlement. Remember, no one in Egypt is in a hurry, least of all in the Mouski.

SPECTATOR SPORTS . . . A great number of sporting events are held in Egypt. Championship matches take place among the various teams in the Mediterranean and Arab countries in soccer, swimming, tennis and basketball. Regattas and sailboat races are held regularly on the Nile.

SPORTS . . . Egypt is a sportsman's paradise. Its climate makes it ideal for tennis, badminton, golf, squash, sailing, fishing, horseback riding and water skiing the year round. Most sporting activity centers at clubs such as Gezira Sporting Club, National, Maadi and Heliopolis sporting clubs in the Cairo area. All have excellent facilities and large playgrounds for children. Meals and refreshments are served on the terrace of the clubhouse. Temporary membership for tourists may be obtained at reasonable fees.

Camping trips to the Red Sea are great fun. Sleeping and eating facilities have been developed in the area of Ain Suhna and Hurghada. The area is excellent for fishing and skin diving. On the Mediterranean beautiful white sand beaches stretch from Alexandria to the Libyan border. In Cairo you may swim in a pool at one of the sporting clubs, the Mena House and the Nile Hilton Hotel.

Good horses, with or without guides, are available near the Mena House by the Pyramids. A moonlight ride across the desert is great sport in Egypt, though not advisable for a novice. Overnight or longer camping trips in the desert may be arranged through local travel agencies.

You may enjoy sailing or motorboating in Cairo on the Nile the year round, and in Alexandria on the Mediterranean all months except winter. Cairo, Alexandria, Ismailia and Maadi Yacht Clubs have their own boats where visitors are welcome. Water skiing is popular in Alexandria. Sailing on the Nile in a feluka, the graceful sailboat often pictured in scenes of Egypt, is delightful. Boats with crew may be rented inexpensively at the dock near Shepheard's Hotel.

Tennis is one of Egypt's most popular sports and there are many courts in Cairo and Alexandria. Tourneys by local participants as well as visiting international groups are held often throughout the year.

THEATERS . . . Cairo is the center of theatrical activity in the Arab world. Three theaters—Ezbekiyah, Gumhuriya and Pocket —stage high-quality productions regularly throughout the year. These productions include translations of American and European plays as well as original Arabic ones. The Pocket Theater is considered Egypt's avant-garde group.

TIME . . . Greenwich Mean Time plus two hours. Noon in Cairo is 5 A.M. in New York. Daylight saving time is observed from May 1 to October 31.

TIPPING . . . Hotels and restaurants add a 10% service charge. Tip luggage porters 5 piasters per bag. Tip 5 to 10 piasters for small services. In restaurants, hotels, etc., droves of men hover about to give you service. If you have been served well, a little *baksheesh* (small tip) is appreciated. Don't overdo it, though. Four or five piasters in Egypt will go a long way. Carry a change purse for coins and always ask for change in small denominations when paying a bill. As a rule of thumb, your total tips should not exceed 10% of your bill before the service charge is added.

TOURIST TAXES . . . At Luxor and Aswan, a 5% tax is added to hotel bills. Airport departure tax is 50 piasters ($1.15).

TRANSPORTATION . . . Taxis are inexpensive. Deluxe air-conditioned express trains and Misrair for quick transport. But if you have the time, Nile steamers are recommended for travel from Cairo to Luxor and Aswan. (See Chapters XV and XVI.)

WATER . . . Tap water is safe in cities and tourist resorts. Bottled water is available in better hotels and restaurants throughout Egypt.

WHAT TO BUY . . . The Mouski overflows with Egyptian handicrafts which will tempt even a disinterested visitor, and a tour through the old bazaars is high on the lists of musts during a visit to Cairo.

Several stores are authorized to sell Egyptian antiquities such as pedestal-mounted statuary and small antique amulets that are representations of the ancient gods. The smallest statues and amulets are sometimes encased or mounted in gold and worn as charms. Charms, cuff links, brooches and earrings are made from ancient fused mosaic glass. The lovely designs run through the entire thickness of the piece and resemble abstract designs of modern ceramics. For Islamic antiquities and copies of Pharaonic and Islamic furniture, *Hatoun and Sons,* Mouski Street, has a wide selection. You may also visit their workship.

Alexandrites, aquamarines, topaz and pearls are made into earrings, rings, pins or bracelets at reasonable prices. Peridot from St. John Island in the Red Sea is scarce and available only in Egypt. Turquoise from Sinai is of good quality. *Onnig Alexanian,* perhaps the most famous gemologist in the Middle East, has a shop in the Mouski and at the Semiramis Hotel. He designs jewelry often inspired from Pharaonic design.

Egypt is the place to buy the camel saddle you always wanted. Many new types are made, but the old kind, free of brass designs, are nicest. There is also a good assortement of poufs or ottomans, sandals and inexpensive leather suitcases.

The Mouski is filled with tempting objects of brass and copper. The new ones have Pharaonic designs; the old ones are engraved with arabesque. Copper plates encrusted with metal or silver, tall pitchers, vases, candle sticks, samovars and braziers are among the best selections.

Gold and silver are sold by weight, and the workmanship is good. You can buy charms of the Pyramids or Sphinx or cuff links and charms with your name inscribed in Arabic or in hieroglyphics. Also popular are the thin, gold bracelets used by native Egyptian women for their dowry. Bedouin jewelry, filigree silver and gold, a variety of necklaces and bracelets, which are copies or adaptations of the ancient Egyptian jewelry, are available. Especially attractive is a choker of mummy beads and a wide gold bracelet with multicolored semiprecious stones—Onnig's copy of the original one worn by Cleopatra.

On tours of old mosques, houses, churches and palaces, you will see examples of intricate woodwork called *mushrabbiyah* (sometimes identified as harem screens). These and other exquisitely carved woods make nice tables and screens.

Needless to say, Egypt is the place to buy cotton. Shirts made to order and dress fabrics are inexpensive. *Galabiyah* cloth, an inexpensive fabric used for the long, outer robe worn by native-dressed Egyptian men, comes in soft colors, is very sturdy and is excellent for draperies and upholstering.

Trays, jewelry and cigarette boxes inlaid with ivory and ebony are attractive. Alabaster vases, ashtrays, lamp bases and figurines are available in Cairo or you may buy from the factory in Luxor.

Leading department stores in the modern shopping district of Cairo are *Chemla,* 11, 26th July Street; *Cicurel,* 3, 26 July Street;

Egyptian Products Sales Co., 2, 26th July Street, *Hannaux,* Kasr al Nil Street; and *Salon Vert,* Kasr el Nil Street.

Downtown Cairo and residential areas have many bookshops which stock books in English. For old and rare editions, *Orientalia,* Kasr al Nil Street (next to American Express), is the best. This store also sells old maps and the famous Robert's prints of old Egyptian scenes. Magazines and newspapers are sold by vendors.

WHAT TO WEAR . . . For ladies, cotton and Dacron dresses are comfortable during spring, early summer and fall. In summer, only cotton dresses and lingerie are advisable. December through February you need light wool suits and dresses with jackets or long sleeves, a lightweight coat or jacket, warm housecoat and slippers. Remember to include a stole for evenings the year round. Temperatures may drop 20 degrees at night.

For men, Dacron and cotton suits will be comfortable. In winter you will need light wool suits, a light topcoat for the coolest days and a warm dressing gown. Most first-class hotels and restaurants require a tie and jacket during meals.

Comfortable walking shoes are essential. Sunglasses are a must, and you may want a shade hat for sightseeing rounds in the open and for the beach. Other useful items are small binoculars, a flashlight (especially for visiting tombs and temples), a wash cloth, disposable premoistened face cloths, insect repellent, collapsible hanger, face soap, packaged soap powders, a collapsible drinking cup, and always have a supply of Kleenex.

WHERE TO GO—SIGHTSEEING . . . The main organization to facilitate tourism is the UAR State Tourist Administration, head office, 5 Adly Pasha St., Cairo. (Tel. 79394.) Tourist officers are stationed in ports, airports, hotels and major tourist areas to assist tourists on arrival and during their visit. English-speaking guides are available through hotels, travel agencies or the State Tourist Office. Fees vary from 2—5 £.E. per day.

In Egypt the handsomely robed and turbaned gentlemen who guide tourist around antiquity sites and the bazaars are called *dragoman.* The word is a corruption of an Arabic word, *terjiman,* meaning interpreter. These men are as characteristic of Egypt as the Nile.

What to see in Cairo depends largely on the length of your visit. Itineraries can be based on visiting the sites in order of their historic, artistic and archaeological importance, or by exploring one district of Cairo at a time. On your first visit, you might prefer to join organized tours. In the long run, it is less costly.

Descriptions of the major sites listed below are available in Chapters XVI and XVII. The country is so rich in antiquities, you could spend months sightseeing.

Special admission cards, valid for one year from June 1 to May 31, entitle holders to visit all ancient monuments in Upper Egypt, including Saqqara. (Price: 180 piasters.) These may be purchased in Cairo at the Egyptian Antiquities Museum.

SOURCES OF FURTHER INFORMATION . . . For hire of Pan Am's official guide, Pan American's office, Continental Hotel, Cairo (Tel. 911233). In New York the United Arab Republic Tourist Office is at 630 Fifth Avenue. For complete details of practical information and on sightseeing, read *Travel Egypt* by Kay Showker (Librairie du Liban, Beirut, 1966). *History of Egypt from Earliest Time to the Persian Conquest* by James Breasted (Scribner's, New York) is a classic work on ancient Egypt.

Cairo by the Nile.

CHAPTER XV

EGYPT: THE COUNTRY AS A WHOLE

TYPES OF ACCOMMODATIONS

HOTELS

An Old World elegance, bright spacious rooms and service by handsomely robed Nubians are the characteristics of most Egyptian hotels. Accommodations range from luxury palaces to cozy pensions. Cairo hotels are very crowded, especially during the winter season. You must make reservations in advance. Hotel prices may vary 10 to 15% according to the season. A 10% service charge is added throughout Egypt, and in Luxor and Aswan there is a 5% city tax. Reductions in hotel rates are given for children under 12. A 10% reduction will be given to a guest after a 16-day stay. Except for those in Cairo, Luxor, Aswan and Alexandria, there are no deluxe or first-class hotels in Egypt. With a few exceptions, noted in Chapter XVI, other towns in Egypt do not have new hotels, and the old ones tend to be second or third class.

PENSIONS

Most hotels not in the deluxe or first-class category are usually run on a pension basis—i.e., room rates include breakfast and one other meal. In Cairo there are several acceptable pensions, but in other towns they tend to be substandard.

YOUTH HOSTELS

There are youth hostels in most of the major towns of Egypt. Accommodations are inexpensive but rudimentary. For details write to the Youth Hostel Association, 7 Sharia Doctor Abdel Hamid Said, Maarouf, Cairo. The association will also assist students in arranging a tour of the country.

CAMPSITES

There are no organized camping sites in Egypt. If you have the necessary equipment you may camp in the desert outside Cairo or any town along the Nile, on the Red Sea and Mediterranean shores. Travel agents in Cairo can arrange camping trips also. The price is determined by the degree of luxury desired.

TOURING

AUTOMOBILES

A tourist entering Egypt with a car registered in a foreign country is exempt from local customs duties for a period of 90 days. The owner must hold a triptych from a recognized automobile club and an international driving license valid for the 90-day period. Customs officials must verify that the owner has no fixed residence in Egypt. By law all car owners must carry third-party personal liability insurance. Good insurance coverage is highly advisable. If you remain in Egypt longer than 90 days, a UAR driver's license is necessary and is issued upon presentation of three photographs, a certificate of medical examination, U.S. or international driver's license and payment of a small fee.

Through airline offices, hotels or travel agents you may rent a car usually with a driver, and may pick up the car at the airport on arrival. The average rent is £.E. 10 per day, including driver and fuel, for driving in the metropolitan area of Cairo.

Certain parts of Egypt have regulations banning motoring. Find out these regulations from the Automobile Club before starting out on a trip. Always carry your passport with you.

Roads in Cairo and Alexandria are good, as are major highways connecting the larger cities of Lower Egypt. Secondary roads, however, are often dusty and filled with donkey carts and people. Most distance and location signs are posted in Arabic throughout

Egypt. There are very few caution signs. You should always drive with great care, as pedestrians often walk in the street. In cities, parking lights only are used for night driving.

Gasoline and service stations are plentiful in Cairo and Alexandria but scarce elsewhere. Before starting on a long trip, be sure to get all necessary information from the Autombile Club, 10 Kasr el Nil St. (Tel. 77243). On the desert road to Suez and on the autostrade to Alexandria there is a midway resthouse with gasoline pumps. Gasoline costs about 50¢ per gallon.

BICYCLES

Can be rented from dealers at about 25 piasters an hour. Generally not recommended.

AFOOT

In towns and cities only. Good maps of Cairo, Alexandria and Luxor are available from the Tourism Administration, bookshops and travel agencies.

PLANES

Misrair operates between the major cities of Egypt and has daily flights from Cairo to Alexandria, Port Said, Luxor and Aswan, and several weekly flights to Mersa Matruh (in summer). The airlines will arrange combined air-and-hotel tickets to Luxor.

TRAINS

Egypt has an extensive network of trains connecting Cairo with the major cities of the Delta, the Mediterranean and Suez, and with the major sites of antiquity in Upper Egypt. Second class is adequate for short trips. On one's first trip to Egypt, first-class travel by express trains is recommended. First- and second-class Cairo–Alexandria passengers may reserve seats in air-conditioned cars. Sleeping cars and a dining car are attached to the express night train from Cairo to Luxor and Aswan. The train station in any major city is well located in the center of town.

Passengers in transit who wish to tour Egypt may get reduced fare on round-trip tickets from Port Said and Alexandria to Cairo. Reductions for students are also granted on train tickets and at youth hostels in major cities. Check with the Tourist Administration for specific information.

BUSES

Daily desert bus service is available between Cairo and Alexandria, Port Said, Ismailia, Suez and Fayum. Schedules of local and desert buses are available at hotels and travel agencies. Fare from Cairo to Alexandria: first class, £.E. 1.15.

NILE STEAMERS

A voyage up the Nile by steamer is one of the most delightful trips in Egypt. Eastmar has four Nile steamers, which during the winter season go from Luxor to Abydos, Dendara and return, and from Luxor to Esna, Edfu, Kom Ombo, Aswan and return. Rates on an all-inclusive 10-day trip begin at £.E. 72 for a double room. The *Isis* and the *Osiris* (under the management of the Nile Hilton Hotel) are new German-built boats, complete with swimming pools and offering deluxe travel. Other steamers at slightly lower prices are also available. At the beginning of the winter season (late November) you may board a steamer in Cairo for the initial voyage. Afterward you must take a train or plane to Luxor or Aswan, where you board a boat for the journey to sites in Upper Egypt. During the season, steamers sail several times weekly between Luxor and Aswan. In planning a Nile steamer trip make reservations in advance. On the other hand, if upon arrival in Cairo you decide to make a voyage, deal directly with one of the companies in charge of the steamers.

For the full excursion in Upper Egypt, a prearranged trip may be bought in Cairo. It includes round-trip train or plane fare, food, hotel accommodation, steamer fare and guides. For most people a prearranged tour organized through a reliable travel agent is probably the most satisfactory way to see Upper Egypt.

MENU TRANSLATOR—See Chapter XXII.

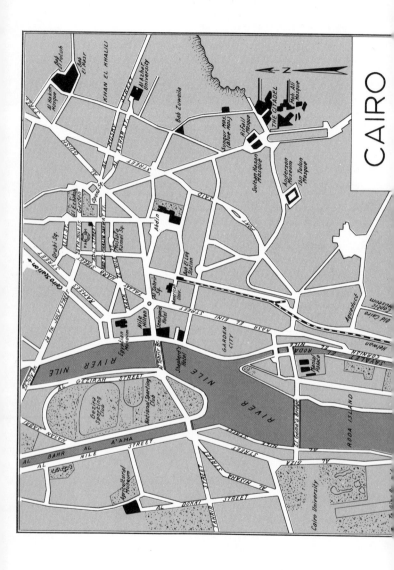

CHAPTER XVI

CAIRO

CAIRO INTERNATIONAL AIRPORT

Cairo has an elegant new airport, well arranged to receive incoming and outgoing passengers, and it includes a 50-room hotel for direct in-transit passengers. Major airlines, tourist agencies and the State Tourist Administration have offices in the new building. Shops, several comfortable lounges and food are available.

Before leaving the plane, your hostess will give you an entry form and customs declaration to be filled in and presented to the airport officials. Keep your customs declaration in a safe place, along with your passport. You will need this form to leave the country. Upon departure there is an airport tax of 50 piasters.

Taxis or buses into town are available in front of the airport building. The drive to downtown Cairo is about 15 miles, and the taxi fare is about 70 piasters ($1.68). Bus fare is 20 piasters (46¢). If you arrive by day, the drive through the suburbs of Heliopolis, Abbassiya and along the Corniche Drive by the Nile is a pleasant introduction to Cairo.

HOTELS

Cairo has a wide range of hotels, but unless you are a seasoned traveler it is worth the extra expense to stay in one of the best ones, such as the Nile Hilton, Shepheard's, Semiramis or El-Borg. These offer the best locations, service, standards and atmosphere—with delightful panoramic views thrown in.

Name (Tel.)		Single w/bath	Double w/bath	Rooms/	Baths
Nile Hilton (811811) Corniche		$ 9.20–$11.50	$12.65–$16.10	432	432
Shepheard's (33800) Corniche		$ 9.20–$11.20	$11.50–$13.80	285	285
Semiramis (22800) Corniche		$ 5.30–$ 7.47	$ 9.20–$12.65	193	193
Mena House (894610) Pyramids		$ 4.60	$ 8.63	120	120
El-Borg (816060) Gezira		$ 6.00–$ 9.20	$ 7.48–$11.50	75	75
Nile Palace (23878) On the Nile	with breakfast	$ 7.56–$ 9.20	$11.50–$12.40	216	216
Omar Khayyam (819910) Palace		$12.80		28	28
Zamalek	Bungalows	$ 6.90	$11.40	232	232
Manial Palace (844659) Roda Island		$ 5.17	$11.40	183	183

Name (Tel.)	Single w/bath	Double w/bath	Rooms/Baths	
Cleopatra (70420) Tahrir Square	$ 7.30–$ 9.20	$10.12–$11.50	84	84
Scheherazade (819896) El Nil, Agouza	$ 6.90	$ 9.20	80	80
Cairo Airport (62581) Cairo International Airport	$ 6.90	$ 8.63	50	—
Continental-Savoy (911197) 10 Opera Square	$ 3.68–$ 4.50	$ 5.75–$ 6.00	208	150
Cosmopolitan (78531) 2 Ibn Saalab St.	$ 3.71–$ 4.50	$ 6.44	94	94
Lotus Pension (70360) 12 Talaat Harb	$ 3.57	$ 5.75–$ 6.21	50	20
May Fair Pension (807315) 9 Aziz Osmar St., Zamalek	$ 1.38*	$ 2.30*	23	—
Garden City House (24969) 23 Kamal ed-Din Salah St.	$2.59*–$ 3.80	$ 5.06	39	19

* without bath.

YOUTH HOSTELS — See Chapter XV.

CITY TRANSPORTATION

At Cairo Railway Station you may entrust your luggage to a station porter wearing a plate number. Porter fees: 5 piasters (12¢) per bag. Taxis are available outside the station. The trip to a downtown hotel takes about 10 minutes and costs about 15 piasters. The taxi fares to outlying districts are approximately as follows: Zamalek, 20 piasters (48¢); Heliopolis, 35 piasters (84¢); Mena House (Pyramids), 50 piasters ($1.20).

All Cairo taxis are painted dark blue and white (in Alexandria, black and yellow). The fare is registered on a meter on the driver's right side. The charge is 6 piasters (14¢) for the first half kilometer and 1 piaster each additional 1/3 kilometer. No extra charge for night service. The drivers usually speak a smattering of English. If you do not know how to get to your destination, ask the hotel concierge to instruct the driver and to write the address in Arabic on a piece of paper. If you wish to direct him yourself, learn these words: *doughri* or *ala toul* (straight ahead), *yameen* (right), *shamal* (left), *'andak* (stop).

Cairo has an extensive bus system, but since buses are very crowded a tourist on a short visit will probably want to use taxis, which are plentiful and inexpensive. Bus fares are proportional to the distance. An average ride in downtown Cairo is 2 piasters for first class. Use only first class—i.e., enter the bus by the front door. (Second class is entered from the rear of the bus.) In addition, numerous travel agencies have sightseeing buses.

Mosque of Mohammed Ali near Cairo.

Native freight barges on the Nile.

CITY SIGHTS

Regularly scheduled tours with guides of Cairo and environs are available at leading travel agencies. On your first trip such tours are recommended for major sights, and if your time allows you can explore the lesser ones on your own.

Egyptian Antiquities Museum: Tahrir Square next to the Nile Hilton Hotel . . . The museum contains the world's most important collection of Egyptian antiquities, dating from earliest times to about the 6th century A.D. Through its exhibits, which include some of the art masterpieces of the world, you get a chronological survey of ancient Egypt, beginning with the earliest period of recorded history, the Ancient Empire about 3200 B.C., followed by the sections of the Middle Empire, and the New Empire comprising the XVIII, XIX and XX dynasties. Numerous rooms contain monuments of Ramsessid, Saite, Persian, Greco-Roman and Nubian periods. The fabulous Tutankhamen collection is displayed on the second floor. From the paintings, statues, furniture and models in the museum a vivid impression of ancient Egypt may be gained. At the entrance a guidebook is available for 15 piasters. At least two hours are necessary for a brief glance at the main exhibits. The museum is full of so many marvels, you will want to return several times.

Museum of Islamic Art: Ahmad Maher Square . . . Created in the late 19th century to house the valuable art objects scattered around in various Cairo mosques. The museum's collection is the most valuable and comprehensive one of Islamic art in the world. Exhibits from the 7th through the 19th centuries are displayed in 23 galleries and are grouped according to style and subject. A careful study of these exhibits is useful for visiting the mosques and other Islamic monuments throughout Cairo. A booklet describing the exhibits is available at the entrance to the museum.

Coptic Museum: Old Cairo adjoining the ancient wall of Babylon Fort . . . Founded in 1908 to house the large collection of Coptic art and antiquities previously kept in the Antiquities Museum. Excavation at Baouit and Saqqara resulted in the discovery of two monasteries, St. Appollon and St. Jeremia, from which many of the museum's objects were taken. The evolution of Christian and Islamic art from Pharaonic motifs are in evidence in many exhibits. At the door of the museum, a brief guide is available for 7 piasters.

Abdin Palace: Begun by Khedive Ismail and completed in 1874, Abdin Palace is a community within itself. The main places of interest are the *Salamlek* (ladies' reception rooms), the dining hall and living quarters of the former king and queen, the Belgium wing used for state reception, the Byzantine Hall and, most of all, the gilded bathrooms with their sunken tubs.

Qubbah Palace: Built in 1862 under Khedive Ismail and used as the official residence of his successor, Tewfiq. The palace has some 400 rooms, including a museum. It now houses the Presidency.

Manial Palace and Museum: Built in 1901 by a prince of the royal family, Muhammad Ali. It is located on Roda Island and surrounded by magnificent gardens. The palace is a mixture of Persian, Ottoman, Moorish and Islamic styles. Every inch of the interior is covered with mosaics, *mushrabiyyah* or some intricate work of art. The palace grounds now house a hotel-motel.

The Citadel and Muhammad Ali Mosque: On the slopes of the Muqattam Hills stand the Citadel of Saladin and the Mosque of Muhammad Ali, commanding a complete view of Cairo, the Nile and, in the far distance, the Pyramids of Giza. The Muhammad Ali Mosque (also called the Alabaster Mosque) is an outstanding example of Islamic architecture. Its domed cupola and graceful minarrets are second only to the Pyramids and Sphinx as subjects for picture postcards of Egypt. Its walls, inside and out, are coated with alabaster. The façade is ornamented with quotations from the Koran and with the names of the Caliphs of the Rashid dynasty. The minarets measure 85 meters in height.

The Citadel was built by Saladin as a fortress and was constructed of stones from small pyramids at Giza. In later years the Citadel was used as the headquarters and official residence of the sultans. Muhammad Ali rebuilt much of the inner part and added the mosque bearing his name, the Jewel Palace, the Law Court, the Mint and Archives situated opposite El-Bab el-Gadid (the New Gate). The *Military Museum* houses twelve exhibits pertaining to ancient and Islamic Egypt, modern history, military dress, swords and firearms, and valuable documents through the ages. Adjacent to the museum is a library containing some 5,000 volumes on the military history of Egypt.

The mausoleum at the southwest corner of the mosque contains the tomb of Muhammad Ali, who died in A.D. 1848. In the tower to the west is a clock presented to Muhammad Ali by Louis Philippe of France. *El Gawhara Palace,* within the compound of the Citadel, is now a museum. Guides show visitors the room in which Muhammad Ali feasted the Mameluk sultans before having them beheaded.

A new road to the Citadel from the south passes the remains of a lengthy aqueduct, originally built by Saladin to supply the Citadel and rebuilt by Sultan el-Ghouri in the early 16th century.

A *Son et Lumière* program is presented at the Citadel in English twice weekly. Check locally for the schedule. A bus leaves the Son et Lumière booth at Liberation Square at 7 P.M. in the winter and at 8 P.M. in the summer. Bus and entrance fee: 55 piasters.

MOSQUES . . . The 400 mosques of Cairo represent some of the finest examples of Islamic architecture in the world. Admission to the mosques is not allowed at prayertime. As a compromise with the Moslem tradition of removing one's shoes before entering the sanctuary, visitors are asked to cover their shoes with large cloth slippers provided by the mosque's caretaker. The major mosques are:

Al-Azhar: Located in the district and street with the same name . . . Al-Azhar (the splendid) was completed in 971 during the rule of the Fatimids and has been expanded and restored many times over the centuries. The present entrance dates from the 14th and 15th centuries. Left of the entrance is the library, containing some of the oldest and most valuable manuscripts in the world. The section behind the large inner courtyard is the oldest part of the building. Throughout its long history Al-Azhar has been a seat of learning as well as a place of worship. Its university, considered the oldest in the world, has educated and trained the leading scholars of the Moslem world since the early days of Islam.

Ibn Toulun: Completed in A.D. 879, it is the oldest mosque in Cairo. The mosque was built of brick and coated with stucco. Its special features are the Kufic writing in bold, massive strips along the wall and the detailed stucco carving of its windows and arches. The minaret is said to have been inspired by the minaret of the Samarra Mosque north of Baghdad and is, therefore, an evolution of the ziggurat.

Sultan Hassan: Standing at the foot of the Citadel is the most colossal mosque in Cairo and a masterpiece of Islamic architecture. It dates from the mid-14th century. The gateway alone measures 85 feet in height, and the minarets are the tallest in the city. The mosque was built in the form of a cross, each section representing one of the four schools of Moslem jurisprudence. Behind the diwan (recessed salon area) of the Shafii wing is the room containing the tomb of Sultan Hassan. Note especially the window and ceiling decorations in this room.

Ibn Qalawun: Formerly one of the leading places of worship in Cairo. It was begun by Sultan el Mansur Qalawun in the 13th century and completed by his son, el-Nassir. The mosque was once covered with beautiful marble and mosaic works. The vestibule containing el-Nassir's tomb has lovely stained-glass windows and elaborately decorated walls and ceiling, parts of which have been restored. The interesting feature of this complex of buildings is its architectural resemblance to a Crusader church. The archway entrance was taken from the Crusader Church of St. John in Akka.

El-Hakim bi Amr Illah: Completed by the Fatimite ruler el-Hakim in 1003, this mosque has many features in common with the Ibn Toulun Mosque. At one time it was a grand and graceful structure. Today, most of it is in ruins. The mosque is located next to the old walls of Cairo between Bab al-Futuh and Bab al-Nasr. A boys' school is located in the courtyard.

El-Muayyad: Built in the early 15th century and extensively restored in the late 19th century. The restored walls, ceilings and windows offer elaborate examples of Islamic art during the Mameluk period. The minarets rise high above the mosque on the two bastions of an 11th-century gate known as *Bab Zuweila.*

El-Sunqur (also know as the Blue Mosque or the Ibrahim Agha Mosque): Built in the 14th century, it takes its name, the Blue Mosque, from the panels of blue and green Persian tiles which decorate the east wall.

Amr Ibn el-As: Built at the time of the Arab conquest, this mosque represents the oldest vestige of Islam in Egypt.

OTHER SITES

Babylon Fort: The only Roman vestige in Cairo is situated in Old Cairo. It dates back to the first century A.D. The Romans chose the site because of its strategic location, which in those days overlooked the desert on the east and was guarded by the Nile on the west, north and south. According to historical records Babylon Fort covered an area of one acre. In the 7th century the Arab armies battled for seven months to conquer it. The remains of the fortress walls are in the compound of the Coptic Museum.

Babylon Fort is surrounded by several old Coptic churches. Those most often visited by tourists are:

El-Mouallaqa Church (Church of the Holy Virgin) is called Mouallaqa (hanging) because it is built over the Roman fortress as though suspended from it. The church, located next to the Coptic Museum, is the largest and loveliest church in Old Cairo. It probably dates from the late 4th or early 5th century and was the patriarchal seat of the Bishop of Alexandria.

Abou Serga Church, according to tradition, rests on the spot where the Holy Family lived after its flight into Egypt. The church was founded in the late 4th or early 5th century and was dedicated to Sergius and Bacchus, martyred soldiers who died in Syria early in the 4th century. From the Abou Serga Church a doorway in the garden leads to a Jewish synagogue, which was a Coptic church until the 9th century.

St. Barbara Church, in the vicinity of the Abou Serga Church and the Coptic Museum, was originally built in the late 4th century and rebuilt in the 10th century.

Gates of Cairo: The two most famous city gates are *Bab al-Futuh* (Gate of Conquest) and *Bab al-Nasr* (Gate of Victory). Both were built by Gowhar, the Fatimid general who founded Cairo. Between the two gates run the old city walls, adjacent to the Mosque of Hakim bi Amr Illah.

Anderson House: near the entrance of the Ibn Toulun Mosque. Built by Hajj Muhammad al-Jazzar in the 17th century and restored by Major Gayer-Anderson, a British resident of Cairo during the 1920s. Anderson lived in the house and furnished it with interesting old pieces and *objets d'art*. After his death the house was turned into a museum by the government.

Maison des Arts: The stairs behind the Rifai Mosque lead to Dar al-Labbana, where you may visit a house with old mushrabiyyah doors and painted ceilings in late Mameluk style. Works of Egyptian painters and craftsmen are also displayed. Meals are served upon request in advance.

Zoological Garden: A twenty-one-acre zoo is located on the Pyramids road. It contains a rare collection of African and Sudanese animals and an interesting museum of stuffed animals.

The Nilometer: On Roda Island an ancient column dating back to A.D. 715 was used to measure the Nile water level. According to legend, this is the spot where the infant Moses was found in the bulrushes.

EXCURSIONS

The Pyramids of Giza: 9 miles west of Cairo . . . The gigantic peaks of the three Pyramids of Giza rise in the distance on the western horizon. Close or afar, their majesty and symmetry are overwhelming. The Pyramids, situated on a hill overlooking the Nile Valley, are testimony to the ancients' belief in the immortality of the soul. Building them took twenty years.

Although there are some 80 pyramids in Egypt, the three at Giza are the most important. The first in size and chronological order is Cheops (Khufu), erected about 2690 B.C. Its original height was 481 feet. Cheophren (Kheophren), Cheops' son, built the second pyramid about 2650 B.C. slightly smaller in size. The third pyramid, smallest of the three, was erected about 2600 B.C. and named after Menkaru (Mycerinus).

According to Napolean, the cubic content of the Great Pyramid is enough to build a wall ten feet high and a foot thick entirely around France. The base of the Great Pyramid covers 13 acres—an area sufficient to hold St. Paul's, Westminster Abbey, St. Peter's, and the cathedrals of Florence and Milan all at once.

The interior of Cheops' pyramid has several long, empty corridors without decoration. Visitors may climb the Great Pyramid during daylight hours, escorted by a guide. From the summit one has a superb view of Cairo and the Nile Valley.

East of the Pyramids are the tombs of the princes; to the west, those of nobles and courtiers. Such tombs are known as "mastabas" because their shape resembles a bench (mastaba) still found against the doors of village houses.

At the foot of the Great Pyramid a resthouse in Pharaonic style has been turned into a museum. Its pleasant outdoor restaurant commands a magnificent view of the Nile Valley and Cairo. Here the panorama of the green valley boldly sketched against the barren desert dramatically expresses the meaning of the Nile to Egypt.

The Sphinx . . . 500 feet southeast of the Great Pyramid lies a recumbent lion with the head of a man. The lion—symbol of kingship—represented might. The Sphinx's human head symbolized intelligence. The Sphinx has a total length of 190 feet and is 66 feet tall at its highest point. The face alone measures 16.6 feet. It probably represents the head of King Cheophren, its builder. Successive kings down to Roman times restored, venerated and admired this remarkable statue. Some considered it the "god of Death."

A Sound and Light program at the Pyramids and Sphinx is given nightly. While floodlights play on the Pyramids, a recorded voice, apparently coming from the Sphinx, tells their history. English programs are given twice weekly at 7:30 (winter) and 8:30 (summer). Check locally for the exact schedule. Buses leave nightly from the *Son et Lumière* booth at Liberation Square in front of the Hilton Hotel and return to the same location after the program. Bus and entrance: 65 piasters.

Memphis and Saqqara: 20 miles southwest of Cairo . . . Nothing remains of the ancient city of Memphis, for centuries Egypt's capital, except Saqqara the necropolis. The name Saqqara is derived from the word *sakr* (hawk), the god of necropolis in the nether world. The necropolis contains over 14 pyramids, hundreds of mastabas and tombs, art objects and engravings dating from the I–XXX Dynasties. Here the oldest mummy and the oldest papyrus were found. *The Step Pyramid,* a "staircase to heaven," erected by Zoser, a king of the III Dynasty, dominates the scene. This pyramid was the first major building in stone and was considered the greatest structure known to man at that time. Its architect, Imhotep (later known as the god of medicine), was the first to investigate the mystery of the Nile Flood about 3,000 B.C. The largest and most beautiful mastaba in the necropolis is the *Tomb of Ti,* an important figure at the royal court in the late period of the VI Dynasty. The wall decorations have been extremely valuable to scholars in studying the life and customs of the ancient Egyptians. The *Serapeum,* the most curious tomb in the necropolis, was dedicated to Apis, the ox, who was worshipped and mummified in exactly the same ceremonial fashion as a human being.

Heliopolis . . . In its early history Egypt was divided into kingdoms. Several princes from the West Delta attempted to unify the country and chose Heliopolis as their capital. Ancient Heliopolis is referred to in the Bible as the city of *On.* Its only remnant is an obelisk. The village of Mataria now stands on the ancient site. Located here is the *Tree of the Virgin,* which tradition holds to be the resting spot of the Holy Family on its flight to Egypt. Today Heliopolis is 15 miles from downtown Cairo and is considered one

Hotel (Tel.)	Single	Double	Rooms

of its suburbs. Its wide boulevards, spacious villas and abundant gardens make it one of the loveliest sections of the city.

Helwan . . . A spa, about 15 miles south of Cairo, Helwan may be reached by car or by train from Bab al-Luk Station. Helwan's six sulphur springs, gushing water at 90° F., are considered to have excellent curative powers. Visitors may swim for health or pleasure in open-air pools fed from the springs. Helwan is on a plateau 275 feet above sea level and enjoys a delightful winter climate. The city's main attractions are its Japanese garden, observatory and the *Wax Museum,* in which exhibits depict the highlights of Egypt's history, especially under the Pharaohs and Islam. Near Helwan there is a small, unpretentious home built in 1942 by King Farouq, which is now a museum. It has a wide veranda overlooking the Nile and is surrounded by lovely gardens.

Excelsior (38105)	$ 2.53	$ 3.68	45

   5 Mansour St.

Fayum . . . 75 miles southwest of Cairo, can be reached by train, bus or car. The largest oasis in Egypt, Fayum is a popular hunting and fishing area. It was the center of one of Egypt's most ancient cultures and the earliest known site of pottery-making and soil cultivation. The period of the XII Dynasty was the most prosperous. At that time Lake Qarun occupied almost half of the Fayum depression. Over the years the lake gradually shrank, although it was still large during the period of the Ptolemies.

The Greek capital was called *Crocodilopolis,* after the local god, Sobek, who was conceived as a crocodile. By the 1st century A.D. the oasis had come to be known as Bion in Coptic, which later evolved into Fayum. Among the monuments at Fayum one of the most important is the Pyramid of Amenemhat III (XII Dynasty, 19th century B.C.), located nine miles southeast of Fayum, and the Tomb of Nefru-Ptah, his daughter. At Lahun, 16 miles southeast of Fayum, are other pyramids and many mastabas belonging to princesses and nobles.

Auberge (18)	$ 4.25	$ 6.90	53

CHAPTER XVII

EGYPT: TOWNS AND SITES

PART I: LOWER EGYPT, SUEZ, SINAI

ALEXANDRIA: 110 miles northwest of Cairo . . . When Alexander the Great conquered Egypt in 332 B.C. he founded a city bearing his name on the site of the tiny fishing village of Rakotis, facing the rocky island of Pharos. Under the Ptolemies, the city became a great cultural center and attracted the most famous scientists, scholars and artists of the time. It had two celebrated royal libraries, said to contain 490,000 different scrolls. Around one of the libraries rose what is considered the first university in history. Under Ptolemy II the great Tower of Pharos, one of the seven wonders of the ancient world, was built.

During the time of Julius Caesar Alexandria became the second largest city of the Roman Empire. When Octavian arrived in 30 B.C., after the suicide of Anthony and Cleopatra, Alexandria became formally a part of the Roman domain. Under the Byzantine Empire, Alexandria was one of the great centers of Christendom and seat of a patriarchate. By the time the city fell to the Arabs in 642 A.D., it had declined considerably. In 1798, when Napoleon's troops landed in Egypt, Alexandria was merely a village.

The city regained its importance once more under Muhammad Ali. In 1819 he ordered the construction of the Mahmudiya Canal to the Nile, thus bringing large areas in the city's vicinity under irrigation.

Today Alexandria is Egypt's second largest city, with a population of over two million people. It is one of the chief seaports on the Mediterranean Sea and Egypt's leading summer resort. Remnants of its one-time glory, especially the Greek and Roman periods, are housed in a museum in the center of the city.

Hotel (Tel.)	Single	Double	Rooms
Cecil (23052)	$ 7.00	$10.00	83
Corniche, 26 July St.			
Palestine (66799)	$11.50	$13.80	117
Montazah Palace			
Windsor Palace (28700)	$. 7.00	$10.00	82
Corniche, Shohada St.			
Al-Salamek (65813)	$ 6.90	$11.50	30
Montazah Palace			
Beau Rivage (62187)	$ 7.00	$10.00	53
Corniche al Gueish St.			
Mediterranee (62706)	$ 3.22	$ 6.44	45
Corniche, Ar-Ramleh			
San Stefano (63580)	$ 7.00	$10.00	134
Corniche, Ar-Ramleh			
Le Roy (23090)	$ 2.53	$ 4.03	33
25 Talaat Harb St.			

Restaurants: Pastroudis, tearoom and nightclub; *Petrou,* seafood; *Union; San Giovanni; Santa Lucia,* (also a night club); *Unica; Omar Khayyam,* Egyptian and other Middle Eastern dishes. Along the Corniche facing the eastern harbor there are pleasant sidewalk cafés which serve light snacks, tea, pastries and cocktails.

Night Clubs: Santa Lucia, Romance, Hotel Mediterranee (summer only); *Casino,* Montazah Palace; *La Grenouille,* Hotel Deauville; *Monseigneur;* and *Pam Pam.* Most do not have shows. The atmosphere is European rather than Oriental.

City Transportation: Alexandria has a sparkling new port building, which is one of the best equipped for passenger ships in the Mediterranean. From the main entrance you board a chartered bus or a train (if there are enough incoming passengers) for Cairo. Taxis to downtown Alexandria or the railway station are also available. Fare is about 15 piasters (36¢). A tour of Alexandria may be arranged with a travel agent at the port before proceeding to Cairo.

Daily express trains run between Cairo and Alexandria. The three-hour trip through the Delta region gives you a delightful preview of Egyptian country life. Daily air service is also available. The flight from Cairo to Alexandria takes one hour.

CITY SIGHTS:

Alexandria is different from Cairo—its flavor is Mediterranean rather than Oriental. The city has a charm and romance of its own, and no visit to Egypt is complete without a visit to Alexandria.

Coastal Road and Beaches: The Corniche is a 15-mile east-west road through Alexandria bordering the Mediterranean. From Ras al-Tin, the peninsula which was once the island of Pharos, the road skirts the eastern harbor on the east and north and passes the city's major hotels and cafés on the south. Facing the eastern harbor are Midan Sa'ad Zaghlul, the main square of the downtown area, and Ramleh, the main tram station. On the far side of the eastern harbor the road continues along the Mediterranean, passing the city's string of beaches.

Pompey's Pillar: A column, 84 feet high and about seven feet thick, made of polished rose Aswan granite, was erroneously called Pompey's Pillar by the Crusaders. In fact, it was erected by the Roman Prefect, Posthumus, in honor of the Emperor Diocletian and was part of the splendid Temple of Serapis. Some historians contend that it stands on the spot where tradition places the famous library of Alexandria. West of the pillar a flight of stairs leads into long subterranean chambers which may also have been part of the temple.

Catacombs of Kom el-Shuqafa: In a funerary construction dating from the 2nd century A.D., the dead were lowered through a shaft into catacombs three stories high. A winding staircase leads into the chambers of the first floor. The catacombs are a curious blend of Greco-Roman and Egyptian design.

Anfushi Necropolis: In a park near the entrance to Ras al-Tin Palace is a necropolis dating from the 2nd century B.C. All the tombs are carved out of rock and contain no other building material.

Fort Kait Bey: On the spot where the Pharos Lighthouse once stood,

Hotel (Tel.)	Single	Double	Rooms

a fortress and mosque were built by Sultan Kait Bey in the 15th century. The site commands an excellent view of Alexandria from the harbor.

Greco-Roman Museum: From the displays in the museum a visitor can gain some idea of the grandeur of Alexandria under the Greeks and Romans. Further, it provides a link between the Egyptian Antiquities and Coptic museums in Cairo. The museum has a large collection of coins minted in Alexandria during the Greco-Roman period, an excellent display of Tanagra figurines, exhibits of iridescent and fused glass, and the fragments of Coptic fabrics.

Ras el-Tin Palace: Begun by Muhammad Ali in 1834 and completed in 1845, it was the official summer headquarters of the rulers of Egypt down through the mid-20th century. Its eastern gate is made up of six granite columns topped by the royal crown of Egypt and bearing inscriptions from the Koran. The room in which Farouq signed his abdication is on the ground floor. After the signing, Farouq descended the stairs leading to the wharf below, boarded his yacht and sailed away to Italy.

Montazah Palace: Built by Khedive Abbas in 1892. The estate is located east of Alexandria on the Mediterranean shore and is surrounded by 350 acres of parks and gardens. The main building has been turned into a casino and a museum. The *Salamek* (women's quarters) is now a hotel. Visitors may swim at the palace beach or relax in the gardens.

Hydrobiological Museum: Located next to Fort Kait Bey, the museum houses a collection of colorful and interesting fish from the Mediterranean Sea, the Red Sea and the Nile River.

EXCURSIONS

Abukir: 18 miles east . . . On the site of ancient *Canopus* stands a small fishing port. Here Nelson's fleet defeated the French in 1798. The area contains the remains of ancient baths, a temple dedicated to Serapis and relics of Napoleon's expedition to Egypt. *Zephyron,* a well-known seafood restaurant, is located by the sea.

Al-Agami: 12 miles west . . . The road west of Alexandria passes through Mex, the main industrial center of Alexandria, where two well-known seafood restaurants, *Xenophon* and *Zephrion,* are located. The road continues west to Agami, one of the best beaches in the vicinity of Alexandria. Houses are available for rent during the summer season.

Hotel (Tel.)	Single	Double	Rooms
Al Agami Palace (26301)	$ 2.76	$ 4.95	50
Hanoville (35637)	$ 2.76	$ 6.90	44

Burg al-Arab and Bahig: 27 miles west . . . Near Abukir are the remains of a 3rd century B.C. temple dedicated to Osiris, later turned into a fortress by the Arabs. Also in the area are the ruins of a Ptolemaic lighthouse believed to be one in a chain which stretched from Pharos at Alexandria across the coast to Cyrene. The ruins of St. Menas, once a great Christian city, may be visited.

Rosetta: 35 miles east . . . The town, founded in the 9th century on the site of ancient *Bolbitine,* was once important as a center for commerce with the Orient. In 1799 near Rosetta at Port St. Julien, one of Napoleon's soldiers found the now famous *Rosetta Stone,* a basalt slab inscribed in hieroglyphics, demotic characters and Greek. From this stone Champollion

Hotel (Tel.)	Single	Double	Rooms

found the key to deciphering Egyptian hieroglyphics. The stone, seized by the British in 1801, is now in the British Museum.

PORT SAID . . . 135 miles northeast of Cairo on the Mediterranean . . . The town is provided with a three-mile breakwater to keep away the mud of the Damietta branch of the Nile. A short trip by motorboat from Port Said takes passengers across the canal to Port Fuad. Recently the UAR government announced plans to make Port Said a free port.

United States Consulate, Sultan Husayn St. (Tel. 705)

UAR State Tourist Office, Sultan Husayn St. (Tel. 3100)

Casino Palace (3381)	$ 3.36	$ 5.87	67
23 July St.			

SINAI . . . The peninsula east of Suez between the Gulf of Suez and the Gulf of Aqaba was the setting for many legends of the ancient Egyptians. Isis went there to search for the body of her murdered husband, Osiris. The goddess Hathor, known to the Pharaohs as "Our Lady of Sinai," sanctified the area. The Bible often mentions Sinai: Here Moses received the Ten Commandments, and the Holy Family fled by way of Sinai into Egypt. Later the area became a place of refuge for Christians from Roman persecution.

The best time to visit Sinai is late February to May and October to November. The most interesting excursion is to the Greek Orthodox Monastery of St. Catharine's, built by Justinian in the early 6th century A.D.

After crossing the canal at Suez, the first stop (about 18 miles) is an oasis, the *Wells of Moses,* said to be filled with water which gushed from the rock that Moses struck with his staff. The next stop (about three hours from Suez over paved road) is the resthouse and mining camp at Abu Zenimeh. Farther south in the Wadi Maghara are the famous mines from which turquoise has been taken since ancient times. Here many Pharaohs left inscriptions recording their exploits. The earliest is that of King Snefru, first king of the IV Dynasty.

Firan Oasis (127 miles from Suez) rests at the foot of Mount Serbal, where, according to many authorities, Moses received the Ten Commandments. Beyond at *Jebel Musa* lies the monastery dedicated to Catharine, the Alexandrian saint. It contains a valuable library of old manuscripts and the most valuable collection of icons in the world.

Preparations: A letter of introduction for the Monastery must be obtained from the Bishop of Sinai, in Cairo. A permit from the Frontiers Administration is necessary and may be obtained in Cairo or Suez. A night's stay at the monastery costs £.E. 2. At least two, and preferably three cars, should make the trip in convoy. Food provisions for five days must be taken along. Through travel agents in Cairo and Suez an all-inclusive trip can be arranged for £.E. 35. This is by far the most practical way to visit Sinai.

SUEZ . . . 82 miles east of Cairo at the southern entrance of the Canal on the Red Sea . . . Suez was a town of no consequence until the canal was opened. Today, in addition to its strategic location on the canal, Suez

*Tourist guides
to the Pyramids.*

*Temple of Deir al Bahri
at Luxor.*

*Temple of Abu Simbel
with Ramses II statues.*

Hotel (Tel.)	Single	Double	Rooms

is developing as a Red Sea resort where sailing, fishing and swimming are delightful. The Red Sea is famous for its beautiful coral and variety of exotic fish. Its coastline, backed by barren cliffs of pink, blue and purple hues, has some of the most dramatic scenery in Egypt. Several hotels in Suez are adequate for a weekend stay for those who prefer not to camp on the Red Sea shores. South of Suez at *Ain Sukhna* (50 miles) and *Hurghada* (240 miles) there are new bungalow-hotels.

Hotel (Tel.)	Single	Double	Rooms
Ain Sukhna Motel (3723) at Ain Sukhna	$ 6.90	$ 8.63	96
Bel Air(3711) Suez	$ 3.10	$ 4.83	48
Hurghada Motel (Cairo 72813) at Hurghada	$ 6.90	$ 9.20	106

SUEZ CANAL . . . In ancient times the area of Suez (Goshen in the Bible) was strategically important to the civilizations of the eastern Mediterranean as a bridge between Asia and Africa. Many efforts were made to connect the Mediterranean with the Red Sea, the two great bodies of water separated by this narrow strip of land.

The first attempt, about 2100 B.C., utilized an ancient branch of the Nile. A second and different canal was cut about 1900 B.C. and was used for about a thousand years. The same canal, after centuries of disuse, was redug in 606 B.C. and completed the following century. A third canal was dug about 286 B.C. during the reign of Ptolemy II and was used until the Roman period. In A.D. 98 Trajan changed the canal and made it reach the Nile near present-day Cairo. Apparently, the last effort to use the canal was about the time of the Arab conquest. After the late 8th century A.D. the canal was no longer serviceable.

In 1854 Ferdinand de Lesseps requested permission from Sa'id Pasha to begin work on the canal. Finally, construction of the canal was begun in April 1858. Eleven years later under Khedive Isma'il, the canal was formally opened with a magnificent ceremony attended by royalty from all over Europe. The Cairo Opera House was built to stage *Aïda,* which Verdi had composed for the occasion.

For the next century the Suez Canal, the lifeline of the British Empire, became the pawn of imperial Europe. Finally, 100 years after the date of the concession to de Lesseps, the Suez Canal Company was nationalized by the Egyptian Government.

The Suez Canal from Port Said on the Mediterranean to Suez on the Red Sea is over 120 miles long. The breadth at water level is 200 yards. Transit time for a ship through the canal is about 15 hours.

PART II: UPPER EGYPT

A visit to the Egyptian Museum, to the Pyramids and Saqqara is only an introduction to the antiquities of Egypt. Not until you have made a trip to Luxor, Aswan and the other sites of Upper Egypt does the magnitude of ancient Egypt's civilization become apparent.

Misrair has daily flights in winter from Cairo to Luxor (1½ hours), round trip $31.28. By rail: sleeper or coach twice daily. Double compartment to Luxor—£.E. 4.600 per person; single, £.E. 6.600 double. For Nile steamer, see page 131. The trip from Cairo can be made by car but should be planned carefully with the assistance of a reliable travel agent.

ABU SIMBEL: 500 miles south of Cairo . . . *The Temple of Abu Simbel* is the most colossal one in Egypt. It was carved out of the side of a sandstone rock cliff facing east to let the light of the rising sun penetrate the innermost sanctuary. The temple was built by Ramses II and dedicated to Amen-Ra, the patron god of Thebes, and Ha-Rakhte, a form of the sun god Horus. At the entrance of the temple are four colossal seated statues of Ramses II, each over 65 feet high. To the right and left of each statue are smaller statues of the royal family. To the left of the second colossus is Ramses' mother, Queen Tue, and to the right stands Queen Nefertari, his favorite wife. On the façade of the temple are representations of Amen-Ra and Ra-Harakhte. On the south wall outside the temple is an inscription of a treaty of peace between the Egyptians and the Hittites. It is believed to be the first treaty of its kind in history.

The temple from the façade to its innermost chamber measures 200 feet. The first room, the Great Hypostyle Hall, has a ceiling supported by eight columns faced with huge statues of Ramses II in the position of the god Osiris. The ceiling and walls throughout the temple are beautifully decorated, and the color in many places is in excellent condition. The second hall measures 36 by 25 feet and is supported by four pillars. The reliefs on the walls show Ramses II and Nefertari burning incense before the sacred ship of Amen-Ra. The third hall is the innermost chamber and sanctuary. Four seated figures, Ramses II flanked by the gods to whom the temple was dedicated, keep watch in the Holy of Holies, where only the Pharaohs and the High Priests were allowed to enter.

Near the Great Temple stands the *Temple of Hathor,* also carved out of solid rock. This smaller temple was built by Ramses II for his wife Nefertari and was dedicated to the goddess Hathor. Outside the temple are six large statues, four of Ramses II and two of his wife, and smaller ones of their children. Inside, the Hypostyle Hall has a roof supported by six pillars topped with the head and face of the goddess Hathor and reliefs similar to those in the Great Temple.

Upon completion of the new Aswan Dam, the area between Aswan and the Sudan border will be inundated by the Nile waters. In anticipation, the UAR Government through UNESCO sent a worldwide appeal for assistance in exploring the area and saving the most important ancient monuments which would otherwise have been lost forever. About twenty groups explored the area and made many important finds. In addition, some 30 monuments and temples were dismantled and transported to other sites.

The most difficult of all the projects was the one to save the temples of Abu Simbel. A wall was built around the temple to protect it from the rising water while the temple (400,000 tons) was cut into parts and crated to be reassembled at the top of the mountain cliff in which it stood. The second smaller temple has been saved in like fashion. The project is expected to be completed about 1970. The U.S. has contributed $12 million to the project.

(The work of relocating Abu Simbel is now under way. Check with

Hotel (Tel.)	Single	Double	Rooms/Baths	

the nearest UAR Tourism Office or Consulate to know if it is advisable to make the trip at the time you are planning it.)

ASWAN: 420 miles south of Cairo . . . As the gateway to the south on the trade route from Egypt to Central Africa, Aswan has lived under a combination of Oriental and African influences throughout its history. Today, Aswan is a popular winter resort because of its dry climate and beautiful location. The late Aga Khan maintained a villa in Aswan and asked to be buried there upon his death. His handsome mausoleum facing the Minarets of Bilal stands on a hill behind his villa.

From a hilltop on the west bank of the Nile you get an excellent view of the old Aswan Dam, the lovely landscape around Aswan, and the graceful white sails of feluccas on the Nile carrying visitors to *Kitchner Island* and *Elephantine Island,* the ancient frontier fortress of Egypt. Elephantine Island also has a museum and ancient tombs of the princesses of Aswan. On the west bank overlooking the new High Dam is the *Temple of Kalabsha,* which was dismantled from its original site and moved to its present location in order to save it from future inundation. On the east bank of the Nile south of Aswan are the granite quarries from where stones were cut for use in ancient monuments throughout Egypt.

The *Temple of Philae,* the most interesting of all Aswan's antiquities, is on an island situated between the old and the new dams. The oldest part of the Philae Temple dates from the XXX dynasty (4th century B.C.); the rest was completed during the Ptolemaic and Roman periods. Most of the temple was under water except during the flood months when the old dam was open. When the dam was closed, only the cornices of the two pylons were visible. With the building of the new dam, plans were made to preserve the temple, toward which the U.S. has contributed $6 million. The water level between the two dams will be low enough to enable the temple to be seen the year round.

Before construction on the new Aswan Dam began the population of Aswan was about 50,000. Today its numbers have swollen to 200,000.

By train you arrive in Aswan on the east side of the Nile. By plane you land at the airport on the west side of the river. You cross from east to west by a road over the old dam. The major hotels, travel offices and shops are located on the east side.

If your time allows, a sail in a felucca around the islands at Aswan is delightful. Boats can be hired at the landing dock by the Cataract Hotel for 50 piasters per hour.

HOTELS: (open from Dec. 15 to March 31). Prices include full board.

Hotel	Single	Double	Rooms	Baths
Cataract Hotel (12)	$11.00	$18.00	169	100
On the Nile				
New Cataract Hotel (506)	$14.50	$20.36	144	144
On the Nile				
Kalabasche (902)	$ 9.32	$13.75	120	120
Hotel Amun (816)	$ 7.00	$16.33	—	—
On an island in the Nile				

Aswan High Dam: Building projects of great magnitude—the Pyramids, the Suez Canal and now the Aswan Dam—have been milestones in Egyptian history. But to present-day Egyptians, the new high dam at Aswan is by far the most important undertaking in their history.

Every year since ancient times the flooding of the Nile was Egypt's main concern. The necessity to cope with the inundation led the ancient Egyptians to acquire mathematical, astronomical and engineering knowledge far in advance of other civilizations. Planning for the lean years during the years of plenty established law and order. This continuity of purpose in the 6,000 years Egypt has existed as a nation is unparalleled in history. Now with the building of the Aswan dam, the changeable behavior of the Nile will be a thing of the past.

The new dam is located four miles south of the present one. In the first stage of construction, a diversion channel was cut through the east bank of the Nile. The rock removed in cutting the channel was dumped into the main riverbed to form a cofferdam and to create the foundation of the new dam. Upon the completion of the cofferdam in May 1964, the course of the Nile River was altered by man for the first time in history. Now the river spills into the diversion channel and through tunnels where its water can be controlled.

The second stage of the project is the building of the high dam itself to a height of 364 feet and a width of two miles across at the top. When it is completed in 1970, the billion-dollar dam will have created a lake 300 miles long. Its waters will allow the cultivation of two million additional acres of land—one third more than the present area. The dam's hydroelectric plant, located about halfway up the diversion channel, is expected to triple Egypt's power output and substantially reduce power costs.

EXCURSIONS

Kom Ombo: 30 miles north of Aswan (1 hour by car from Aswan, 105 miles south of Luxor). Entrance fee: 10 piasters . . . Kom Ombo is situated on a hill overlooking the Nile at a point where the river makes a wide bend to the west. In ancient times it was a strategic location on the desert route to Nubia and Ethiopia. The principal deities of the ancient town were Haruar, a hawk-headed god, and Sobek, represented in the form of a crocodile. The *Temple of Kom Ombo* is dedicated to the two deities and is unlike any other monument in Egypt. To avoid offending either god, a twin temple was constructed, the left half dedicated to Haruar and the right half to Sobek.

LUXOR: 450 miles south of Cairo . . . The modern town of Luxor on the east bank of the Nile is situated on the site of ancient *Thebes,* the capital of Egypt at its zenith during the Middle and New Kingdoms. The actual site of Thebes is said to have occupied all the area between present-day Luxor and Karnak, a village a few miles north of Luxor. Today the area contains the ruins of the most gigantic monuments, statues and temples in all Egypt. These represent the greatest artistic accomplishments of the ancient Egyptians from the XIII to the XXX dynasties.

On the west bank of the Nile is the world-famous Valley of the Kings, the burial grounds of the great pharaohs of the empire. In the cliffs nearby are the Tombs of the Nobles. The inside walls and ceilings of these tombs are painted with detailed scenes and inscriptions in colors so vivid they could have been applied yesterday. On the plain at the foot of the

Hotel (Tel.)	Single	Double	Rooms/ Baths

mountains stand the mortuary temples of Deir al Bahri, the Ramesseum and Medinet Habu.

A guide for the day at Luxor costs 2 £.E. and is recommended. Horse-drawn carriages are a popular means of conveyance to antiquity sites. A ride around town should cost 20 piasters.

HOTELS: Prices quoted are with full board, 10% service charge and 5% municipal tax added.

Hotel (Tel.)	Single	Double	Rooms/ Baths	
Winter Palace (2000) El Bahr St.	$10.24	$16.45	135	65
New Winter Palace (2000) El Bahr St.	$14.50	$20.36	144	144
Luxor Hotel (2405) Facing Luxor Temple	$ 7.45	$12.65	89	—
Savoy Hotel (2200) El Bahr St.	$ 5.75	$11.50	144	—

SITES ON THE EAST BANK

Temple of Luxor: Entrance fee: 10 piasters . . . Less than a century ago the temple was completely covered under a hill of rubbish and hovels. It was discovered by accident and took two years to exacavate. The original temple was built during the reign of Amenhotep III and was dedicated to the trinity of the Theban gods: Amen-Ra, Mut and Khonsu. From the North Gate an impressive Avenue of the Sphinxes once connected Luxor Temple with the Temple of Karnak.

Temple of Karnak: Entrance fee 20 piasters . . . Northward two miles through the village of Luxor (a few hundred yards before reaching the Temple of Karnak, the magnificent South Gate of the temple comes in view. The gate, built by Ptolemy III, was the ceremonial gateway through which the festival processions passed from Karnak to the Temple of Luxor.

Another road from Luxor to Karnak along the Nile leads to the North Gate of the great *Temple of Amen-Ra.* In front of it are the ruins of the Avenue of Ram-headed Sphinx. The temple dedicated to Amen-Ra, the patron god of Thebes, was the most important temple in the kingdom. Consequently, each pharaoh enlarged and embellished it as evidence of his faith. From the top of the temple entrance you get a full view of Karnak, Luxor and the west bank of the Nile.

Inside the temple of Amen-Ra an earlier temple built by Ramses III predates the forecourt of the Great Temple. From the forecourt you enter the Hypostyle Hall, reputedly the largest hall of any temple in the world. Its area covers 50,000 square feet. The roof of the hall was once supported by 134 immense columns.

From the Hypostyle Hall you enter the original Temple of Amen-Ra. Here stands the Obelisk of Queen Hatshepsut—97 feet tall, cut from one piece of pink Aswan granite. At the end of the temple is the Festival Hall of Thothmes III, used as a church by the early Christians.

SITES OF THE WEST BANK

For 5 piasters you may ride a motor launch from the landing stage in front of the Winter Palace Hotel to the west bank of the Nile, from where cars may be hired (2 £.E. per day) to drive you to the sites. Distances between the sites are too far to make the excursion on foot. Visitors usually go first to the Valley of the Kings. (Be prepared to do a great deal of climbing, especially up and down stairs inside the tombs.)

Tombs of the Kings: In the Valley of the Kings. Entrance fee: 30 piasters. 64 pharaohs' tombs have been found in the Valley of the Kings. The safest and most interesting are open to the public. The best are listed here in their order of priority:

Tomb 17: Seti I (XIX Dynasty, 13th century B.C.) is considered by many experts to be the most interesting one in the necropolis. It is the largest and certainly the most impressive. The wall decorations begin at the entrance and continue all the way to the bottom of the tomb. The drawings and reliefs are exquisite and in excellent condition.

Tomb 283: Tut-Ankh-Amon (XVIII Dynasty, 14th century B.C.) is the only one so far discovered which escaped the tomb robbers of ancient times. The chambers are small in comparison with other tombs, but the colors of the fine drawings are remarkably well preserved. The gold-masked mummy of King Tut (as he is known in popular writing) lies *in situ.*

Tomb 35: Amen-Hotep (Amenophis) II (XVIII Dynasty, 15th century B.C.) is called the Tomb of Safety because several coffins, moved there by the high priests for safekeeping against the tomb robbers, were found in the tomb. The wall drawings are completely different from those in the tombs of Seti I and Tut-Ankh-Amon.

Tomb 9: Ramses VI (XX Dynasty, 12th century B.C.) has excellent wall drawings, especially on the ceiling and side walls of the last chamber.

Tomb 33: Haremheb (XIX Dynasty, 14th century B.C.): In the small room of the inner chamber, the colors of the drawings are excellent, but some are unfinished.

Tombs of the Queens and Princes: In the Valley of the Queens. Entrance fee: 10 piasters. While over 57 tombs have been discovered in the Valley of the Queens, very few are open. The best are: *Tomb 55: Prince Amenherkhepeshef* (Son of Ramses III), whose wall paintings are in pastel colors used and *Tomb 52: Queen Thyti* (about XX Dynasty).

Tombs of the Nobles: The private tombs of the priests and nobles in the courts of the pharaohs are located in various groups along the edge of the desert. They are famous for their fine wall decorations, which depict scenes from the daily life and customs of the ancient Egyptians. The nobles' tombs are small in comparison to those of the kings, and the wall drawings appear as miniatures. The important tombs, located in the hills between the Ramesseum and the Temple of Hatshepsut, belong to the XVIII Dynasty between the 15th and 14th centuries B.C. These are *Tomb 52: Nakht,* Scribe of the Granaries; *Tomb 69: Menna,* Chief of the King's Estate; *Tomb 96: Sennefer,* Prince of Thebes, Superintendent of the Granaries; and *Tomb 55: Ramose,* Vizir of Egypt (under Amenhotep IV), the largest tomb of the nobles. *Tomb 100 (35): Rekh-mi-ra,* Vizir of Egypt (under Thutmose III and Amenhotep II) contains many famous wall drawings which are often reproduced in art books and in designs using ancient Egyptian motifs. The *Tomb of Sen-Nezem,* XIX Dynasty, located at Deir el-Medineh, is one of the best in the necropolis.

To photograph inside the tombs you need a flash. Only art specialist and professional photographers are given permission to photograph in the tomb of Tut-Ankh-Amon. For maximum enjoyment of your visit to the tombs, you should familiarize yourself in advance with the names of the gods, the pharaohs and their representations in wall paintings.

THE TEMPLES:

Deir al-Bahri: Entrance fee 20 piasters . . . At the foot of the Theban Hills stands the mortuary temple built by Queen Hatshepsut (XVIII Dynasty, 15th century B.C.). It is one of the most handsome monuments in Egypt, enhanced by its location at the foot of towering cliffs. The design of the temple, which incorporates terraces and colonnades, is unique in ancient Egyptian architecture. The chapel dedicated to the goddess Hathor is the best-preserved section of the Temple.

Ramesseum: Entrance fee 20 piasters . . . South of the Valley of the Kings lies a mortuary temple built by Ramses II (XIX Dynasty, 13th century B.C.), one of the largest temples in Egypt. At the front of the temple on the east is the fallen head of Ramses' statue—the largest in Egypt, cut from a solid piece of stone.

Medinet Habu: Entrance fee 20 piasters . . . South of the Valley of the Kings is a mortuary temple built by Ramses III (XX Dynasty, 12th century B.C.). It is one of the most colossal monuments in the world and is considered second only to Karnak in architectural importance. The well-preserved temple is actually a complex of four temples—two built by Ramses III, one by Amenhotep I and another by Queen Amenartas (700 B.C.).

Deir el-Medineh: Entrance fee 10 piasters . . . South of the Valley of the Kings, a temple dedicated to the goddesses Hathor and Maat was built by Ptolemy IV about 210 B.C.

Colossi of Memnon: In an open field south of the Valley of the Kings rest twin statutes representing Amenhotep III in the classical sitting position. Each statue is 64 feet in height. The statues were apparently the entrance to a temple complex which no longer exists.

EXCURSIONS

The Nile steamers from Luxor and Aswan stop at several antiquity sites long enough for passengers to visit the monuments. Or you may travel by train from Luxor to towns near the ancient sites. From the train station you either walk, ride a donkey, hire a carriage, car or boat to the site as the situation requires.

ABYDOS: 90 miles north of Luxor at Balianeh (2½ hours by train; or Nile steamers from Luxor stop on the second day at Nag Hamadi, 19 miles south of Balianeh, from where you proceed by bus to the site for 1½ hours' drive). Entrance fee 20 piasters . . . For centuries Abydos was a place of pilgrimage, as the tomb of Osiris was supposedly located in the area. Abydos is situated on the site of the ancient city of *This (Thinis),* which was one of the earliest sites of man in the Nile Valley. Tombs of pharaohs from the first dynasty have been discovered here.

The most important monument at the site is the *Temple of Seti I,* built on the site of an earlier temple. The temple was later enlarged and completed by Ramses II, son of Seti I. The Temple of Seti I, dedi-

Hotel (Tel.)	Single	Double	Rooms/ Baths

cated to Osiris, is considered one of the most important monuments in Egypt for its artwork. The art of Egypt during this period reached its peak and is unequalled for its beauty and delicacy. The most important feature in the temple is the group of some 70 cartouches of the pharaohs of Egypt arranged in chronological order. Upon discovery of these cartouches Egyptologists, correlating them with information from other sources, were able to establish a definite timetable of the ancient dynasties for the first time.

DENDERAH: 40 miles north of Luxor at Qena (1½ hours by train). Entrance fee 20 piasters . . . Denderah was the capital of the sixth district of Upper Egypt under the Ptolemies. Here you may visit the *Temple of Hathor,* one of the best preserved monuments in Egypt, built in the 1st century B.C. near the end of the Ptolemaic rule. The temple was dedicated to Hathor, goddess of heaven, joy and love, and patron deity of Denderah. The temple took about 100 years to build and some parts were never completed.

ESNA: 30 miles south of Luxor (1 hour by train). Entrance fee 10 piasters . . . The *Temple of Khnum* is Ptolemaic in origin. From other evidence at the site, however, it appears that an earlier temple was constructed by Thutmose III (1500 B.C.) on the same site. Work on the Ptolemaic temple probably began about 180 B.C. and ended in A.D. 250, as the Emperor Decius is mentioned in a relief.

EDFU (Idfu): 70 miles south of Luxor, halfway to Aswan (2 hours by train). Entrance fee 10 piasters . . . The ancient Greeks called the site *Apolonopolis,* after Apollo (or Horus), whose representation is here in the form of an eagle. The *Temple of Horus* is practically intact and is one of the finest examples of Ptolemaic art in Egypt. Its foundation was laid in 237 B.C. under the reign of Ptolemy III, but the temple was not completed until two centuries later.

Hotel (Tel.)	Single	Double	Rooms/ Baths
Edfu Hotel (38)	$ 8.05	$10.35	30	30

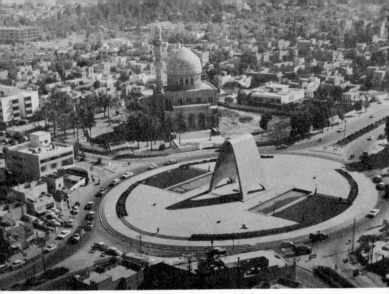

Monument of the Unknown Soldier, modern Baghdad.

CHAPTER XVIII

IRAQ

TRAVEL FACTS

WEATHER IN BAGHDAD—Lat. N33°21′—Alt. 112′

	JAN.	FEB.	MAR.	APR.	MAY	JUNE	JULY	AUG.	SEPT.	OCT.	NOV.	DEC.
Average temp.	49°	53°	60°	71°	82°	90°	94°	94°	88°	78°	61°	53°
Sunny days	26	23	27	27	30	30	31	31	30	30	26	26

LOCATION . . . Iraq lies in a structural depression between the plateaus of Iran and Arabia and extends for 600 miles from the head of the Persian (or Arab) Gulf to the highlands of Kurdistan on the Turkish border. Its mountainous eastern frontier borders Iran. In the great Syrian desert on the west and south it shares common boundaries with Syria, Jordan and Saudi Arabia. The northern plains correspond to ancient *Assyria,* whose historic capital was Nineveh, now modern Mosul. Lower Iraq from Baghdad to the Gulf corresponds roughly to ancient *Babylonia.* Its famous capital, Bablyon, is situated near present-day Hilla.

CHARACTERISTICS . . . Iraq is ancient *Mesopotamia, the land between the rivers*—the Tigris and the Euphrates. Where the two rivers meet in the Shatt al Arab is said to be the site of the *Garden of Eden.* Iraq claims, with substantial archaeological and historical evidence, to be the site of the oldest civilization in the world. Iraq is marked by great extremes in terrain and climate. These extremes manifest themselves in the variety of people and their way of life—rugged mountaineers in the north, nomadic Bedouins in the desert, farmers in the fertile midlands and "Marsh Arabs" in the south. No generalizations hold in describing this diversified land.

POPULATION . . . Approximately 8,000,000. Over two-thirds are Arabs and less than one-third are Kurds, with small minorities of Turks, Persians and other Middle Eastern ethnic groups.

SIZE . . . 171,599 square miles (slightly larger than California).

CAPITAL . . . Baghdad, the exotic city of the *Arabian Nights,* is now a modern city of over a million people.

GOVERNMENT . . . A republic.

HOW TO GET THERE . . . 18 hours by Pan Am Jet Clipper from New York. Baghdad is one hour from Beirut by Iraqi Airways or Middle East Airlines. Iraq can be reached overland from Turkey through Syria and Jordan or from Beirut through Syria and Jordan to Baghdad. From Beirut the drive takes approximately 18 hours. By sea the most practical route would be to Beirut and from there by air or overland to Baghdad.

ACCOMMODATIONS . . . Among the several hotels in Baghdad, the newest are the first class, air-conditioned *Baghdad Hotel* with single rates from about $11., European Plan (without meals) and the *Ambassador* and *Khayam* with rates from about $9, including breakfast. The *Zia* (of Agatha Christie fame) has moved to a new location and costs from $5.60 for a single, while the new *Baghdad Resthouse* offers modern accommodations at $4.20 for a single with bath. In towns and at important sites of antiquity outside of Baghdad, the main accommodations are those provided in rest-houses built by the government or the Iraq Railway Company.

ARTS . . . Several of the leading artists of the Middle East are Iraqis. Exhibits are held frequently in the winter season in Baghdad. For art treasures of the ages a visit to the Iraqi National Museum is first on the list of musts during your stay in Baghdad.

BANKS . . . Commercial banks are government-owned. Several have U.S. affiliations.

CALENDAR OF HOLIDAYS . . . The official weekly holiday is Friday. National holidays include Army Day, January 6; Tree Day, March 21; Labor Day, May 1; Revolution Day, July 14. *Moslem religious feasts* observed as national holidays are Muharram 1, Moslem New Year; Muharram 10, Ashoura, the martyrdom of Hassan and Husayn; Prophet Muhammad's Birthday; Id al Fitr (3 days), breaking the fast at the end of the month of Ramadan; and

Id al-Adha (4 days), the Feast of Sacrifice at the end of the pilgrimage to Mecca. Christmas and Easter are observed by the Christian communities only.

CIGARETTES AND TOBACCO . . . Some American and British cigarettes are available at 58¢ per pack.

CLIMATE . . . The climate varies with the terrain. Winters are cold in the northern mountains and plains and mild in the midlands and south. Summer in Iraq is hot except in the mountain areas of the north. The best times to visit Iraq are the spring and fall.

CLUBS . . . The most popular club in Baghdad is *Alwiya,* which has two swimming pools, children's playground, dining room, bar and game room. Other leading clubs are *Mansur* and *YMCA*. Visitors are welcome, but they must be accompanied by a member.

COMMON COURTESIES AND LOCAL CUSTOMS . . . Iraqis are extremely generous and hospitable. If you are invited to a home for dinner, you will be overwhelmed by the quantity and variety of food, and your host or hostess feels dutybound to see that you eat enormous amounts. You will often use *ashkurak* for "thank you." You can greet a friend with *salam alaikum* or *shlonak,* and they will bid you farewell with *fi aman allah.* Typical of the Iraqi characteristic of extremes is the status of women. Some Iraqi women are completely liberated and very modern; in fact, the first woman lawyer, doctor and cabinet member in the Arab World were Iraqis. Others, however, must adhere to strict traditional behavior. So, unless a gentleman has been introduced to a stranger's wife, sister or daughter, he should not inquire about the women of the family.

CURRENCY . . . The unit of currency is the Iraqi dinar (I.D.), divided into 1,000 fils. One dinar equals $2.80. Money should be exchanged at banks and authorized dealers. You do not need to declare Iraqi dinars under the amount of I.D. 5 and foreign currencies less than the equivalent of I.D. 25. There is no limit on the amount of traveler's checks you may bring into or take out of the country. Upon departure you can take out up to I.D. 5 and up to the amount of foreign currency declared upon arrival.

CUSTOMS REGULATIONS AND DOCUMENTS REQUIRED FOR UNITED STATES CITIZENS . . . To visit Iraq you need a passport, visa and vaccination certificate. Tourist visas are valid for three months from date of issue and can be used for a stay of one month. An *exit visa* is required if you stay over thirty days. You may bring in one bottle of liquor and 200 cigarettes duty free. Personal effects accompanying a tourist are exempt from customs duties. Automobiles, motorcycles, carriages, recorder players, records, radios, tape recorders, binoculars, typewriters and cameras could be subject to duty, although a tourist is seldom required to pay any. You should obtain a receipt upon arrival for such items so that when you depart there will be no problem about taking them out of the country. There is an airport departure tax of 500 fils ($1.40).

DRUGSTORES . . . Some American and British medicines and medical products are available at pharmacies. Cosmetics and toiletries are sold at grocery stores, department stores and specialty shops. At least one pharmacy in Baghdad is open all night.

ELECTRIC CURRENT . . . 220 volts, 50 cycles, A.C.

FAUNA . . . Horses, donkeys, sheep and goats are the most common; camels in the desert. Partridges, ducks, wild boars, gazelles, wild pigs and rabbits also.

FLORA . . . The most famous palm tree in the world is the date palm of Iraq. These trees supply 90% of the dates on the world market. In the northern plains and foothills there is a profusion of fruits and flowers characteristic of the Middle East.

FOOD . . . Leading hotels serve European cuisine as well as Iraqi specialties. The most famous Iraqi dishes are *masgouf,* broiled fish prepared in a special way, and *Quzi,* stuffed roasted whole lamb. (For other dishes, see Menu Translator, Chapter XXII). Milk should be boiled, except the bottled milk obtained from the government dairy in Baghdad.

LANGUAGE . . . Arabic is the official language of the country. English is the second language and is widely used by the educated class.

LAUNDRY AND DRY CLEANING . . . A suit cleaned and pressed costs $1–$1.40. The cleaning plant at the Baghdad Hotel is recommended and is available for non-patrons as well. Or inquire at the Pan Am office.

LIQUOR . . . American drinks are available in all hotels. Scotch and gin prevail; bourbon is hard to find. *Araq,* an aperitif made from dates, is a potent drink. The local beers *Diyana* and *Farida* are good. Local wines are made in Mosul and Shaqlawa. A variety of familiar American bottled soft drinks are plentiful.

MEDICAL FACILITIES . . . There are a number of public and private hospitals in Baghdad with modern facilities. The newest and best equipped is Ibn Sina Hospital (Tel. 34828). Most Iraqi doctors are British or American trained.

MOTION PICTURES . . . The main movie theaters in Baghdad which show American films are *Nasr, Khayyam, Roxy, Rex, Sindbad, Watani, Aladdin* and *Granada.* Seats should be reserved in advance. Shows begin at 4:30, 7:30, 9:30 P.M.

MUSIC . . . Concerts are held by the Baghdad Symphony Orchestra at Al-Khuld Hall. Periodically visiting artists perform at the German and British Cultural Centers. The Baroque Ensemble plays monthly at the Red Crescent Society.

NIGHT CLUBS . . . The leading night clubs are the *Select* and the *Embassy* (which are also restaurants). Arrive about 10 P.M. for dinner and floor show. The *Embassy* usually has a belly dancer on the program. Other night clubs are *Baghdad, Caravan, Sheherazade* and *Al-Hurriyah*. These are frequented mainly by men.

PHOTOGRAPHY . . . Film for movie and still cameras is available in color and black-and-white. Only black-and-white film can be developed locally. Prices are only slightly higher than in the States. Be cautious about photographing religious shrines or Shiite mosques. Men should refrain from photographing Iraqi women in native dress without having secured their permission or the permission of a male member of their family.

RELIGION . . . Over 95% of the population is Moslem, divided into the two major divisions in Islam: Sunni and Shiite. The largest Christian group is the Assyrians (not to be confused with the ancient Assyrians), who are Nestorians. About 100,000 indigenous "Chaldeans", who were originally Nestorians, joined the Uniate churches in the 19th century. Other Christian sects include Jacobites, Catholics and Orthodox. There is a small minority of Jews and of the ancient sect of the Sabeans.

RESTAURANTS . . . In addition to hotel dining rooms and night clubs, European food is available at *Hammurabi, Mataam al Mataam,* the *Three Sevens* and *Hammourabi Gardens* (an outdoor garden located east of Baghdad beyond the Army canal). The first two are also among the leading Baghdad restaurants for Arabic food. *Baghdadi* specializes in Oriental food and is notable for its attractive Oriental decor. *Taj Mahal* offers good Indian food. Places serving European food in modest surroundings are *Flight* and *Golden Nest*. Inexpensive places specializing in Iraqi cuisine are *Faraj* (known for its *Kubbah Mosul*), *Mina, Shtora, Yildizlar, Gondola, Gardenia, Baghdad Nights* and *Asia*. The latter four are located along the riverbank and specialize in *masgouf*.

SHOPS AND STORES . . . The main shopping district is Rashid Street in downtown Baghdad and the bazaars nearby. A newly developed area is Saadun Street near the Baghdad Hotel and Pan American's office. Store hours are from 8 or 9 A.M. to 1 P.M. and from 3 or 4 to 6 or 7 P.M. The leading department store is Orosdi-back, Rashid Street.

SPECTATOR SPORTS . . . Soccer games, swimming and tennis tournaments are held throughout the year at Baghdad University, schools and clubs.

SPORTS . . . You can swim at the public Baghdad Pool run by the Tourism and Resorts Administration (where certain days are reserved for ladies only), at private clubs (when accompanied by a member) and at Habbaniya Lake (51 miles west-southwest of Baghdad). Horses for riding are available in Mansur, which is also the district of Baghdad where the golf course is located.

TIME . . . Greenwich Mean Time plus 3 hours. When it's noon in New York it's 8 P.M. in Iraq.

TIPPING . . . A 10%–12% service charge is usually added to hotel and restaurant bills. If so, a 5% additional tip is adequate. If not, a 10% tip is customary.

TRANSPORTATION . . . In Baghdad, buses and taxis are plentiful. Average taxi ride in town should be 200 to 300 fils. Between Baghdad and the other major cities of Iraq the most convenient means of travel is by train. Air service is available daily to Basra.

WATER . . . Tap water in Baghdad is safe. In outlying areas you may prefer to drink bottled water or soft drinks, although it is seldom necessary. For excursions in the desert you should carry along drinking water.

WHAT TO BUY . . . Iraq goods, such as brassware, rugs and blankets, are found in the bazaars, where bargaining is the normal practice. The most famous craftsmen in Baghdad are the coppersmiths, whose tradition has been handed down for tens of centuries. They are located in the bazaars. Rugs and blankets in traditional Kurdish and Turkish designs are quite nice. Silver work by the Sabeans is primitive but amusing, as is the pottery made in the north. For antiquities, there are no authorized dealers, although Oriental shops usually have a small selection. The most interesting items are "cylinder seals," which are found frequently in excavations of antiquity sites in Iraq. These, however, can and have been copied, so you run the risk of buying a fake.

WHAT TO WEAR . . . From May through October, cottons only. A sweater or light jacket is advisable for evenings, especially for outings in the desert. From November through April medium and lightweight wool dresses and suits are sufficient. In December and January you will need a warm coat, especially in the evening. Throughout Iraq ladies should dress as they would in any large American or European city. Near holy shrines your dress must be conservative. Slacks are acceptable for picnic and desert outings but should not be worn on the streets in town. Sunglasses and comfortable walking shoes are vital.

WHERE TO GO SIGHTSEEING . . . See Chapters XX and XXI for details. Unless you are a seasoned traveler, your tour of Iraq should originate from Baghdad under the guidance of a competent travel agency or the Pan American office. Distances are deceptively long in Iraq, and tourist facilities are not always available.

SOURCES OF FURTHER INFORMATION . . . Pan American's office is located on Saadun Street (Tel. 88300) near the Baghdad Hotel. Recommended reading is *Ruined Cities of Iraq* by Seton Lloyd (Oxford University Press, London, 1943).

Date palms of southern Iraq.

CHAPTER XIX

IRAQ: THE COUNTRY AS A WHOLE

TYPES OF ACCOMMODATIONS

HOTELS

Outside of Baghdad most hotel accommodations are resthouses at major railway junctions, built by the Iraq railway company prior to World War II, and new hotels or resthouses near major antiquity sites and at leading summer resorts, built in the last decade by the Tourism and Summer Resort Administration of the Iraqi Government. They have simple, clean facilities with basic amenities. These accommodations are noted at each locality in Chapter XXI.

YOUTH HOSTELS

The YMCA, Saadun Street, Baghdad (Tel. 81362), maintains a hostel where the rate for a single with breakfast is $2.80 per day. The YWCA, Damascus Road, Mansur (Tel 33994), has single accommodations with breakfast at $3.36 per day.

CAMPSITES

The only organized campsite in Iraq is just outside Baghdad by the Army canal connecting Diyala with the Tigris. It is a trailer camp with basic facilities (Tel. 28861).

TOURING

AUTOMOBILES AND MOTORCYCLES

Private cars and motorcycles belonging to foreign tourists must have a certificate from an international automobile association recognized by the Iraqi Automobile Association or the owner must post a deposit upon entering Iraq. The car is allowed to stay six months and permission can be obtained to extend the stay up to one year. Customs duty is imposed after expiration of one year. An international driver's license is necessary. Self-drive cars and cars with drivers are available in Baghdad. Inquire at Pan American.

Some road signs are in English but most are in Arabic. Traffic moves on the right. Main roads in general are passable in all seasons, but secondary ones may not be. Gasoline costs 120 fils per Imperial gallon. Gasoline stations sell gasoline only; they do not perform any services. Outside of the cities, night driving is not recommended.

The Iraqi Automobile Club Association is located at Battaween, Saadun Street (Tel. 81170). The association can issue triptych and international driving license, and they have good road maps.

BICYCLES

Bicycles can be rented in Baghdad. Ask at your hotel for details. Generally their use in Iraq is not recommended because of long distances between towns, villages and sites of antiquity.

AFOOT

Advisable only in towns. Distances between towns and villages are too great to attempt long hiking expeditions. Walking in the downtown sections of Baghdad is easy, but from the downtown area to outlying residential sections bus or taxi is recommended. Baghdad spreads quite far on both sides of the Tigris River and distances are deceiving.

TRAINS

Iraq is served by an extensive network of trains. It is by far the best and least expensive way to travel around the country. Schedules of trains and fares are available from the Iraq Republican Railways (Tel. 86566), the Tourism Office and hotels. There are three main lines: the Baghdad–Basra line (341 miles), which has branch lines to Karbala and Ur-Nasiriyah. On this line visits to Bablyon, Karbala, Al-Ukhaidar, Eridu and Ur can be made by taxi from the train station of the town nearest the site. The Baghdad–Kirkuk–Erbil line (256 miles) has a branch line to Khanaqin. On the Baghdad–Mosul–Tel Kotchek line (319 miles) visits to Samarra, Hatra, Nimrud and Nineveh can be made by taxi from the train station of the town nearest the site. This line continues to Aleppo, Syria, and Istanbul, Turkey.

BUSES

In Baghdad the bus system is good, though buses tend to be overcrowded. Buses run between the major towns but they are not recommended for tourists. If you are traveling in a group, note that the Government Tourism Bureau has an 18-passenger bus which can be rented for I.D. 6 per day including driver and gas.

AIRPLANE

Iraq is served internally by Iraqi Airways. There are daily flights from Baghdad to Basra and weekly flights to Mosul.

TRANSPORTATION TO NEARBY COUNTRIES

Beirut is one hour flying time, 18 hours by bus. Cairo is two hours by air, Teheran two hours by air, 12 hours driving. Between Baghdad and Damascus and Beirut, air-conditioned desert buses operated by Nairn Company offers service several times weekly. From Basra to Kuwait there is regular taxi-*service* (shared taxi).

MENU TRANSLATOR—See Chapter XXII.

Arch of Ctesiphon, 20 miles from Baghdad.

CHAPTER XX

BAGHDAD

BAGHDAD INTERNATIONAL AIRPORT

The airport is located on the west side of town about 20 minutes from the downtown area and the Pan American office. Taxis are available at the airport, and a ride into town costs about 300 fils, but be sure to agree on the price beforehand. There is an office of the Tourism Bureau immediately outside the airport terminal. There is a new Baghdad airport southwest of the present one. Opening date: late 1967. The new terminal building is expected to be in operation by 1969.

HOTELS

Hotels in the city tend to be expensive. From May through October be sure to book into an air-conditioned one. You should make reservations in advance. A 10% service charge is added to the hotel bill. For information on hostels and campsites, see Chapter XIX.

Hotel (Tel.)	Air-conditioned	Single	Double	Rooms/	Baths
Baghdad (89031) Saadun St.	yes	$11.20	$14.00	200	200
Ambassador (86105) Abu Nawas St.	yes	$ 8.40	$11.20	65	65
Khayam (87141) Rashid St.	yes	$ 8.40	$12.60	56	56
Zia (4808) Saadun Park	air-cooled	$ 5.60	$ 9.80	25	25
Sinbad (86181) Rashid St.	air-cooled	$ 4.20	$ 9.80	42	42
Semiramis (86191) Rashid St.	air-cooled	$ 3.50	$ 6.00	90	90
Opera (93008) Alwiya	no	$ 5.60	$11.20	100	42
Baghdad Resthouse (86430) Saadun St.	yes	$ 4.20	$ 8.40	16	16

CITY TRANSPORTATION

Baghdad is amply served by buses and taxis. Buses run from 6 A.M. to 12 midnight. Bus fare is 15 fils. City buses are crowded. The average taxi ride in the downtown area costs 200 to 300 fils. The official fixed price for a taxi's waiting time is 500 fils per hour. There are no metered taxis in Iraq, so it is important to settle the price in advance. You can also phone for a taxi.

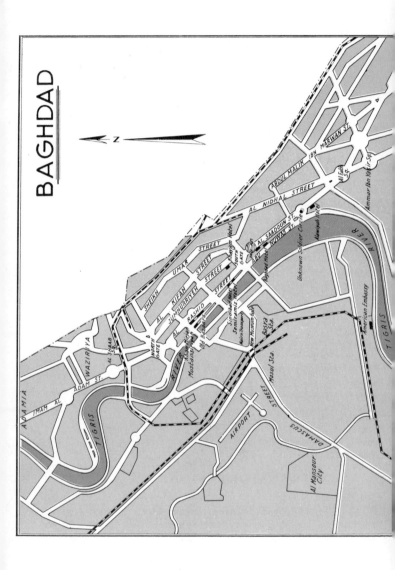

CITY SIGHTS

The capital of Iraq is situated on the Tigris River, 40 miles from the Euphrates River. From ancient times it was the focal point of desert travel and trade. The present city was founded by the Abbassid Caliph Mansur in A.D. 762 on the west bank of the Tigris. It rose to its height as the fabled city of the *Arabian Nights,* under Harun al-Rashid in the 10th century. The city was devastated by the Mongols under Hulagu Khan in the mid-13th century and again in the 14th and 16th centuries. After 1638, when it became part of the Turkish Empire, Baghdad remained insignificant until the 20th century, when once again it was the capital of independent Iraq.

The center of town is on the east bank of the Tigris at the circle known as *South Gate.* Rashid Street is the main business and commercial street of the downtown area. There are now five bridges across the Tigris leading to the newly developed residential areas and the new home of the Iraq Museum on the west bank.

Few of Baghdad's antiquities remain. These sites and the museum can be visited in a day.

Abbassid Palace, according to tradition, once belonged to the son of Harun al Rashid. It probably dates from the mid-13th century. It has been partially restored.

Mustansariya (or Khan el Ortma), located near Bank Street, dates from the early 13th century. Originally the building was probably a school. In 1823 it became a customs house. The building has been restored extensively and is now the main ancient monument in Baghdad.

Khan Mirjan, Bank Street, is a 14th-century caravanseria which now houses the *Islamic Museum.* The exhibits are made up of pottery, wood carvings, copper vases, tiles, and stuccos found at Islamic sites in Iraq.

Bab Wastani, one of the ancient gates of Baghdad, has been restored and now houses a small museum of old weapons. Hours: 9 A.M. to 1 P.M., closed Thursday.

Kadhimain Mosque, located about five miles from downtown, is one of the most celebrated Shiite monuments in the world. Although it was built at an earlier period, the mosque was fully restored in the 19th century. Its golden domes and minarets dominate the northern skyline of Baghdad. It houses the tombs of two important Shiite imams. Non-Moslems are forbidden to enter the mosque.

Iraq National Museum: The exhibits in the Iraqi Museum are some of the most interesting and important discoveries that have been made over the past century of excavations in the Middle East. Many are art masterpieces. These exhibits, more than any of the historic sites themselves, will help you understand the importance of

Hotel (Tel.)	Air-conditioned	Single	Double	Rooms/Baths

the civilizations in ancient Mesopotamia and the high degree of culture they achieved. Items of the Sumerians, for example, are far more delicate and refined than anything found at sites contemporary with them in other countries.

The relics date back 50,000 years, and every important archaeological site in Iraq is represented. One of the most famous pieces is the *Sumerian harp,* found at Ur. The exhibits of Sumerian jewelry and the ivories from Nimrud are also outstanding. A brief look at all the exhibits takes about two hours. A visit to this museum is by far the most important one to be made in Iraq. *Hours:* 8:30 A.M.–1:30 P.M., closed Thursday.

Iraqi National Gallery (Gulbekian Museum) is a modern building housing contemporary paintings by Iraqi artists. It is located near South Gate, the main traffic circle in downtown Baghdad.

EXCURSIONS

Aqarquf: 20 miles west of Baghdad . . . Built on the site of ancient *Dur Kurigalzu,* which was founded in the early 15th century B.C. by a Kassite king, Kurigalzu. The ruins include several temples and a ziggurat modeled after the one of Babylon. About a ½ mile north of the ziggurat are the ruins of a palace. Three different layers of ruins dating from the 15th to the 12th centuries B.C. have been excavated at the site.

Ctesiphon: 20 miles south-southeast of Baghdad . . . On the site of the ancient winter capital of the Parthians stand the remains of a gigantic Sasanian arch, said to be the widest single-span vault of unreinforced brickwork in the world. It once formed part of the façade of a palace. Some authorities credit Chosroes II, the famous Sasanid king who reigned from A.D. 590 to 628, with building the arch. Others claim that it dates from the 4th century. Ctesiphon was founded by the Parthians around 144 B.C. opposite the famous Greek city of Seleucia (now Tell Omar). Ctesiphon was the first important Persian city conquered by the Arabs after the birth of Islam and opened the way for their expansion to the East. The town of Salman Pak, named after the first Persian convert to Islam, is located ½ mile from the arch.

Salman Pak Resthouse (18)		$ 2.80	$ 5.60	5	5
Ctesiphon—Salman Pak		WITH BREAKFAST			

Tell Harmal: 6 miles south of Baghdad . . . Excavations at the site uncovered the world's oldest book of law, the code of Eshnunna (c. 2000 B.C.) and thousands of clay tablets. One of the most significant tablets pictures a geometric-algebraic problem involving a theorem of Euclid (3rd century B.C.) and shows that the principle was in use centuries before Euclid's time.

CHAPTER XXI

IRAQ: TOWNS AND SITES

BABYLON: 57 miles south of Baghdad . . . Four miles from Hilla is the site of the famous ancient capital of Hammurabi and later of Nebuchadnezzar. Its Hanging Gardens were one of the seven wonders of the ancient world, and the ziggurat is known to us as the Tower of Babel.

As early as 2400 B.C. the Akkadians built a temple here to the goddess Ishtar. Two centuries later Babylon came under the control of the Sumerians of Ur. When northern Mesopotamia was invaded by Semites from Amurru, who established their capital at Babylon, they founded what history knows as the first Babylonian dynasty. Hammurabi (1792–1750 B.C.), the great lawgiver and the greatest of the Babylonian kings, established order and unified the country under a strong central power. Babylon flourished until the 16th century B.C., when it was attacked by the Hittites and later the Kassites, who placed themselves in power. In the 12th century the Kassites were replaced by the Assyrians, whose empire dominated Mesopotamia until 612 B.C., when the Assyrian capital of Nineveh was destroyed.

The new period, known as Neo-Babylonian, is best remembered in the name of Nebuchadnezzar II (605–562 B.C.), who in 586 captured Jerusalem and took the Jews captive to Babylon. The great dynasty of new Babylon ended in 539 B.C. with the conquest of the city by Cyrus the Great. It declined steadily until its conquest by Alexander the Great in 331 B.C., who made it the capital of his Asian empire. Eight years later Alexander died here.

A visit to the ruins might begin with the museum, where small models will help you understand the excavations. The major portion of the ruins date from the 7th – 6th centuries B.C. At one time the city was surrounded by two walls with nine gates. Legends say that the inner wall was wide enough for two chariots to ride abreast on it. The decorated *Ishtar Gate* opened onto the main street of the city, which ran along the east side of the palace. The *Lion of Babylon,* near the gate, is Hittite in origin. The great palace of Nebuchadnezzar had five large courtyards and a throne room. Its walls were 20 feet thick. In the northeast side are ruins of a well and pavement which might possibly be the location of the famous *Hanging Gardens.* Beyond the Ishtar Gate is the *Temple of Ishtar,* one of the most important sanctuaries of Mesopotamia. Southwest of the temple stood the great ziggurat, the Biblical *Tower of Babel.*

Hotel (Tel.)	Single	Double	Rooms/Baths	
Babylon Resthouse	$ 2.80	$ 5.60	3	3

BASRA: 364 miles south of Baghdad, 2 miles from the Shatt al Arab, population 100,000 . . . The only seaport of Iraq is located at the head of the Persian Gulf. Basra was founded in the 7th century soon after

Hotel (Tel.)	Single	Double	Rooms/Baths

the Arab conquest and was important throughout the early history of Islam. North of the city on a pleasant drive through miles of the famous date palm groves, you come to the point where the Tigris and Euphrates rivers meet to form the *Shatt al Arab*. Here, according to some legends, was the *Garden of Eden*. Small canoes (and small boys to row them) can be hired for a few fils to take a boat ride around the area. Basra has an airport which is served by Iraqi Airways.

ROOM AND BREAKFAST

Shatt Al Arab (7-7083)	$ 6.44	$11.82	88	88

DIWANIYA: 121 miles south of Baghdad, population 10,000 . . . This small town is the starting point for excursions to Nippur and Warka/Larsa.

ROOM AND BREAKFAST

Diwaniya Resthouse (375)	$ 2.80	$ 5.60	11	11

EXCURSIONS

NIPPUR (Naifar), 28 miles from Diwaniya . . . The ancient Sumerian city of Nippur was an important religious capital from the end of the 4th millennium B.C. and held a sanctuary dedicated to the god Enlil, the chief Sumerian diety. The tell is dominated by the ruins of a ziggurat. walls and a temple.

WARKA, about 80 miles from Diwaniya . . . Warka is the site of Uruk of antiquity, which is mentioned in the Bible as *Erech*. The site was occupied from the Neolithic period and became known as Uruk about 3400 B.C. The ruins of its ziggurat, the city and many temples are in evidence. Some scholars believe that the people of Uruk were the first to introduce the art of writing. Uruk possessed a mythical dynasty of twelve kings who reigned over 2,000 years. One of these kings was the famous hero of Sumerian literature, Gilgamesh. About 2400 B.C. when Sargon of Agade united Sumer and Akkad, the dynasty of Uruk came to an end. Around 2146 B.C. the city fell to Ur, and finally to the Amorites, after which it merged into a Sumerian–Babylonian culture along with most of southern Mesopotamia. Later Uruk was dominated by the Kassites, followed by the Assyrians. Throughout the ancient period and even up to the Persian conquest, its temples were important.

ERBIL (Arbil): 56 miles east of Mosul, 189 miles north of Baghdad, population 50,000 . . . The modern town rests on the site of *Urbillum*, noted in Sumerian writings of the 3rd millennium. Erbil was an important religious shrine in the pre-Assyrian period and claims (as does Damascus) to be the oldest continuously inhabited city in the world. Here, in 331 B.C., Alexander the Great defeated the Persians in the most decisive battle of his Asian campaign. There is a modern resthouse near the railway station. Erbil is the starting point for excursions to Salahuddin and other leading resorts in the Kurdish mountains.

Hotel (Tel.)	Single	Double	Rooms/ Baths

EXCURSIONS

The narrow, winding road climbs for 20 miles northward up the Kurdish mountains through the Khanzad Pass to the small resort village of Salahuddin (altitude 3,500 feet). The resort hotel is located on a knoll surrounded by green scenery and commanding a magnificent view of the snow-capped mountains across the border in Iran. The hotel has a large restaurant, outdoor cinema and swimming pool.

ROOM AND BREAKFAST

Salahuddin (1)	$ 2.80	$ 5.60	30	30

SHAQLAWA, 12 miles beyond Salahuddin, is another popular resort. It has a small airport. From Shaqlawa along the Ruwandiz Gorge, the countryside is green and picturesque with fresh, rushing streams. This is the favorite fishing area of Iraq and is ideal for picnics and hiking.

ROOM AND BREAKFAST

Khanzad (9)	$ 2.80	$ 5.60	9	8

GALI ALI BEG, 35 miles beyond Shaqlawa, is the loveliest waterfall of the Kurdish mountains. There is a small restaurant and garden at the foot of the falls. The drive from Salahuddin to Gali Ali Beg covers some of the most beautiful scenery in Iraq.

Beyond Ruwandiz at the village of Khalifan a road on the left proceeds to Shanidar (29 miles) along the valley of the Greater Zab River. The valley varies from a half mile to one mile wide and is enclosed on both sides by high rocky mountains. From the Shanidar police station you need to walk about two miles (up about 1,200 feet) to reach the famous Shanidar Cave on the side of the mountain. Here, archaeological excavations found evidence that man has lived for 60,000 years. The entrance of the cave is in the shape of a rough triangle, 82 feet wide and 25 feet high. Inside it broadens suddenly to 175 feet and 130 feet in depth and 45 feet in height. The excavations reached bedrock at 45 feet, or approximately the 60,000-year level. An abundance of artifacts were discovered, the most important of which was the skeleton of a Neanderthal man. About one mile from the cave a village 10,000 years old was uncovered. Experts think that in ancient times the inhabitants of the village used the Shanidar Cave in winter in much the same way as do the seven families who inhabit it today.

HABBANIYA LAKE: 51 miles west of Baghdad . . . A new holiday resort has been developed in the past few years around the lake. Tourist facilities include 50 cabins of the Tourism and Summer Resorts Administration, a restaurant, and swimming, boating and water-skiing equipment.

HATRA (Hadhr): 83 miles south-southwest of Mosul, 30 miles west of Sharqat . . . The exact origins of Hatra are unknown. It is believed to have been founded in the 1st century A.D. and was for most of its history under the domination of the Parthians. The Romans tried twice without success to seize it. It was finally captured by the Sasanids in the mid-3rd century.

Waterfall of Gali Ali Beg, Kurdish mountains.

Note regarding words used in this chapter.

ziggurat: a temple tower consisting of a lofty pyramidal structure built in successive stages with outside staircases and a shrine at the top. The ziggurat was a religious structure characteristic of ancient Mesopotamia and served a similar purpose to the temple of other ancient cultures.

tell (tal):   a high mound. Often in Iraq and throughout the Middle East, a tell marks the site of an ancient city. The site might have been a natural rise in the land, or it might have been made high over the centuries by the presence of successive civilizations one on top of the other.

Hotel (Tel.)	Single	Double	Rooms/Baths

Apparently, Hatra, like many ancient cities on the edge of the Syrian desert, was an important junction for the caravans and at the same time a military outpost between the rivalling powers of East and West.

The outline of the city walls (two miles in diameter) can be traced. The town center was further enclosed by a wall with seven gates. The ruins include a temple to the sun and other religious structures. Many statues were discovered in the excavations (now in the Iraq Museum) and, in all, twelve temples have been uncovered. The desert area where Hatra is located is also the home of the Shammar, one of the most famous tribes of Iraq

	ROOM AND BREAKFAST			
Hatra Resthouse	$ 2.80	$ 5.60	8	8

HILLA: 71 miles south of Baghdad, population 55,000 . . . The modern town of Hilla, partially built from materials of the Babylon ruins, is an agricultural center of a fertile region watered by the Euphrates River. It has been important since the 12th century as a stopping place for pilgrims from Baghdad en route to Kufa. Hilla is the turn-off point for Babylon (four miles) and the starting point for excursions to Kish, Kufa and Najaf, Diwaniya and Nippur. The trip to Karbala and El Ukhaidar can also be made from here. There is a resthouse at the Hilla railway station.

KARBALA (Kerbala): 95 miles south of Baghdad, population 65,000 . . . As a holy shrine for the Shiite sect of Islam, Karbala is second only to Mecca. The *Abbas Mosque* marks the place where in A.D. 680 the supporters of Ali, led by his son, Husayn, fought the partisans of the Umayyads over the question of the rightful successors to Muhammad as the Caliph of Islam. In the battle Husayn and his family were killed. Their martyrdom split Islam irrevocably into two sects: the Sunnis, who believed in the Caliphate as an elective office, and the Shiites, who recognized only the right of the direct descendants of the Prophet Muhammad to the Caliphate. Under the golden domes of the *Mosque of Husayn* in the center of Karbala rests the tomb of Husayn. Non-Moslems are not allowed to enter these mosques, nor should they attempt to photograph them at close range.

	ROOM AND BREAKFAST			
Karbala Resthouse (82)	$ 2.80	$ 5.60	37	37

EXCURSIONS

A desert track from Karbala leads (32 miles) to the Castle of El-Ukhaidar. The exact origins of the castle are unknown, but most authorities think it was built in the 7th century after the Arab conquest. The ruins are extensive and the outer walls in particular are well preserved. The site is one of the most impressive antiquities in Iraq. In her writings Gertrude Bell eloquently describes the sight of the lonely castle in the midst of the empty desert. In the Abbassid Palace Museum in Baghdad there is an excellent model of El-Ukhaidar.

Hotel (Tel.)	Single	Double	Rooms/Baths

KHANAQIN: 112 miles northeast of Baghdad . . . This small town is located on the main road from Baghdad to Kermanshah, Iran. It is the last town before the Iranian border where customs and passport formalities are arranged. The border is five miles farther east.

KIRKUK: 173 miles northeast of Baghdad, altitude 1,000 feet, population 100,000 . . . Kirkuk is the center of the oil industry of Iraq. From these fields oil is piped over 600 miles to ports on the Mediterranean Sea. The Iraq Petroleum Company was founded in 1925. Its installations now cover an area of about 50 miles and can be visited after securing permission from the headquarters office. *Baba Gurgur,* where oil was struck for the first time in 1927, is said to be the burning furnace into which Nebuchadnezzar ordered Shadrach, Meshach and Abednego, as the Bible account relates. The Eternal Fire, as it is called locally, is kept burning by escaping gases. Near the modern town of Kirkuk there is an artificial mound known as El Qalaa, the citadel of Kirkuk, on which there is a mosque dedicated to Daniel (of the Bible). Kirkuk was *Arrapkha* (and later Karka) of antiquity. Scholars say it was built by Sardanopolus, the last king of the great Assyrian empire.

Kirkuk is the starting point for trips into the Kurdish mountains to Sulaimaniya and to the famous Jarmo excavations.

	ROOM WITH FULL BOARD			
Kirkuk Resthouse (2048)	$ 6.30	$ 9.00	13	13

EXCURSIONS

TEPE JARMO (37 miles) is an artificial mound perched on a hill on which fifteen different strata of civilization have been excavated. It was one of the earliest inhabited places in the world. The layers of the upper third of the mound date from the Neolithic period (6000 B.C.). Zarzi (65 miles), another important archaeological site, is a grotto where traces of human occupation dating back 10,000 years were discovered.

KUFA: 28 miles southwest of Hilla, population 15,000 . . . The town was founded in 638 soon after the Arab conquest. When Ali came here to live in 657, Kufa became the capital of the Shiites. In 661 Ali was assassinated in the Mosque of Kufa. From Kufa the road continues five miles to Najaf.

MOSUL: 256 miles north of Baghdad, 421 miles east of Aleppo, population 200,000 . . . The modern city of Mosul is the largest town in northern Iraq and the second largest city in the country. It is located on the right bank of the Tigris River at the site of the great Assyrian capital of Nineveh. Mosul was an important town of the earlier Islamic period until it was devastated by the Mongols in the mid-13th century. Throughout its history Mosul has been an important agricultural and commercial center because of its location on the river, at the head of the fertile plains and at the foot

Hotel (Tel.)	Single	Double	Rooms/Baths

of the Kurdish mountains. The city was once known for its fine cotton goods, from which the name "muslin" was derived.

Interesting sites in town include the *Archaeological Museum,* Jamhuriya Street (near the new bridge), which contains exhibits from excavations in northern Iraq. Especially important are the Assyrian pieces from Nimrud, statues from Hatra, artifacts from prehistoric sites such as Shem-Shemal, Zarzi and Jarmo, and a collection of Islamic antiquities. Guides are available for tours of the Mosul area for reasonable fees.

The *Great Mosque* of Mosul stands on the site of a church. All that remains of the ancient mosque is the minaret, known as the "Leaning Tower." Its apparent tilt is caused by erosion of the brickwork by the prevailing winds. Other sites include several old Assyrian (Nestorian) churches, the *Mausoleum of Yahia* topped with an octagonal pyramid, and the *Qara Serai,* the palace of Badr ud-Din Lu'lu, who ruled Mosul from A.D. 1234 to 1258.

The main antiquity near Mosul is Nineveh at the tell known as *Kuyunjik.* Nineveh was occupied as early as the 5th millennium. Under the Assyrian empire it became the capital of the domain and was especially important under the rulers of the 7th century B.C. In the great palace of Assuribanipal 25,000 cuneiform texts were found (now in the British Museum). To Assurbanipal, who had his scribes collect and transcribe the literature of his day, we owe our knowledge of the Sumerian epic of Gilgamesh and the Babylonian version of the Deluge. The fall of Nineveh in 612 B.C. marked the end of the Assyrian empire, and within 300 years even its site was lost until its discovery in the mid-19th century. At the entrance to the ruins there are diagrams which help explain the excavations of the temples, palaces and gates.

WITH FULL BOARD

Mosul Resthouse (3083)	—	$14.00	20	20
Railway Station				

EXCURSIONS

Mosul is the starting point for excursions to several important archaeological sites and to leading summer resorts in the Kurdish mountains.

KHORSABAD (13 miles north) is the site of *Dur Sharrukin,* founded by Sargon II (721–705 B.C.). It once had a splendid palace surrounded by a city wall with seven gates ornamented by sculptured figures. Today the site is distinguished by a tell. As in the case of many archaeological sites in Iraq, the ruins are a mass of rubble due to the nature of the building material. In most cases buildings were constructed with sun-dried mud bricks. Consequently, many of the ancient sites in Iraq have not been preserved as have those in other countries where more durable materials were used, and they are often confusing, if not disappointing, to the average visitor. Jerwan, 20 minutes by car north of Khorsabad, is the site of an aqueduct built by Sennacherib in the early 7th century to bring water from a tributary of the Great Zab to Nineveh over a distance of 50 miles. It is

Hotel (Tel.)	Single	Double	Rooms/Baths

the oldest aqueduct in the world of which remains have survived. At the *Bavian Gorge* (a three-hour hike from Ain Sifni) there are eleven steles which describe the building of the dam and waterworks as well as bas reliefs of Sennacherib and other Assyrian figures and gods.

From Mosul a road north into the Kurdish mountains leads to the summer resorts of Swaratouka (4,430 feet), where there are a few cottages and a large restaurant, and to Sirsang (84 miles, 3,670 feet), the leading resort of the area. Amadiya, 18 miles beyond Sirsang, is a picturesque Kurdish village set in a natural fortress. It rests on a high bluff in a long valley surrounded by snow-capped peaks. All these resorts have serene settings surrounded by wild natural beauty. They seem almost untouched by the 20th century.

	ROOM AND BREAKFAST			
Swaratouka Resthouse (6)	$ 2.80	$ 5.60	12	3 (not priv.)
Sirsang Hotel (14)	$ 2.80	$ 5.60	61	61

NIMRUD, 25 miles south of Mosul, was the capital of the Assyrian empire for many centuries. It is known as *Calah* in the Old Testament. Excavations have revealed settlements as early as the 4th millennium B.C., but the main period of Nimrud was under Shalmaneser I in the early 13th century B.C. The city was apparently destroyed about 614 B.C. just before the fall of Nineveh. The ruins are extensive and cover an area of five miles. They include many palaces, temples, houses and fortress walls. There are two reconstructed gates with huge winged bulls and lions, and a frieze of colossal figures bearing gifts to Assurnazirpal.

ASHUR, 70 miles south of Mosul along the west bank of the Tigris (six miles south of Shargat), was the first great capital of Assyria. The site commanded a strategic position on the Tigris and was occupied as early as the Neolithic period. As a city it was first important under the Sumerians about 3000 B.C. The city was known by the name of its supreme god Ashur, whose temple was the largest and most beautiful religious shrine of the region. Ashur fell to Hammurabi in the early 18th century B.C. It was again important about the 13th century B.C. and later under Shalmaneser III (853–834 B.C.), Sargon II (721–705 B.C.) and Sennacherib (705–681 B.C.). In 614 B.C. Ashur was attacked by the Medes from Persia and the Chaldeans from Babylon. On its ruins the victorious kings strengthened their alliance by giving a Median princess in marriage to the Chaldean Crown Prince Nebuchadnezzar II. For his Persian princess, history records, Nebuchadnezzar built the Hanging Gardens. Ashur was later seized by the Parthians in 140 B.C. and the Romans in A.D. 116 and 198. The ziggurat dominates the site. The Temple of Ashur, founded in the 3rd millennium B.C., was rebuilt many times. There are ruins of several temples dedicated to Ishtar as well as remains of Assyrian palaces and a necropolis.

NAJAF: 33 miles southwest of Hilla, population 80,000 . . . Najaf is one of the holiest cities of the Shiite sect of Islam. Here rests the tomb of Ali, the son-in-law of the Prophet Muhammad, who the Shiites believe was the

Hotel (Tel.)	Single	Double	Rooms/Baths

rightful successor to Muhammad as the Caliph. The town is built around the mosque, which is dominated by a golden dome and two minarets. Inside, the tomb of Ali, enclosed by a decorative iron fence, rests in the center. The tomb is laden with precious gold, silver and jeweled gifts which have been offered by pilgrims over the centuries. Non-Moslems are not allowed in the mosque, nor is it advisable for them to take photographs of the mosque at close range.

NASIRIYAH: 236 miles south of Baghdad, 128 miles north of Basra, population 40,000 . . . The village was founded in the last century by Sheikh Naser Pasha As-Sadun, head of the Muntafiq tribe, who was persuaded by Midhat Pasha to turn his sheikdom into a governorship. A Belgian architect, invited by Naser Pasha, planned the city. The area around Nasiriyah contains some of the most important antiquity sites in Iraq. It is the starting point for excursions to Ur and Eridu.

	ROOM AND BREAKFAST		
Nasiriyah Resthouse (279)	$ 2.80	$ 5.60	6	6

RAMADI: 47 miles west of Baghdad . . . This small town is the first important place in Iraq on the drive from Damascus and Amman to Baghdad. There is a restaurant, resthouse and gasoline station.

	ROOM AND BREAKFAST		
Ramadi Resthouse	$ 2.80	$ 5.60	9	9

RUTBA: 259 miles west of Baghdad . . . The town is located near the Jordanian frontier and is the Iraqi customs and passport station. A gas station is located at the east end of town; the customs office and resthouse are at the west end.

	ROOM AND BREAKFAST		
Rutba Resthouse (16)	$ 2.80	$ 5.60	16	16

SAMARRA: 110 miles north of Baghdad . . . The short-lived capital of the Abbassids was founded in 836 by the Caliph Mu'tasim, the son of Harun al-Rashid. Each of the seven caliphs who followed added new palaces and mosques and enlarged the city until its great central boulevard extended twenty miles in length. After forty years of splendor Samarra was abandoned, and the capital was moved back to Baghdad.

The famous *Friday Mosque* with its spiral minaret dominates the scene. This mosque is one of the oldest in Iraq. Its plan was simple but colossal. Only the buttressed walls remain standing. The minaret known as *Malwiya* in Arabic is said to have been an evolution of the ziggurat. Steps, which can be climbed, wind around the minaret to the top, from where there is a splendid view of the mosque, present-day Samarra and the ancient ruins.

Other important ruins are the main palace, called *Beit al Khalifa*. Its vast halls and reception rooms were once profusely decorated. It was surrounded by flowering gardens and pavilions skirting an artificial lake.

Hotel (Tel.)	Single	Double	Rooms/Baths

The ruins of another extensive palace, called *Balkuwara,* can be seen on the south, where there is also the remains of a large arch. Farther on, another building, called *Qadisiyah,* is set in a large octagonal enclosure. On the north side the Caliph Mutawakkil built an entirely new quarter, including an enormous canal to bring water from the Tigris to this part of the city. The canal, however, was never made to work. There is another mosque, *Abu Dulaf,* which also has a spiral minaret. Its interior is better preserved than the Friday Mosque.

The modern town of Samarra, located near the ancient site, contains the tombs of two of the twelve Shiite Imams and a shrine dedicated to the twelfth one, the Mahdi. Its 14th-century doorway, according to the Shiite belief, will be the place where the Mahdi will make his Second Coming. One of the city gates of Samarra has been restored and extended to house a small museum. In the museum there are plans and pictures of ancient Samarra and exhibits from the excavations. The museum is a good place to begin your tour.

	ROOM AND BREAKFAST			
Samarra Resthouse (24)	$ 2.80	$ 5.60	6	4

SULAIMANIYA: 71 miles east of Kirkuk, population 50,000 . . . The village is a summer resort and winter ski area. It has a charming setting in an amphitheater-shaped mountain.

	ROOM AND BREAKFAST			
Sulaimaniya Resthouse (100)	$ 2.80	$ 5.60	12	12

UR ((Tell Muqayyar): 10 miles southwest of Nasiriyah, 1¼ miles west of Ur Junction . . . Although Ur was occupied as early as the Neolithic period, its historic importance dates from the First Ur Dynasty, about 2700 B.C. Ur succeeded the older Sumerian dynasties of Kish and Uruk and became the leading city of southern Mesopotamia. Its fame in history was as *Ur-of-the-Chaldees,* the home of Abraham. Under Sargon (c. 2400 B.C.), Ur, along with other cities of Sumer, was united with Akkad. About 2131 B.C. Ur-Nammu, King of Ur, defeated the King of Uruk and took the title of "King of Sumer and Akkad." The kings who followed from 2123–2015 B.C. constituted the Third Ur Dynasty, which was the most glorious period of Sumerian history. Later Ur became part of the Babylonian empire. Under the Kassites many of its sanctuaries were restored, yet from this period it began to decline. Although it had a brief revival under Nebuchadnezzar, by 400 B.C. Ur no longer existed. The site was discovered in the mid-19th century but was not scientifically excavated until after World War I.

The ziggurat of Ur was one of the earliest in southern Mesopotamia and became a prototype for those built afterward. It was built about 2700 B.C. under the First Ur Dynasty on the site of earlier sanctuaries. Northeast of it was the *Court of the god Nannar,* which dates from the Kassite period. Southeast of the ziggurat is the *E-Dub-Lal-Markh,* which dates originally from about 2124 B.C. and was a passageway to the ziggurat. It was reconstructed by the Kassites as a chapel. In the *Royal Tombs,* located

The Ishtar Gate of Babylon.

Courtyard of the Muslansariya, Baghdad.

on the southwest side of the ruins, a vast quantity of exquisite jewelry and artifacts were found intact. These finds (now in the Iraq Museum) were significant aids to archaeologists in helping them form a picture of the Sumerian civilization and in understanding the high level of development their culture had reached.

Four miles northwest of Ur is Tell el Obeid. The prehistoric period (4000–3000) is called *El Obeid (Ubaid)* after the site and pertains mainly to the civilization found in southern Mesopotamia. *Eridu,* 14 miles south-southwest of Ur at Tell Abu Sharain, is one of the oldest sites in southern Iraq. It was occupied as early as 4000 B.C. and probably earlier. In antiquity, Eridu was reputed to be the most ancient city in the world.

CHAPTER XXII

MENU TRANSLATOR

Middle Eastern food is based largely on rice or cracked wheat and lamb or beef and chicken. Many exotic vegetable dishes are also prepared. Butter and olive oil are used lavishly. Herbs, nuts, sesame, lemon juice, the essence of orange blossoms or roses are used frequently for flavoring. Lebanon, Syria and Jordan have similar cuisine with the addition of local specialties. Iraq has many of the same dishes plus a variety of Persian, Turkish and Kurdish specialties not found in the other countries. Egypt has less variety, but certain dishes are typical of the country. Names of food sometimes vary from one country to another. These are indicated by (E) for Egypt, (J) for Jordan, (I) for Iraq, (L) for Lebanon and (S) for Syria. The letters are also used to indicate specialties of a particular country.

In most hotels throughout the area breakfast will be the usual European repast of coffee, rolls, butter and jam. Juice and eggs are extra. Generally Middle Easterners have their lunch at 2 P.M., though it might be as early as 1 P.M. or as late as 3 P.M. Dinner is never served before 8 P.M. unless you specially request it. When you are invited to someone's home or to a restaurant or night club, dinner will probably not be served before 9 or 10 P.M.

Menus in most restaurants where foreigners are likely to dine are written in French and sometimes in English. Those in Arabic will be written in Arabic script. Seldom will they be transliterated into Latin characters. Except for your personal enjoyment of knowing the names of food, the list below will probably not be as helpful in reading a menu as would brushing up on your French.

Throughout the Arab world the greatest expression of hospitality that can be shown by a host to his guest is the generosity of food he offers. In turn the guest is expected to eat heartily, lest he offend his host. But since eating is the favorite pastime throughout the Middle East, a major problem for a visitor is overeating. The cuisine is excellent and tempting, but it is rich and loaded with spices. You should sample a little of each, and remember—what often appears as the main dish is only the beginning! There will probably be four or five more courses to follow.

FOOD TERMS

ADAS: Lentils.
AHWI: Coffee.
AIYSH: (E) Bread.
ARAQ: Aperitif made from grape alcohol and flavored with anis. It looks like water, but when water is added, as it should be, araq turns a milky-white. In Iraq it is made from dates.

ASAL: Honey.

ASHA: Dinner.

AWAMATI: (S) Fried batter, similar to donuts.

BABA GHANOUJ: Baked eggplant, seasoned with TAHINI, lemon, garlic and olive oil. In Syria it is called MUTABAL.

BAID: Eggs.

BAID BRISHT: Soft-boiled eggs.

BAID MASLOUQ: Hard-boiled eggs.

BAKLAWA: Layers of paper-thin crisp pastry filled with pistachio, walnuts or pine nuts, baked in syrup.

BANADURA: Tomatoes.

BARAAQI: (S) Biscuit covered with sesame seeds.

BASAL: Onions.

BATARIKH: (E) Egyptian caviar, pressed and dried, and preserved in salt and oil.

BATANJAN: Eggplant.

BATEEKH: Watermelon.

BIRA: Beer.

BORT'AN: Orange.

BOUZA: Ice cream.

BURGHUL: Cracked wheat.

CASTALETTA: Cutlet of beef or lamb.

DAFAD'A: (S) Frog's legs. A specialty of Damascus.

DAUD PASHA: (J) Stew of meat balls, onions, pine nuts cooked with tomatoes and served with rice.

DJAJ: (L) Chicken.

DONDURMA: (E) Sweet milk sherbet.

DURRAK: Peaches.

ENAB: Grapes.

FALAFEL: Patties of mashed fava beans with finely chopped parsley, highly seasoned and fried in deep oil.

FARROUJ MESHWI: Chicken broiled over charcoal; can be eaten with a garlic paste.

FARIDAN: A white, meaty fish from the Mediterranean (red mullet).

FATAYIR: Small pieces of baked dough stuffed with chopped onions, spinach or meat and pine nuts.

FATAYIR ZALATIMO: (J) A pastry to be eaten at Zalatimo's in the Old City of Jerusalem. It is a paper-thin dough with corners folded in and filled with cheese or walnuts. The pastry is baked in a brick oven situated in the original wall of ancient Jerusalem before the time of Christ. The pastry is made prior to 10 A.M. and should be eaten in the morning.

FATOORA: The bill.

FATTET EL-HUMMOS: (J) Bed of Arabic bread chips covered with chick-peas and their juice, and topped with yogurt, garlic and roasted pine nuts.

FAWAKEH: Fruit.

FATTET MAKKADEM: (S) Lamb knuckles baked in yoghurt with chips of Arabic bread.

FILFIL: Black pepper.

FILFIL HELLU: Sweet pepper.

FOOL: Fava beans.

FOOL MUDAMMAS: (E) This is the national dish of Egypt. Fool is cooked with spices, and sometimes tomatoes, into a thick sauce (something like chile con carne without meat). It is often eaten with a fried egg on top for breakfast, or without for other meals.

FREEK: (S) Green wheat cooked with chunks of meat.

FURTAIKEH: (L) Fork.

FUSTUQ HALAB: Pistachio.

FUSULYA: White beans.

GEBNA: (E) Cheese.

GHADA: Lunch.

HALEEB: (L) Milk.

HAMAM: (E) Pigeons broiled on open spit.

HUMMOS: Chick-peas.

HUMMOS BI-THINI: Mashed chick-peas seasoned with garlic, sesame paste, lemon and olive oil.

IJJE: Omelet.

INJAS: Pears.

JIBIN: (L) Cheese.

KAFTA MESHWIYEH: Minced lamb mixed with chopped onions and parsley, and broiled on skewers.

KARABEJ HALAB: (S) Small sweet pastry stuffed with pistachio nuts and eaten with meringue.

KASHTA: Thick whipped cream used as filling in desserts. A specialty of Tripoli.

KANAFA: Sweet cake filled with cheese and served with hot, clear syrup. Eaten for breakfast or as dessert. Available in all countries but specialty of Nablus, Jordan.

KATAYEF: A thin pancake filled with cheese, KASHTA or nuts and topped with syrup.

KEBAB: *See* Shishkebab.

KESH AL-FA'ARA: (S) A dessert or pastry.

KHALL: Vinegar.

KHAROOF: Lamb.

KHAROOF MESHWI: Roast stuffed lamb. Same as Mansaf.

KHASS: Lettuce.

KHIYAR: Cucumber.

KHUBZ: Bread.

KHUKH: Plums.

KHUDRA: Vegetables.

KIBBEH: Ground lean lamb or beef and cracked wheat pounded with cumin, minced onions, pine nuts and salt.

KIBBEH ARNABIYA: KIBBEH stuffed with pine nuts and meat, cooked in a sauce of sesame paste and chick-peas flavored with lemon and served over rice.

KIBBEH BI-SANIYEH: KIBBEH baked with a layer of sautéd ground meat, onions and pine nuts. This is the national dish of Lebanon and Syria.

KIBBEH LABANIYA: KIBBEH stuffed with pine nuts and cooked in yogurt.

KIBBEH NAYEH: Fresh raw lamb pounded with cracked wheat and seasoned with onions, pepper, cumin and salt. (Similar to steak tartare.)

KIDREH BIL-FURN: (J) (pot-in-oven) Cubed meat, rice, chick-peas and spices are placed in an earthen jar and baked in an oven. A specialty of Hebron, Jordan.

KOOSA: Squash.

KOUBEH: (S) Small KIBBEH balls stuffed with meat and pine nuts and fried in olive oil.

KUBAIYEH: Glass.

KUBBAH MOSUL: (I) Large KIBBEH balls stuffed with meat, pine nuts and almonds, and roasted.

LAHM: Meat.

LAHM BAQAR: Beef.

LAHM BI AJEEN (or Sambusik): A closed version of SFEEHA.

LAHM 'IGL: Veal.

LAHM MESHWI: Shishkebab.

LEBAN: (L) Yogurt; (E) Milk.

LEBAN ZABADI: (E) Yogurt.

LIMON: Lemon.

LUBIYA: Green beans.

MADLUQA: (S) Dessert of KANAFI with KASHTA.

MAHSHI: Vegetables such as eggplant, squash, cabbage, grape leaves and peppers stuffed with chopped meat and rice, usually cooked in tomato sauce.

MAL'AQA: Spoon.

MALFOOF: Cabbage.

MANAQUEESH: Bread baked with finely minced thyme, sesame seeds and olive oil.

MANSAF: (J) Roast lamb stuffed with rice, highly spiced with cinnamon and served with makheedh (beaten yogurt combined with the butterfat of mutton). This is the traditional feast of the Bedouin when a lamb is slaughtered for a guest or a special occasion. For such a ceremony the whole lamb is served atop a huge tray of rice, and the honored guest is often presented with the eye of the lamb (although not in a restaurant).

MAQLOUBA (means literally "upside down"): A stewlike dish of vegetables, usually cauliflower or eggplant, and meat served on rice. (Yogurt is sometimes added on top.) A specialty of Jerusalem.

MAT'AM: Restaurant.

MASQOUF: (I) Fish from the Tigris, roasted on a pole by an open fire. A specialty of Baghdad.

MESHWI: Broiled.

MEZZAH: The equivalent of hors d'oeuvres, but much more generous. The spread of forty different dishes usually includes stuffed grape leaves, TABOOLI, HUMMOS BI THINI, BABA GHANOUJ, KIBBEH NAYEH, a variety of pickled vegetables and cold meats. ARAQ is served with the MEZZAH and is an excellent complement to it.

MILH: Salt.

MISHMISH: Apricot.

MOOZ: Banana.

MOULUKHIYA: (L) Sliced chicken on a bed of rice and toasted bread chips, covered with a sauce of marinated onions and topped with a steamed herb (Moulukhiya). (E) Steamed herb is used as sauce for many dishes. (S) Cooked with rice.

MUGHLI: A spicy rice pudding topped with bleached nuts.

MUGHRABIYA: Cracked wheat cooked with chunks of meat, chicken and a variety of beans.

MUHALLABIYA: Cream of rice pudding.

MURABBA: Preserves; jam.

MUSAKHAN: (J) Chicken, previously steamed in a sauce of olive oil, onions and sumak, is baked on specially prepared bread and covered with a layer of onions marinated in oil and sumak. A specialty of Tulkarem, Jordan, and borrowed by Ramallah and Jericho. Several restaurants in the latter two towns specialize in it. The dish is very rich, highly seasoned and one of the most delicious in the Middle East.

MUTABAL: (S) *See* Baba Ghanouj.

MYE: Water.

NBEED: Wine.

OUZI: (I) same as MANSAF. (S) Large round pastry stuffed with rice, lamb, pine nuts and almonds.

ROSTO: Roast meat.

RUZZ: Rice.

SAHN: Plate.

SALATA: Salad.

SALATA BI-TAHINI: (J) Finely chopped tossed salad seasoned with the paste of sesame oil.

SAMAK BI-TAHINI (samak tajen): Fish baked in sesame paste.

SAMAK-HARRA: Baked fish dressed with a thick sauce of crushed almonds, colander, peppers and herbs.

SAMAK TAJEN: (S) Fish baked with onions in sesame paste.

SAMAK MESHWI: Grilled fish, often served with TARATOUR.

SAMAK NAHRI: Trout.

SAYYADIEH: Fish cooked with onions and pine nuts and served over brown rice.

SFEEHA: (L) Open-face patties baked with ground meat, onions and pine nuts. (S) long-shaped pastry stuffed with meat, onions, pines and yogurt.

SHAKRIYA: (S) Any dish cooked with yogurt, such as meat and rice.

SHAMMAM: Yellow melon.

SHANKLEESH: Dried yogurt with chopped tomatoes and onions combined as a salad.

SHAWARMA: Slivers of highly seasoned lamb, cooked on a pole beside a charcoal fire.

SHISHKEBAB: Chunks of lamb or beef on a skewer.

SHOWRABA: Soup.

SHY: Tea.

SIKKIN: Knife.

SNOBAR: Pine nuts.

SULTAN IBRAHIM: (L) A small fish similar to sardines, fried in deep oil.

TAAMEYYA: *See* Falafel.

TABOOLI: A salad of cracked wheat, tomatoes, parsley, onions, lemon juice and olive oil.

TAHINI: Oil paste of the sesame seed. Taheena (E): preparation includes a variety of herbs and served as a cocktail dip.

TALJ: Ice.

TARATOUR: A sauce of sesame paste, lemon juice, garlic, chopped parsley, olive oil and salt.

TARWIQA: (L) Breakfast.

TASQIA: (S) Toasted bread, chick-peas, pine nuts cooked with lemon juice.

TEEN: Figs.

TOOM: Garlic.

TURSHI: (E) Mixed pickled vegetables served with cocktails.

WARAQ AREESH (Waraq enab): Rolled grape leaves stuffed with rice and meat or lentils.

ZAIT: Olive oil.

ZAITOON: Olives.

ZEBDA: Butter.

ZNOOD ES-SIT: Thin, crisp pastry roll filled with KASHTA and topped with syrup. A specialty of Tripoli, Lebanon.

INDEX

LEBANON Currency Converter

Rate of exchange based on rate of LL 3.05 equals U.S. $1

COINS	
5 piasters =	$.01½
10 piasters =	$.03
25 piasters =	$.08
50 piasters =	$.16

Notes are in Bold Type

LL	$
.10	.03
.25	.08
.30	.10
.50	.16
.75	.25
1	**.33**
1.50	.49
1.55	.50
1.65	.55
2	**.65**
2.50	.81
3	**.96**
4	**1.28**
4.50	1.44
5	**1.64**
6	**1.96**

LL	$
7	2.26
8	2.56
9	2.88
10	**3.28**
12	3.92
13	4.26
14	4.60
15	4.91
16	5.25
17	5.41
18	5.90
19	6.23
20	6.56
21	6.84
22	7.21
23	7.54
24	7.86
25	**8.20**
30	9.84
40	13.11
50	**16.31**
60	19.67
75	24.59
80	24.51
90	28.80
100	**32.80**

SYRIA Currency Converter

Rate of exchange is based on the market rate of L.S. 4 equals U.S. $1

COINS	
.05 piasters =	$.01¼
.10 piasters =	$.02½
.25 piasters =	$.06¼
.50 piasters =	$.12½

Notes are in Bold Type

L.S.	$
1.00	**.25**
1.50	.38
2.00	.50
2.50	.63
3.00	.75
3.50	.88
4.00	1.00
4.50	1.13
5.00	**1.25**
5.50	1.38
6.00	1.50
6.50	1.63
7.00	1.75
7.50	1.88
8.00	2.00

L.S.	$
8.50	2.38
9.00	2.50
9.50	2.63
10.00	**2.75**
11.00	2.88
12.00	3.00
13.00	3.25
14.00	3.50
15.00	3.75
16.00	4.00
17.00	4.25
18.00	4.50
19.00	4.75
20.00	5.00
25.00	**6.25**
30.00	7.50
35.00	8.75
40.00	10.00
45.00	11.25
50.00	**12.50**
60.00	15.00
70.00	17.50
75.00	18.75
80.00	20.00
90.00	22.50
100.00	**25.00**

JORDAN Currency Converter

Rate of exchange based on official rate of J.D. 1 equals U.S. $2.80

COINS
10, 20, 50, 100, 500 fils

Notes are in Bold Type

J.D.	U.S. $
.010	.03
.020	.06
.030	.08
.040	.11
.050	.14
.060	.17
.070	.20
.080	.22
.090	.25
.100	.28
.150	.42
.200	.56
.250	.70
.300	.84
.350	.98
.400	1.12
.500	**1.40**
.550	1.54
.600	1.68
.750	2.10
.800	2.18
.900	2.52
1.000	**2.80**
1.200	3.36
1.500	4.20
1.750	4.90
2.000	5.60
2.100	5.88
2.200	6.16
2.500	7.00
3.000	8.40
3.500	9.80
3.750	10.50
4.000	11.20
5.000	**14.00**
6.000	16.80
7.000	19.60
8.000	22.40
9.000	25.20
10.000	**28.00**
20.000	56.00
25.000	70.00
30.000	84.00
40.000	112.00
50.000	140.00
100.000	280.00

EGYPT Currency Converter

Rate of exchange based on L.E. 1 equals U.S. $2.30

COINS
Silver—
50, 25, 20, 10, 5, 2 piasters
Copper—
1 piaster (10 milliemes),
½ piaster (5 milliemes)
Brass—
20, 20, 5 piasters
(milliemes)

Notes are in Bold Type

Piasters	U.S. $
.01	.023
.02	.05
.03	.07
.04	.09
.05	**.12**
.06	.14
.07	.16
.08	.18
.09	.21
.10	**.23**
.15	.35
.20	.46
.25	**.57**
.30	.69
.35	.80
.40	.92
.45	1.04
.50	**1.15**
.55	1.27
.60	1.38
.65	1.50
.70	1.61
.75	1.73
.80	1.84
.85	1.96
.90	2.07
.95	2.19
1.00	**2.30**
2.00	4.60
3.00	6.90
4.00	9.20
5.00	**11.50**
6.00	13.80
7.00	16.10
8.00	18.40
9.00	20.70
10.00	**23.00**
15.00	34.50
20.00	46.00
25.00	**57.00**
30.00	69.00
35.00	80.50
40.00	92.00
45.00	103.50
50.00	**115.00**

IRAQ Currency Converter

Rate of exchange based on official rate of I.D. 1 equals $2.80

COINS			I.D.	U.S. $
10, 20, 50, 100, 500 fils			.800	2.18
			.900	2.52
			1.000	**2.80**
Notes are in Bold Type			1.200	3.36
I.D.	U.S. $		1.500	4.20
.010	.03		1.750	4.90
.020	.05		2.000	5.60
.030	.09		2.100	5.88
.040	.11		2.200	6.16
.050	.14		2.500	7.00
.060	.17		3.000	8.40
.070	.20		3.500	9.90
.080	.23		4.000	11.20
.090	.25		**5.000**	**14.00**
.100	.28		6.000	16.80
.150	.42		7.000	19.60
.200	.56		8.000	22.40
.250	**.70**		9.000	25.20
.300	.84		**10.000**	**28.00**
.350	1.00		20.000	56.00
.400	1.12		25.000	70.00
.450	1.25		30.000	84.00
.500	**1.40**		40.000	112.00
.600	1.68		50.000	140.00
.750	2.10		100.000	280.00

OTHER PAN AM BOOKS

This book is one of a series of guides on individual European countries which include "Complete Reference Guide to Britain . . . to France . . . to Scandinavia . . . to Spain and Portugal . . . to Austria and Switzerland . . . to Germany . . . to Italy . . . to Low Countries."

Inquire also about these other authoritative Pan Am Books:

New Horizons World Guide. Best selling travel book with over a million copies sold. Covers details important to the traveler on 36 subjects on each of 112 countries in its 640 pages.

New Horizons U.S.A. Similar to the World Guide in its comprehensive factual information — covers 100 U.S. cities and resorts in 50 states plus Puerto Rico and the Virgin Islands. 540 pages.

New Horizons Living Abroad. Even if you have no plans to live abroad, you'll want this fascinating encyclopedia of living conditions in 90 countries, a *must* for military families, students, retirement planners or anyone living overseas or considering it.

Round the World Cookbook. Includes 600 easy-to-follow recipes for exciting dishes from 81 foreign countries. 480 pages.

Golf New Horizons. New guide to golf courses in 52 countries near and far with thousands of facts from playing tips to nearby attractions.

The Whole Wide World. This huge book is filled with beautiful 4-color photographs and 200,000 words of text of 57 top contemporary authors.

New Horizons in Education. Detailed information on 200 universities as well as boarding schools, day schools and summer sessions; accommodation, costs and credits; educational opportunities abroad.

New Horizons Maps of Europe. New book with 47 city streets maps and 24 country maps all in color with cross references to capsule sketches of sightseeing highlights.

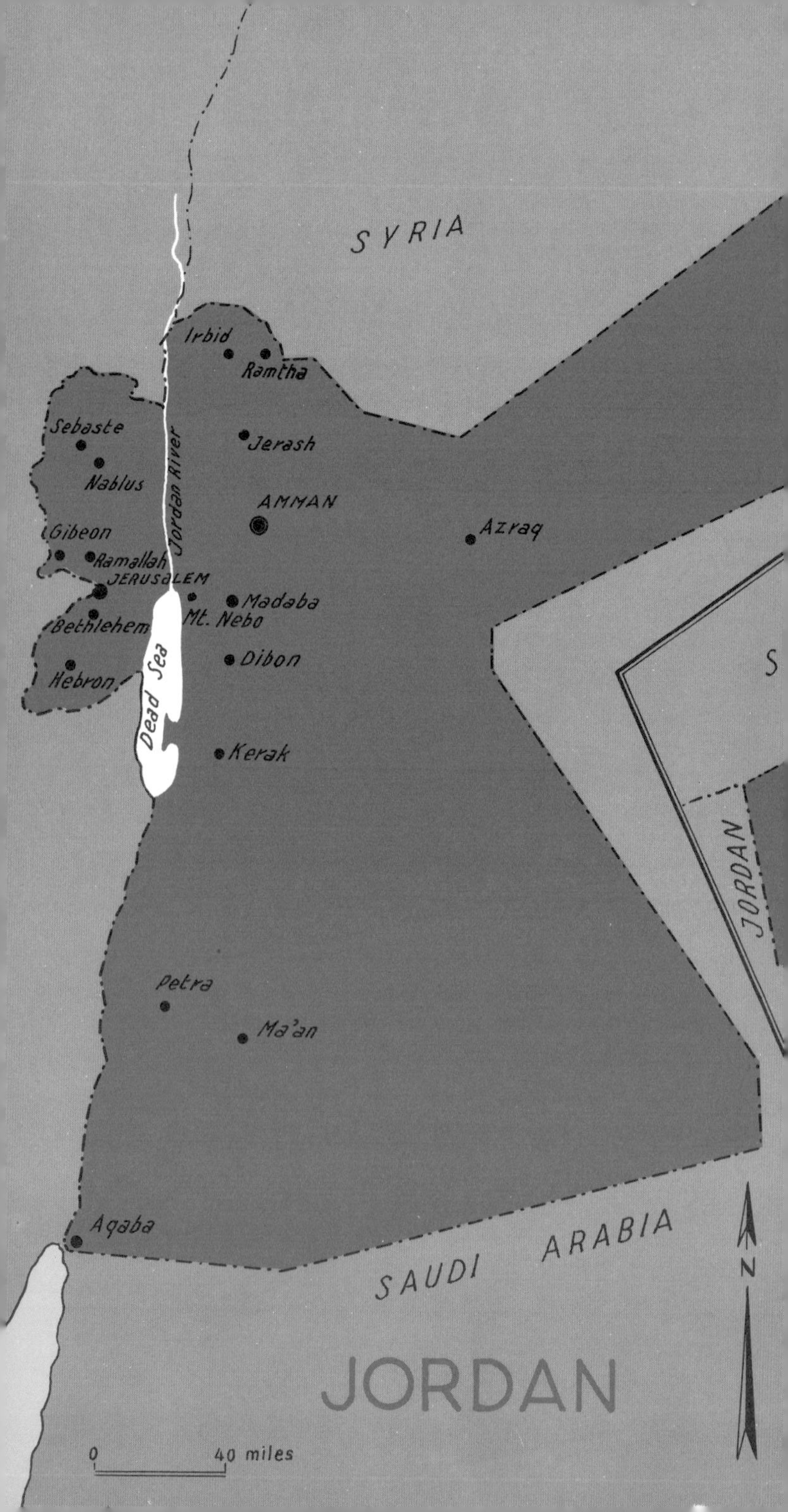
SYRIA
Irbid
Ramtha
Sebaste
Nablus
Jerash
AMMAN
Jordan River
Azraq
Gibeon
Ramallah
JERUSALEM
Madaba
Mt. Nebo
Bethlehem
Dibon
Hebron
Dead Sea
Kerak
S
JORDAN
Petra
Ma'an
Aqaba
SAUDI ARABIA
N
JORDAN
0
40 miles